NEW ECCLESIAL MINISTRY

LAY PROFESSIONALS SERVING THE CHURCH

REVISED AND EXPANDED

New Ecclesial Ministry
LAY PROFESSIONALS SERVING THE CHURCH

Zeni Fox

SHEED & WARD

Franklin, Wisconsin
Chicago

As an apostolate of the Priests of the Sacred Heart, a Catholic religious congregation, the mission of Sheed & Ward is to publish books of contemporary impact and enduring merit in Catholic Christian thought and action. The books published, however, reflect the opinions of their authors and are not meant to represent the official position of the Priests of the Sacred Heart.

2002

Sheed & Ward
7373 South Lovers Lane Road
Franklin, Wisconsin 53132
1-800-266-5564

Printed in the United States of America

Cover photo by © S. Meltzer/PhotoLink/ PhotoDisc/ PictureQuest
Cover and interior design by Robin Costa Booth

Library of Congress Cataloging-in-Publication Data

Fox, Zeni.
    New ecclesial ministry : lay professionals serving the church / Zeni Fox.—
    [Rev.ed.].
    Includes bibliographical references and index.
    ISBN 1-58051-122-8 (pbk.)
        1. Lay ministry—Catholic Church. 2. Catholic Church—United States—
        Clergy. 3. Catholic Church—United States-Government. I. Title.

    BX1916 .F.68 2002
    262'.15273-dc21

                        2002070526

CONTENTS

PART II: PERSPECTIVES FROM THE TRADITION

Section One: Scripture

Part III: An Agenda for the Future

PREFACE TO THE 2002 EDITION

For you, the reader, this preface is the first part of the book; for myself it is the last part to be written. For me, it is an opportunity to acknowledge the many people who have contributed to my work, directly and indirectly; for you, it is an opportunity to trace the influences on my thought.

Of course, there is a sense in which all of my life has influenced what I think, even what I see. The spiritual life of my childhood was nurtured through immersion in communities of lived faith at home and in my parish and schools. My search for meaning was deepened at the College of Mt. St. Vincent, and there excellent theology courses opened the door to the Church's intellectual life. At Fordham's Graduate School of Religion and Religious Education, studying newspaper texts of Vatican II documents, Scripture, the Church Fathers and theologians old and new, my vision of a hoped-for future of the Church, rooted in the legacy of the centuries, was forged. Later, doctoral study of theology at Fordham allowed fuller exploration of our Christian tradition, as well as other religions, shaping a deeper and more inclusive vision. Developments in the life of the Church and my own desire to share what I had learned brought me, a layperson, into the life of ministry. At St. Mary's parish in Greenwich, the two pastors (Monsignor John Toomey and Reverend Martin Hitchcock), the priests, the sisters, the people, and I learned together the what and how of my new role as director of religious education. Shared work and many conversations with other DRE's of the town, the diocese, and the country heightened awareness and increased understanding of laypeople involved in ministry. Later, work as a staff member in the archdiocese of New York, teaching in the graduate program at Fordham, serving on the staff at the Center for Youth Ministry Development (CYMD), and in recent years, teaching and serving as Director of Lay Ministry at Immaculate Conception Seminary, Seton Hall University, have given me the opportunity to experience the Church in many diverse and wonderful ways, and to encounter countless people who have enriched my life inestimably. All of these experiences are remote influences on this book, and I stand ever indebted, ever grateful to the countless family members, teachers, priests, colleagues, friends, parishioners, and students who have given me more than I can name, even for myself.

More direct influences on the evolution of my work begin with an experience in a pastoral ministry class I was teaching at Fordham in 1976. My class was composed mostly of young adults, eager to learn, eager to serve, faithful, committed. One day I realized: these are the young men and women who, when I was their age, would have gone into the novitiate, the seminary. I began listening in a new way to stories of laypeople preparing for and involved in ministry. My work with the youth ministers in New York, and my students at Fordham and throughout the country in certificate programs sponsored by CYMD, gave me many opportunities to do this. (You will meet some of these lay ministers, their names changed, in the pages of this book.)

In 1983, when I was seeking a dissertation topic, my former teacher and colleague, Dr. John Nelson, suggested that I do it in the area of lay ministry. Further conversations with him, and with my mentor, Reverend Sabbas Kilian, led to the study I undertook. It began with an extensive national survey of lay ministers, shaped with the guidance of sociologist Dr. James Kelly. The questions emerged from my knowledge of the lay ministers; many respondents expressed gratitude for the survey, which they said helped focus sometimes inchoate understandings of themselves. Some of this work is reported again in this volume. The data from the survey yielded a picture of the present reality, which was then evaluated theologically by drawing on the tradition of the Church. That framework informs this volume as well.

In more recent years, my thinking about lay ministry has continued to be shaped by my experiences. Teaching, my lay formation responsibilities at the seminary, interaction with professional colleagues in lay ministry education and formation, and participation in faculty committees and exchanges continue to pose questions to me and deepen understanding. Particularly valuable has been my participation as an advisor in the work of several NCCB committees that have focused on the issue of lay ministry—the Committee for Pastoral Research and Practices, the Committee on the Laity, and the Subcommittee on Lay Ministry. As this manuscript was completed, the latter committee was planning a theological colloquium, "Toward a Theology of Ecclesial Lay Ministry." Chapters 1–4 of this book were summarized as a paper, "Ecclesial Lay Ministers," for the colloquium.

The writing of this book would never have been possible without the sabbatical granted me for 1994-95 by Seton Hall University. My ability to focus this writing project was helped by participation in an Association of Theological Schools invitational seminar, "The Role of the Teacher as Scholar," as my sabbatical began. The production of the manuscript was aided by the extensive computing skills and patient understanding of Mrs. George (Linda) Bindhammer and Ms. Ewa Bracko. Throughout the period of research, writing, rewriting, correction, the support of my family (patient with my absences, enthusiastic about my efforts, always ready to celebrate life's journey) was my mainstay.

It is the community we call Church which has taught me and in its life raised the questions which I try to explore. It is my hope that my work will assist our life together in some small way.

Again, the addition to the Preface for this revised edition is the last part to be written. A sabbatical, generously granted by Seton Hall, has made it possible to do this work. And again, the work has made me more aware of the ways in which my perspectives are rooted in my experience as teacher, formator, and colleague, and my journey sustained by these relationships, and those of family and friends. The publication of the original book was the catalyst for my inclusion in many conversations, with varied individuals and groups, which have richly gifted me. I am particularly grateful to Robert Heyer, then editor of Sheed & Ward, who saw a value in publishing my work, and now to Sheed & Ward for their decision to produce this new edition.

INTRODUCTION

In the closing chapter of the first epistle of Paul to the Thessalonians, we have an interesting clue to the slow unfolding of ministry in the earliest period of the Church's life. Depending on the translation, we hear of "those who labor among you and who are over you" (Douay-Rheims), "those who are working among you and are above you" (Jerusalem Bible) or "those who work with you and who lead you" (Chicago Bible) (1 Thes. 5:12). The account tells us that some ministers are active in the community, and Paul implores the Thessalonians to appreciate them, to hold them in esteem, to show them affection. But they do not yet have titles for their roles nor precise names for their functions. They labor, they lead, but their ministry is not yet defined and delineated. The later books of the New Testament will name many ministers and ministries with more precision, but in this first book of the Christian Scriptures we have only the functions named, and those in a very general way. It is the thesis of this book that we are encountering a similar reality today, in regard to new ministers emerging in the life of our communities. Because of the lack of definition, at this point in this analysis it is only possible to say that these new ministers represent a not yet clearly differentiated group of people who are not ordained, but who are engaged in ministry with stability and specificity, which is different from the general church ministry of the lay faithful. In 1980, the U.S. Catholic bishops named them "ecclesial ministers," laypersons who have prepared for professional ministry in the Church,[1] and in 1999 they further specified them as "lay ecclesial ministers."[2]

Both ordinary Catholics and leaders in the Church in the United States recognize that something new has been unfolding. Parishioners note that parish bulletins have a variety of titles and names listed under the heading "parish staff." The titles are diverse, and the persons filling the roles include more than priests. Bishops observed the varieties of people serving in their parishes, and therefore the National Conference of Catholic Bishops (now the United States Conference of Catholic Bishops) requested that a study be done of the "new parish ministers." More recently, a subcommittee for lay ministry was formed, to determine what leadership actions should be recommended to the conference and to individual bishops. Their report represents the first comprehensive official statement about these new "lay ecclesial ministers."[3] Many national organizations, such as the National Conference of Catechetical Leadership and the National Association for Lay Ministry, have worked to assist an adequate naming of these ministers. Other groups such as the Canon Law Society of America and the National Association of Church Personnel Administrators have addressed issues of concern to the ministers, and the Church which employs them.

At the present time, there are not yet precisely evolved definitions which would serve to differentiate these new ministers in a practical way. Lacking precise definition, it is difficult to resolve many other issues, such as what kind of education and formation these men and women need, what type of support is just, what manner of designation is appropriate and what forms of relationship with other ministers, including bishops, are desirable. This book will explore these new ministers and these issues. It will do so by drawing on various sociological studies of the ministers, and on the work of many individuals and groups in the Church, including theologians and organizations addressing pertinent concerns. The exploration is framed by my own experience with these ministers, who have included colleagues, students, teachers, and friends. The purpose is to draw together a range of perspectives which have not yet been collated. While conclusions will be drawn and recommendations made, they are offered as another voice in the conversation.

The first section of the book will examine our present situation. The first part will describe the new ministers, using both sociological and theological categories. The second part will report on various ways the Church has been responding to this new phenomenon, both pastorally and theologically. The second section will explore these developments in light of the scriptural and theological tradition of the Church. The final section will present conclusions and recommendations, proposals for an agenda for the future.

In the five years since the publication of the original book, the number of new ministers has increased greatly, and more attention has been given by many individuals and groups to the issues this new reality presents to the community of the Church. This revision demonstrates these developments, providing a clear indication that the original premise, that the Church *was* responding in many and diverse ways to the new ministers, was true, and is even more true today. While the process of integrating these new ministers into the life of the Church is far from complete, the actions of the last five years demonstrate that the vision and energy of many are engaged in the effort of doing so. This chronicling of developments also demonstrates that much more still needs to be done.

It is my hope that this book will heighten understanding of these new ministers, and of the implications of their presence in the Church. This embraces the self-understanding of the ministers, that of their colleagues in ministry, including bishops, and of the communities in which they work. From understanding will come, I trust, action to further integrate these ministers into the official life of the Church.

In the epistle quoted above, Paul continues his exhortation to the Thessalonians: "Be at peace among yourselves" (5:14); "never try to suppress the Spirit" (5:19). It is the intent of this book that it further Paul's wish for his community, certainly a wish shared in today's Church.

NOTES

1. *Called and Gifted: The American Catholic Laity* (Washington, D.C.: United States Catholic Conference, 1980), p. 4.
2. *The State of the Questions* (Washington, D.C.: United States Catholic Conference, 1999), pp. 7–8.
3. Ibid.

✣

PART ONE

THE PRESENT REALITY

Section One

The New Ministers

INTRODUCTION

In attempting to write about the Church's new ministers, the lack of precise definition and definitive delineation presents an immediate problem. What criteria can be used for deciding who should be included in the study? Existing research uses varied categories, precisely because clear differentiation has not yet occurred in the Church. Employment (part time and full time), not being a member of a religious community, exercising leadership in the community and holding a particular role are all categories used—sometimes. To underline the complexity, it is helpful to contrast this situation with that of another new ministry in the contemporary Church, the permanent deacon. Who the deacon is is clearly defined and delineated; an exact count of deacons in each diocese is possible. The permanent deaconate was established by the Church, officially, and then training programs were developed, candidates were recruited and eventually men were deemed suitable and were ordained. By comparison, in many ways the new ministers are like Topsy; they "just growed."

Because the intent of this section is to describe the *multi-faceted* present reality, a definition as such will not now be attempted. Rather, various studies of the new ministers will be used as resources, despite the fact that one includes vowed religious, another doesn't, one examines those filling a certain role, another is inclusive of many roles, etc. A further complication arises from the fact that some groups of ministers have not yet been studied. Nonetheless, a picture emerges from the various studies which invites further definition, but the community has not yet determined what differentiations to make. In the second part of this section, responses by various groups and individuals, in the church community, to the new ministers will be described. Again, this exploration will proceed without a specific delimitation of the new ministers.

CHAPTER ONE

WHAT THEY DO AND WHO THEY ARE

ROLES IN MINISTRY

FORMAL STUDIES

Early efforts to study the new ministers in the Church focused on professional religious education coordinators/directors. A review of articles in the *Catholic Guide to Periodical Literature* suggests that these were, indeed, among the first roles filled by new ministers, beginning in the 1960s. As early as 1970, an attempt to define the role states, "The extent of his *(sic)* training and experience will determine the extent of his work . . ."[1] An effort was made to differentiate the roles of directors, coordinators, and parish helpers, indicating expected functions and educational preparation for each category.

A 1983 study commissioned by the National Conference of Diocesan Directors of Religious Education continued this kind of analysis by defining those to be studied as professionals, persons "with a Master's Degree in theology, religious education or an approved equivalency and at last three years of administration or teaching experience who has demonstrated skills in organization and is a salaried, full-time member of a parish staff."[2] In preparation for the study, diocesan directors had been asked in 1981 how many DRE's met the definition; they responded—4,685.

A study in 1986 also focused on parish ministers.[3] Names of "lay people professionally employed as pastoral ministers in parishes" were requested from diocesan staff in nine representative dioceses. The largest group responding to the survey were directors or coordinators of religious education. Coordinators of youth ministry/youth ministers, pastoral ministers, directors of liturgy, and directors of social concerns were also represented. In addition, 7 percent of the respondents named unique roles, for example director of finance and administration, and parish coordinator of canonical marriage cases. Many people recorded combination titles. The data demonstrate that parishes define needs differently, and seek ministers to meet the needs they have.

A 1992 study of parish ministers also finds that the ministry of religious education is the most prevalent, with titles including DRE, CRE, and adult education coordinator.[4] However, the second most prevalent role was the more recently developed one of pastoral associate or pastoral minister. Murnion notes that people who once were DRE's often now are in this broader role, in part because of their desires, in part because more parishes want a generalist.[5] The study posited that there were 20,000 new ministers, part time and full time, lay and vowed religious, working in parishes.[6]

The most recent national study finds that religious educators (including directors and coordinators of religious education and adult education directors) are 36.3 percent of the total, a decline from the 41.7 percent of five years earlier, but still the largest single group. General pastoral ministers (sometimes called pastoral associates) are 24.7 percent of the total, down from 27.4 percent in 1992. Liturgy and music directors hold 14.9 percent of the positions, an increase from 11.7 percent. Youth ministers, too, increased, from 7.5 percent to 10.7 percent. A small but significant group, the parish life coordinators, present where there is no resident priest pastor, increased from .8 to 2.1 percent. A wide range of other titles are each held by less than 1 percent of the ministers, but a total of 5 percent of those employed, and some roles are so idiosyncratic as not to even form a category in the study. The number of all parish ministers has increased by 35 percent, to 29,146, of whom 20,402 are full time.[7]

While the major studies have focused on parish ministers, there are other new ministers serving in various roles and settings. A survey of lay professional ministers conducted by the National Association for Lay Ministry had respondents from parishes (36 percent), diocesan offices (41 percent), and other agencies and organizations (23 percent).[8] Another, of graduate ministry students, found that of those who want to work in ecclesial settings, preferences were pastoral administrator (25 percent), pastoral care/counseling (14 percent), retreats/spiritual direction (13 percent), and religious education (22 percent).[9] A recent study of diocesan directors of religious education reports that 60 percent of the directors are lay, 29 percent vowed religious, and 11 percent ordained (priests and deacons).[10]

Finally, a study of Catholic institutional ministries, specifically higher education, health care, and social services, provokes thought. While the focus is on the institutions *qua* institutions, the questions raised are pertinent. The study named as one of its working assumptions: "While recognized as Catholic, they are heavily influenced by secularizing factors. There are few priests, sisters or brothers active in these ministries." It then raised the question, "Must there be many priests, sisters and brothers involved in providing service?" in order that an institution be Catholic.[11] Summarizing the perspective of the Delphi study, which was the starting point for the broader study and symposium, Bishop Sullivan observed: "All ministries [in the study] seem acutely aware of the feasibility of lay leadership to assure Catholic identity, but they concur in the need for both formation and education of lay leaders."[12] (Although the study did not examine this issue, increasingly laypersons are serving as chaplains in hospitals and nursing homes, Catholic and otherwise, but this group has not been studied. In 2002, 32 percent of the membership of the National Association of Catholic Chaplains was lay.)[13]

Implicit in the Delphi study is the question: what roles within Catholic institutions are ministerial? And, consequently, what formation and education is needed to assure the "Catholic identity" and "Catholic culture" of these institutions? The relationship of the institutions to the local diocese and the parish is also a question. A related question is, what is the relationship of the individuals who work in the institutions to the diocese and the parish, and to the ministry of the Church. Both priests and vowed religious worked within structured patterns of relationship to the official Church; lay leaders, even chaplains, in institutional ministries do not.

INFORMAL PORTRAITS

Studies of new ministers give a broad picture, each representing a particular moment in time. The stories of particular ministers give glimpses of the ways roles evolve and are combined, and of the ways individuals move from one role to another.

Dot, a single mother with previous experience as a volunteer, served her rural/suburban parish as a DRE. She struggled to develop a viable religious education program for teenagers, drawing on the gifts of committed parishioners. However, they did not experience much success. In the early years of the development of youth ministry, Dot took a course to help her reorganize parish efforts with teens in this new model. Eventually, she was designated as the DRE/Coordinator of Youth Ministry. Some years later she was invited by a religious community to help staff a regional youth center. When the center closed, she assumed responsibility for the youth ministry of several clustered parishes. Dot's journey was primarily defined by a discernment of need within her parish and region.

Jim, as a young man just out of college, was a DRE for a number of years, serving a poor parish and living in the inner-city. When his first child was a year old, he concluded that playing on a glass-strewn city street was not what he wanted for his son, and so, sadly, left his position and moved into a secular field. But he missed the work he had done. When a bequest left him the owner of a small suburban home, in another state, he again thought about church work. He took a position as campus minister in a small Catholic high school, and a second as part-time youth minister in a nearby parish. Economic necessity, especially the needs of his children, influenced Jim's decisions about ministry.

When Dolores began her work as a DRE, one of the first in her diocese, she had many years experience teaching religion and English in high schools staffed by her community. While working in the parish, she decided to leave her community. After several years, she took a position in a national church office; eventually, she moved into human resource development work in the secular arena. Recently, she took CPE training, and drawing on both her church and secular work, took a position as a chaplain in a secular hospital. Through the years, her own gifts caused her to seek new and varied ministry and other positions.

Sally and John met in graduate school, when they were pursuing degrees in theology. After graduation, they married, and each took a position as a DRE. When their children were born, Sally moved to a smaller parish, to work part time. They bought a home in a somewhat depressed area, so each could continue to work in ministry. As her children grew, Sally put added time into family ministry efforts, working especially with young mothers. She partnered with two other professional women to develop new models for meeting the needs they perceived. Eventually, Sally pursued a second degree in social work, and moved into secular work. John pursued a doctorate, and continued in church work. A significant number of couples like Sally and John work together to discern how to use their gifts for the service of people, in the Church and in the world.

When her children were little, Joan volunteered extensively in the parish. When the DRE left, the pastor asked her to take the position. While working, she pursued an M.A. A primary area of interest was spirituality and spiritual formation. Some years later, a retreat center staffed by a religious community of men invited Joan to join their staff. She serves now as an administrator, retreat director, and spiritual director. The desire of the religious community to work collaboratively with laypeople led to the invitation to Joan to move into a new area of ministry.

Jack studied for the priesthood, but left the seminary before ordination. He had been hearing about the newly emerging role of DRE, so he completed his graduate degree in theology, and applied to a diocese which mandated that all parishes hire a professionally prepared educator for the role. After a few years, he assumed responsibility for a regional religious education office in another state. A few years later he moved again, to become a diocesan director of religious education. After a time, Jack became the director of the Office of Christian Formation in that diocese, with responsibility for Catholic schools, religious education, and some other ministries. Deeply committed to the ministry of religious education, each of Jack's changes of position represented a move to greater responsibility and greater financial remuneration.

Conclusion

Implicit in this overview are various questions which an eventual definition will need to answer. Does the role define the minister? When people change roles, do they become another kind of minister? Does the category "ecclesial lay ministers" include vowed religious? Does the designation "minister" remain when an individual does the same work begun in a parish, but now in a secular setting? What are the implications of minister couples? Is ministry a career? Do ministers work in parishes? parishes and dioceses? parishes, dioceses, and other Church-related institutions such as retreat houses? Is being a minister about what you do? who you are? where you work?

FUNCTIONS AND RESPONSIBILITIES

FORMAL STUDIES

The titles people hold are suggestive of what they do, but studies show that there is considerable latitude in respect to the actual functions and responsibilities of each individual. For example, the overall responsibility of the DRE, the oldest and most clearly defined role is "the design, implementation and direction of educational programs as opposed to programs for pastoral ministry." Most DRE's are responsible for catechist training, three-fourths for parent programs, and a third for programs for mentally and physically handicapped. By age groups, over 90 percent work with elementary school children, 80 percent with adult education, about two-thirds with high school students, and less than 20 percent with young adults,[14] showing a range of responsibilities for individual DRE's.

In profiling pastoral associates or general pastoral ministers, Murnion notes that there is no particular ministry for which more than half of those in the sample are leaders. However, by combining leadership and participation categories, he indicates that roughly three-quarters are involved in evangelization, prayer/reflection groups, religious education, and ministry training—all activities that two-thirds or more of the DRE's are also involved in.[15]

Furthermore, the responsibilities of ministers are evolving. Walters compared data he gathered in 1989 with his 1986 survey; he reports, among other changes, that 11 percent fewer DRE's were responsible for youth retreats, while 8 percent more were responsible for the RCIA.[16] However, Murnion stresses that there is considerable variation which the statistics alone do not identify. Both individual pastors and parishes, and individual ministers shape the defining of the tasks and responsibilities performed.[17]

Another approach to analyzing what new ministers do involved presenting survey participants who were lay with a list of eighteen functions performed by parish ministers. They were asked to assess these in various ways: which were essential to their own role and which to a priest's role, which were inappropriate for lay ministers, and which three were most important for their own role, and for the priest's role.

In terms of essential functions, respondents tended to check many items. At least 70 percent checked ten as essential for their own work, and sixteen for the priests' work. For themselves, greatest weight was given to teacher, community builder, leader, and enabler. In terms of primary function, the overwhelming majority indicate that Eucharistic celebrant is primary for the priest. Community builder is ranked a distant second; no other function has a significant preference. For themselves, community builder, enabler of leaders, administrator and teacher are the functions ranked as primary. The study suggests that respondents see some differentiation of their own ministry from that of priests, in terms of the particular functions which most shape their ministry. However, it also indicates that they perceive many functions as shared by both themselves and priests.[18] Just as roles do not yield a sharply defined picture of what new ministers do, this study of functions also does not.

TWO PORTRAITS

A description of the evolution over a period of a few years in the work of two DRE's, within that role in their respective parishes, captures something of the diverse responsibilities and functions assumed by new ministers.

Roberta was the first DRE in her parish. Her initial work involved the organization of an elementary grade religious education program, with responsibility for recruitment of needed teachers, choice of texts, etc. Working with some area DRE's, all new, a joint teacher training program was planned. Working with a parish priest and a liturgist, new programs of preparation for Eucharist, Reconciliation, and Confirmation—all involving parents—were developed. An education committee was formed. In the ensuing years, the models begun in the first two years expanded. The area DRE's worked together to plan and present various adult education programs. The elementary program expanded to include high school grades. Roberta became involved in an ecumenical educators group; teachers' workshops and an ecumenical vacation church school were jointly presented. Concern about world hunger led her to plan various educational efforts, some developed with the parish staff for the Sunday Eucharistic gatherings. Also with the staff, a baptism preparation program was begun. Eventually, Roberta complemented her parish ministry with part-time university teaching. Out of the needs of the parish, the resources of colleagues on the staff and in area churches, the gifts and talents of particular parishioners, and her own concerns and interests, a set of responsibilities evolved over time.

Patti took on the role of DRE in a parish where the position was already well established. She continued administering the elementary and high school programs, and the sacrament programs. Because of her background in and love for Scripture, Patti formed several Scripture sharing groups. Because most of her teachers were certified, she planned monthly enrichment sessions for them. Some sessions she presented with a neighboring DRE. That collaboration led them to plan some women's retreats together. As she became aware of the desire of the Catholic school teachers to do more in the area of social justice in the school, she assumed responsibility for guiding them in their efforts, presenting models and identifying resources. She was invited to join the area Fellowship of the Clergy, and subsequently asked to preach at an ecumenical Thanksgiving service. Eventually, Patti complemented her parish ministry with writing a column for the local diocesan paper. Again, parish needs, the resources of particular people in the area, and the minister's own concerns and interests defined what the role actually encompassed.

CONCLUSION

Again, several questions emerge for consideration. Are there particular functions proper to the new ministers? Is function a fruitful way to try to define this new reality? Should individual ministers be assuming responsibilities based on interest and/or concern? Are certain functions essential for the life of a parish? Should ministry be defined functionally?

DEMOGRAPHIC DATA

MORE WOMEN THAN MEN

Overwhelmingly, the new ministers are women. The most recent national study of parish ministers indicates that 82 percent are women,[19] and approximately the same percentage has been found in other studies.[20] However, a study of diocesan directors of religious education found that 44 percent are men,[21] suggesting that proportionately more men move into diocesan administrative roles. And, in certain ministries, the proportion of men is higher, notably full-time youth ministry (41 percent) and music ministry (52 percent).[22]

Murnion has concluded that there is a stronger feminine dimension in parish life today. This is so not simply because of the presence of significant numbers of women in ministry. Changes in the larger culture and in the Church have led to a shift in parish focus to activities that are more nurturing and supportive. Furthermore, women are more likely to desire collaborative efforts, to focus on relationships as well as tasks, and so new styles of ministry are more relational and communal. These create a stronger "feminine dimension."[23]

Why are so many more women employed than men? Perhaps it is, as Murnion suggests, that the increased focus of parish work on children and the elderly, teenagers and the homebound, has contributed to this pattern. In our culture, it is more often women who work with these populations. Furthermore, a significant proportion, though a diminishing one, of the new parish ministers are women religious. Some other clues to the large number of women are found in comparing the responses of men and women to the question, "if you were to leave Church work, what would be the reasons?" For men, the reason ranked first was inadequate salary; for women, this was third.[24] The issue of income is different for single persons and those who are married. Generally, for single men and women their ministry is their only source of income. For married women, on average their salary represents 38 percent of the family income, 41 percent for those working full time. For married men, on average their income is 59 percent of family income, 68 percent if they are full time.[25] In our society, men continue to earn significantly more than women, and more often are the primary breadwinners in their families. Since the salaries of church ministers are substantially lower than that of other professionals, it is not surprising that salary is an important issue, especially for men.

Another difference between men and women in ranking reasons for leaving is that men ranked "lack of security" third and "lack of advancement possibilities" fifth. For women these concerns were not significant.[26] Both could be linked to salary issues, but advancement suggests the idea of achievement. In our culture, men are socialized more to value personal achievement. Yet another difference between men and women is that for women, "lack of support from the pastor" is ranked fifth; men do not give this a significant ranking at all.[27] In our culture, women are socialized more to value relationships. Cultural norms may be more supportive of women being involved in ministry than of non-ordained men being involved.

Finally, one could ask whether the call of many women to participate in ministry is not a sign of the times. Throughout the world, women have moved into many arenas of work which were once thought not to be women's place. Throughout the world, there is movement toward a fuller working together of men and women in partnership. Perhaps the large numbers of women coming forward to work with ordained men is the work of the Spirit.

Many Are Married

In a Church in which pastoral leadership has long been provided by celibate male priests, with additional ministry by celibate men and women religious, married ministers are certainly new. Some studies include vowed religious in their population; they represent a significant proportion of the new parish ministers. Other studies do not report whether respondents are married or not. However one national study which excluded vowed religious found that almost two-thirds of the lay ministers were married; 6 percent were widowed, divorced, or separated. Furthermore, 71 percent of the group have children; family size is slightly higher than in the population in general.[28]

The implications of the presence of married people among the Church's ministers has not yet been adequately assessed, nor sufficiently planned for in the organizational life of the Church. In terms of assessment, many questions arise. How will married ministers affect Catholics attitudes toward human sexuality? What effect will they have on the development of family ministry? (Parishioners report that one of the most important improvements in parish life brought by the new ministers is increased sensitivity to family needs.)[29] Will the demands of family life place limits on ministry? Will the children of lay ministers experience the kinds of difficulties experienced by those of Protestant ministers? What models of ministry are needed for married persons with families, especially since existing models were developed with celibate leaders? Experience is needed for answers to these questions to begin to emerge.

Organizationally, there are many implications. Our society is very mobile; workers are transferred by employers, or themselves move to other areas for reasons of work. As ministers follow their spouses to new locations, issues such as portability of ministry "credentials" and health benefits and pensions become important. The patterns of hiring are also of significant importance. Presently, the laywomen hired by pastors are usually parishioners whom they know already, often people who are not credentialed when they begin.[30] With such a hiring practice, experienced and credentialed ministers may find it quite difficult to find another place to minister. Experienced workers are one of the greatest assets in any setting; how to utilize well this resource of the Church needs attention.

MANY ARE MEMBERS OF RELIGIOUS CONGREGATIONS

Many sisters, and a much smaller number of brothers, who once were involved in other ministries now serve on parish staffs. They represent 29 percent (a decrease from 42 percent five years earlier) of the new parish ministers. Pastors are almost evenly divided on whether they prefer laypersons or vowed religious for these positions.[31]

The numbers of vowed religious are declining, and yet there are some trends that suggest many will continue to seek opportunities to serve in pastoral roles. The three trends most strongly noted in a Leadership Conference of Women Religious (LCWR) survey are each relevant to this issue: trends from serving children to serving adults, from works owned or sponsored by the institute to ministries not owned or sponsored by the institute, from administration to direct service.[32] Furthermore "compensated positions as pastoral associates, parish administrators and pastoral ministers were most frequently cited as ministries which members desired but for which they could find no opportunity."[33] There is also expectation of "increased involvement of sisters" in adult education.[34]

There are also some trends to suggest that vowed religious will move away from religious education roles, and assume more generalist roles. Studies of professional religious educators done in 1983, 1986, and 1992 find that the percentage of vowed religious declines from 54 percent to 31 percent to 25 percent over that period.[35] Murnion indicates that a shift from religious education to more generalist positions is occurring, because of the desires of both the individuals and of the parishes.[36]

On the other hand, in addition to the fact that in the future there will be fewer sisters, the religious congregations are placing their strongest emphasis on "a preferential option for and solidarity with the poor."[37] However, poorer parishes, in rural areas and inner cities, and smaller parishes presently are significantly less likely to have parish ministers than are large, suburban parishes.[38] The question of how the needs of these parishes are to be adequately met in the face of declining numbers of clergy is a pressing one. Religious congregations are important partners in the conversation that must ensue to address this need.

OF VARIOUS AGES

The median age of the lay ministers is 50, of the vowed religious 60 years of age.[39] There are also variations according to role. Two-thirds of the youth ministers are under 35 (although there are also a significant number who are over 50, and have begun their jobs in the past five years).[40] Liturgists also tend to be younger than the general group of parish ministers.[41]

The profile of graduate students in ministry shows that the majority are between 35 and 50 years of age, with the median age of incoming students being 42.5.[42] A survey of Catholic students at ecumenical divinity schools found a slightly younger population: the mean age of the women was 34.5, of the men 30.8.[43]

The fact that there are relatively few people in their twenties is worth considering, especially since the usual pattern for ordained and vowed religious had been to begin ministry at this age. Research by Dean Hoge found a very high level of interest in lay ministry among Catholic college students, especially those involved in campus ministry. Sixty-four percent of women campus ministry student leaders and 53 percent of men student leaders indicated they were seriously interested in devoting their careers to the Church. Interest among students as a whole was almost as great. Hoge concludes that the number interested in lay ministry is about fifty times as large as those interested in ordination or religious life.[44] In light of this high degree of interest, one would expect that in graduate school programs and ministry positions there would be more people in their 20's. Is it that college students don't know about actual possibilities for employment in the Church? Is any encouragement offered to them to pursue a vocation as a lay minister? Do any mechanisms exist on campuses, in dioceses, to assist students in exploring such an option? And related to these questions is another: are all ministry positions potentially "entry level" ones? This entire area has not been explored.

NOT CULTURALLY DIVERSE

Many studies note that the overwhelming majority of the new ministers are white. An older study found that in Catholic graduate ministry programs 87.7 percent were so; other students included: Asian-Pacific, 3.7 percent; black, 3 percent; Hispanic, 3.2 percent, and Native American, 1 percent.[45] At ecumenical schools, the ratios were similar: white, 89 percent; black, 2 percent; Hispanic, 4 percent; Asian and other, 5 percent.[46] In ministry programs (degree and non-degree) in 1986, three quarters of the participants were white, 15 percent Hispanic, and 2 percent black.[47] In 1999, 71 percent were white, 23 percent Hispanic/Latino, 3 percent black, 2 percent Asian, and 1 percent Native American.[48] In studies of parish ministers, in 1992 there were fewer than 5 percent who were Hispanic, African-American, Asian, Native American, or Pacific Islanders. "As of 1997 it appears that these groups are only very slightly better represented."[49] What is more complex in trying to assess diversity is that studies of leadership in African-American, Hispanic, and Asian communities have not been done. The Notre Dame study of the parish chose to exclude Hispanic communities, on the grounds that they were unique.[50]

This is an issue which the Church in the U.S. has pondered in relation to priests, vowed religious, and permanent deacons. In general, traditional church leaders from minority communities are not being successfully recruited by the Church, nor are ecclesial ministers being successfully empowered by the communities. To date, lay ministry has not been a route to more formal minority leadership, but whether it can be has not yet been fully explored.

BEYOND STATISTICS

Studies give a helpful overview of a total population; they do not allow individuals in their uniqueness to stand before us. They also do not account for significant transitions from one "category" in a study to another.

Certainly, year by year, ministers get older; sometimes this affects ministry.

Matthew provided leadership for a multi-parish youth ministry. As a young adult, he began the program with a handful of friends; twenty years later there were over one hundred trained leaders, many of them former participants, and scores of volunteers. Classes, retreats, service projects, youth and adult leadership training, social gatherings, personal relationships with teens, leaders and many former participants, gradually filled every hour of every day. As he moved into midlife, slowly, sadly, Matthew realized that he simply could not continue the pace. He chose to move into public school administration.

On the other hand, at midlife, Miriam reflected on the fact that her children were grown. She looked about to see where she might invest her energies. She noted that her parish had no programs for teens. She heard about some youth ministry courses, being offered at the diocesan seminary. She thought: I have always enjoyed teenagers. So, Miriam began her studies, volunteered to begin a youth ministry program and eventually was hired as a youth minister. In her mid-50's, she was providing vibrant leadership, and enjoying every minute of it.

Other transitions also occur. Single lay ministers sometimes marry; this raises many questions for them. Sally had been a youth minister for several years; she was deeply committed to her work. Many evenings and weekends, she was at the parish or away with teens for retreats, service efforts, or social trips. She was also dating, and the relationship was becoming more serious. She asked herself, "Can I be married and be a youth minister?" Her reflection process was helped by taking that question as a topic for a theological reflection paper. She researched the issue of women and work in our society, as well as topics related to ministry itself. She concluded that yes, marriage and ministry could both be possible—providing she determined various boundaries, and discussed them with her by then fiancé. Sally was able to make a successful transition because of her prayerful reflection beforehand.

A more painful transition is that of divorce. Sometimes the divorce itself gives rise to ministry. Jean had four young children when her husband divorced her. She realized that she would have to be a primary breadwinner for them, and herself, and so went to graduate school. Geri planned to build on her volunteer work at the parish and, with the degree, seek a position as a DRE. However, in graduate school she did research on ministry with divorced and separated persons. One day she declared: "My family is not broken. We were broken, but with God's grace we are now healed." With that conviction she designed a program for divorced and separated which her diocese eventually hired her to administer on an ongoing basis.

People also make the transition both into and out of religious life. As recounted above, Dolores left her religious community, while she continued in her role as director of religious education in her parish. On the other hand Barbara, who had been a DRE for several years, entered a religious community. Until the time of her canonical novitiate, she continued on in her position in the parish. In both cases, the women received support from many parishioners in the time of their transition. Angelo, a parish youth minister for several years, entered the seminary. After three years, he decided he was not ready for ordination, and returned to a parish to serve again as youth minister for a time. When he was eventually ordained, he brought with him the prior experience of ministry as a layperson in the Church. Statistics show that a significant proportion of lay ministers had been priests, religious, or seminarians before,[51] but there are no statistics on how many have made the opposite transition. What is significant is that the church community is supportive of individuals in these transitions. And that their ministry is not contingent on their church status.

Some lay ministers make the transition to being clerics by being ordained to the permanent deaconate. William had been involved in family ministry for three years before deciding to seek ordination. He did so because he thought it would help his ministry, a new one in his diocese, by giving him clearer authorization. Ray had been a DRE for many years. He decided to become a deacon because it provided a way of symbolizing the permanence of his commitment to work in the Church. Both men said that while what they do did not change, their communities received their ministry more fully. They felt more effective.

NOTES

1. Dolores Gerken, *The Emerging Role of a Director of Religious Education* (Rockford, IL: CORED, Fall 1970), p. 2.
2. Thomas P. Walters, *National Profile of Professional Religious Education Coordinators/Directors* (Washington, D.C.: NCDD, 1983), p. 4.
3. Zenobia Fox, *A Post-Vatican II Phenomenon: Lay Ministries: A Critical Three-Dimensional Study* (unpublished dissertation, Fordham University, 1986). A summary of the sociological data (one part of the larger study) is found in "The New Parish Ministers," *Church*, Spring 1991, pp. 16–21.
4. Philip J. Murnion, *New Parish Ministers* (New York: National Pastoral Life Center, 1992), p. 43.
5. Ibid., p. 45.
6. Ibid., p. v.
7. Philip J. Murnion and David DeLambo, *Parishes and Parish Ministers: A Study of Parish Lay Ministry* (New York: National Pastoral Life Center, 1999), pp. 45–46 and iii.
8. Marian Schwab, "Career Lay Ministers," *Today's Parish*, October 1987, pp. 9–10.
9. Barbara J. Fleischer, *Ministers of the Future: A Study of Graduate Ministry Students in Catholic Colleges and Universities* (New Orleans: Loyola Institute for Ministry, 1993), p. 19.
10. Thomas P. Walters and Rita Tyson Walters, *National Profile of Diocesan Directors of Religious Education* (Washington, D.C.: National Conference of Catholic Leaders, 1998).
11. Charles J. Fahey and Mary Ann Lewis, *The Future of Catholic Institutional Ministries* (New York: Third Age Center, Fordham University, 1992), pp. 6–7. For a fuller exploration of these issues, see Zeni Fox, *Laity in Leadership Roles in the Church in the United States Today: A Theological and Pastoral Overview* (Washington, D.C.: FADICA, Inc., 2000). In this white paper, Catholic institutional ministries are part of what is explored. See pp. 20–21, 24–27.
12. Ibid., p. 148.
13. National Association of Catholic Chaplains Statistical Reports 5 and 6, Membership Demographics, October 1996.

14. Walters, pp. 21, 23–24. Their most recent study is *Catechetical Leaders: A Statistical Profile* (Washington, D.C.: NCEA, 1998).

15. Murnion, pp. 48, 50.

16. Thomas P. Walters and Rita Tyson Walters, "NPCD Membership Survey: 1989 Final Report," circulated to the membership, July 5, 1989.

17. Murnion, pp. 53–54.

18. Fox (1986), p. 234; pp. 242–245.

19. Murnion and DeLambo, p. 23. The percentage of men increased from 15 to 18 percent in the five years between the two studies.

20. Walters (1983), 83 percent, p. 10; Walters (1989), 87 percent, p. 1; Fox (1986), 80 percent, p. 152.

21. Joseph P. Sinwell, Thomas P. Walters, and Rita T. Walters, *National Profile of Diocesan Directors of Religious Education* (Washington, D.C.: National Catholic Educational Association, 1989); the Schwab study also suggested a higher percentage of men in diocesan ministry (p. 10).

22. Murnion, p. 27. In a study of youth ministers only, one-third were men. Zeni Fox, "Research Report on Youth Ministers" and "Youth Ministers and Work Issues" in *Vision and Challenge*, February and April 1994.

23. Ibid., pp. 11–13.

24. Fox (1986), pp. 200–201. A helpful analysis of the possible relationship between salary, gender, and staying in ministry is given by Murnion; he concludes, "That the majority found their compensation 'fair' to 'good' in meeting their family needs is somewhat encouraging. But that nearly one in four found their compensation poor suggests there is real need for improvement, for one must keep in mind that these responses tell only half the story: the story of lay parish ministers who have been able to make ends meet. Those who have not have already left ministry (as the demographics suggest). In essence those in ministry right now are those that can *afford* to be in ministry," pp. 128–129.

25. Murnion and DeLambo, p. 60.

26. Fox (1986), p. 201. Murnion and DeLambo explored why people left their prior ministry position and found that only 5 percent did so for financial reasons, p. 43. But, see note 24 for a reflection on the limitations in this data.

27. Ibid.

28. Ibid., pp. 156–157. Murnion and DeLambo, too, found almost two-thirds of the lay ministers to be married (p. 26).

29. Murnion, p. 83. See also Murnion and DeLambo, p. 52.

30. Ibid., p. 37. This pattern is affirmed in Murnion and DeLambo, pp. 23–24.

31. Murnion and DeLambo, pp. 23 and 41, ". . . 41 percent of the pastors favor a layperson (indeed 38 percent favor a parishioner) while 38 percent favor a religious."

32. Anne Munley, *Threads for the Loom: LCWR Planning and Ministry Studies* (Silver Spring, MD: Leadership Conference of Women Religious, 1992), p. 123.

33. Ibid., p. 194.

34. Ibid., p. 193.

35. Walters (1983), p. 11; (1989), p. 2; Thomas P. Walters, Wayne Smith, and Sylvia Marotta, *A Hopeful Horizon* (Washington, D.C.: National Catholic Educational Association, 1993), p. 8.

36. Murnion, p. 45. However, in the later study, there are fewer general pastoral ministers; "This is related to the fact that there are fewer religious among the parish ministers" (Murnion and DeLambo), p. 46.

37. Munley, p. 195.

38. Murnion and DeLambo, pp. 34–35.

39. Ibid., p. 26.

40. Fox (February, 1994), p. 15.

41. Murnion, p. 50.

42. Fleischer, p. 11.

43. Henry Charles, Dean R. Hoge, Francine Cardman, *Partners in the Conversation: The Role of Ecumenical Divinity Schools in Catholic Theological Education* (New Haven: Catholic Task Force of Yale Divinity School, 1992), p. 16.

44. "Attitudes of Catholic College Students Toward Vocations and Lay Ministries," unpublished report, 1985, p. 9.

45. Fleischer, p. 12.

46. Charles et al, p. 20.

47. Suzanne Elsesser and Eugene Hemrick, *Preparing Laity for Ministry* (Washington, D.C.: United States Catholic Conference, Inc., 1986), p. 17.

48. Bryan T. Froehle, ed., *Catholic Ministry Formation Directory* 1999 (Washington, D.C.: CARA, 1999), p. 187. The researchers note that they received information about race and ethnicity from only about 65 percent of program participants and state: "Because of this relatively low response rate, these percentages should be treated with caution."

49. Murnion and DeLambo, p. 24.

50. "Spanish speaking parishes were not included because Hispanic Catholicism has such unique qualities that a scientific team, field researchers, computer encoders, and others who know Spanish and Hispanic religio-culture would have been needed. Also, Spanish copies of all survey materials would have been necessary." *Notre Dame Study of Catholic Parish Life*, Report no. 1, David Leege and Joseph Gremillion, eds. (Notre Dame: University of Notre Dame, 1984), p. 3.

51. In 1986, 10 percent. Fox (1986), p. 166. "The percent of former religious among the fully laypeople has increased significantly, from about 5 percent of the total in 1992 to almost 13 percent in 1997." Murnion and DeLambo, p. 26.

Chapter Two

Preparation, Education, and Formation

Paths to Ministry

What is it that has brought people into their work of ministry? Different studies throw light on this question in different ways.

Why Ministry?

Over a period of many years now, this question has been asked. It is worth tracing the history of the responses, to note the similarities over time. One study focused on professional DRE's, that is, those with a master's degree and at least three years experience in administration or teaching. The question posed was open-ended. For them, the category "sharing the faith" describes the responses most often given (22 percent of the sample). The researchers state: "Individuals in this group indicate the desire to preach the Gospel, to spread the kingdom and to serve the Church by sharing the good news of salvation." For vowed religious, serving public school students, whom they viewed as "short changed," was the second strongest response (22 percent). For laypersons, being asked by the pastor was second (15 percent). Other reasons, for both groups, included that they fell into it (often after leaving religious life or the seminary), the work uses their creativity and talents, they like working with adults and families, they were assigned, they were called by God, they enjoy theology and working with people.[1]

Another study whose population was employed lay ministers who were not vowed religious asked, who was most directly influential in the choice of church work? A strong majority indicated that an individual priest was most influential. Second was the individual's spouse. (Since a third of the sample was unmarried, this had greater importance than the statistic alone suggests.) Almost as important were lay ministers and women religious; mothers, friends, teachers, and various others were much less influential. Of particular interest in terms of this volume was the fact that 28 percent of the sample indicated that a lay minister was influential in the choice of lay ministry employment.[2]

A third study, of lay and vowed religious ministers, offered a dozen reasons why persons enter church ministry; respondents were asked to rank the three most important for them. Vowed religious had as their primary choices: growth in spirituality, relationship with God, and desire to live in religious community. Laypeople most often named a call to church service, the desire to "serve people" and "be part of church life in a more active way," and the pastors' invitation.[3]

The most recent national study states that half of the laypeople surveyed said that they have experienced a call by God; this is even more true for full timers. The opportunity to be more active in the Church's service to people drew 18 percent, and the desire for various forms of personal fulfillment (for example, integration of faith and work in their lives) drew 23 percent.[4] It is worth noting that the idea of a response to a call by God seems to be articulated more over the years.

An indirect commentary on why people chose ministry is provided by response to the question, why would you stay in ministry work? Lay ministers were asked to rank in order thirteen possible reasons. Three reasons emerged clearly as most important: they enjoy the work, feel called to it, and think it utilizes gifts God has given them. Somewhat less important was the judgment that they contribute to a need which must be addressed. Other reasons given some importance were that the work is challenging and exciting, that the Church and church work are important to them, that the work utilizes skills and experience, and that the people worked with are liked. All other reasons were far less significant; ranked lowest of all were "I need the salary" and "my position has security."

Looking at the commonalities in these studies, it is possible to summarize the findings in terms of internal and external factors which lead to a choice of ministry. The primary external factor is the invitation to church ministry extended by a priest, or sometimes by a lay minister or vowed religious.[5] Other external realities such as salary are not significant. The inner motivation of the ministers could be summarized in traditional church language: they feel a vocation to the work ("a call to church service," "the desire to preach the Gospel"), they have been given charisms to do it ("the work uses their creativity and talents"), they are responding to the needs of others ("the desire to serve people," and "to serve the Church"). Vocation. Charism. Service. Long the language of ministry.

PRIOR TO MINISTRY

One study asked lay ministers what they were doing before their first salaried ministry position. Sixty percent indicated that they were involved as volunteers (some, while studying, some, while working).[6] Another found that about nine out of ten laypersons had volunteered before being hired,[7] and a number had been ministering in a Catholic school.[8] Twenty-eight percent of the ministers were studying before they began; of these, 10 percent were only studying. (Among youth ministers, 32 percent were studying before they began, 20 percent explicitly for church work.)[9] Another 10 percent were involved as a priest, seminarian, or vowed religious.[10] Sisters come to parish ministry with a broad range of prior experience. More than two-thirds of the laypeople had been employed, in profit and non-profit settings, before coming to church work.

The hiring process of sisters and of laypeople is somewhat different. Almost half of the sisters come via their congregation's clearing house services or contacts, or diocesan clearing house efforts. Almost a quarter had some personal contact with parishioners, staff members, or the pastor. Only 2 percent had responded to a national newspaper ad or organizational network.[11]

With the laypeople, prior involvement in the parish as a volunteer had often led to their being invited by the pastor to assume a position. And sometimes, the layperson had suggested establishing a particular ministry and the pastor agreed. Pastors indicated that by far their most important recruitment strategy is to turn to people they know already (87 percent). Certainly, there are many strengths in hiring a parishioner—someone who knows the parish and its people, and who is known by the pastor and the people. However, there are weaknesses as well: their vision can be too parochial, and firing them becomes more complex.[12]

Another aspect of the hiring process is significant. While the pastor is the most important person, councils and their committees or other committees of parishioners also play a role, and contribute to defining both the position and the qualifications.[13] The associate pastor, the entire staff, and the diocesan office also are sometimes involved in the process.

And, although usually the parish minister is directly responsible to the pastor, here, too, occasionally this authority is shared with another staff member or a committee.[14]

INFLUENCES TOWARD MINISTRY

The question of what draws individuals to religious life and priesthood has long been pondered, but no clear-cut answers have emerged. Their families, schools, parishes, acquaintances, and the activities they were involved in were found to have some influence, but no data was conclusive. Very little study has been done of the lay ministers, and here, too, nothing is conclusive.

The central role of invitation by a priest, or a lay minister or vowed religious, has already been named above. Education for ministry is certainly a factor; that will be discussed below. What other influences have been identified?

Youth ministers were asked to identify factors that influenced their choice of ministry. The overwhelming majority indicated it was concern about youth and their needs (87 percent). Their own lack of opportunities as a youth for involvement in the Church was named by 27 percent. All other choices had less than one-fourth response: high school retreat (22 percent), experience as a parent (16 percent), college campus ministry program (14 percent), college theology classes (12 percent), Catholic high school experience (11 percent), parish high school religion classes (9 percent), and college retreat (7 percent). Since they could check all that applied, the fact that church formation/education efforts in high school and college were named by relatively few is significant.[15]

The new parish ministers have been influenced by various church movements, including Marriage Encounter, the charismatic renewal, Cursillo, the Christian Family Movement, Search and Renew. Among lay parish ministers, Renew, Marriage Encounter, and various youth movements were most frequently named. However, Murnion and DeLambo note that fewer report such involvement in their 1997 survey than in 1992. They express concern about the impact on vocations of the decline of the movements.[16]

Lay ministers were asked whether they had a model for their role in the Church. Slightly more than half said they did; of these, more than half said their model was a layperson employed in a parish. Almost a third indicated their model was a vowed religious, and the same number that the person worked in a diocesan office.[17] It would appear that the fact of laity engaged in ministry in parishes and diocesan offices itself influences other laity in becoming involved.

CONCLUSION

There is much discussion in the Church today about a "vocation crisis." The limited data available about the new ministers involved in parish work suggests that they very often have a clear sense of their own call to work within the Church. Furthermore, the call has most often been tested through prior involvement as a volunteer in ministry and, in a sense, validated by the recognition of pastors who hire these volunteers. The desire to serve God and God's people is nurtured through many aspects of the Church's life: retreats, religious education in parishes and schools, campus and youth ministry experiences, various movements, and family life, including the influence of spouses on their lay minister partners.

EDUCATION

The Church has a long history of educating its ministers. In Europe and the U.S., many ancient universities were begun as schools for the education of the clergy. In this country, many colleges were started to educate sisters and brothers for their ministries. Since Trent, seminaries have provided both education and formation of men preparing for priesthood; in recent decades, attention to formation has been more intentional and comprehensive. The Program of Priestly Formation guidelines carefully delineate areas of study that must be included, and norms for formation of men for priesthood. In light of this legacy, what are the educational and formational backgrounds of the new ministers?

　　The education of the new ministers is varied, both in nature and content. It is worthwhile to contrast this fact with cultural norms for other professionals in the United States today. We presume that doctors, priests, and teachers have certain specific degrees. These represent an important credential for their work and assure that a certain body of knowledge and skills has been taught.

Although the credentials do vary, generally speaking, the new ministers are well educated, certainly more so than the population in general. Among the vowed religious, 83 percent have a master's degree, and 41.6 percent of the lay ministers do. Of full-time lay parish ministers, 47.5 percent have a master's degree, an improvement from the 38.2 percent in the 1992 survey. Interestingly 2½ percent of the laity hold doctorates, and 1.7 percent of the vowed religious. Overall, although the decline in the number of vowed religious has led to a slight decline in the educational level of the new ministers, the trend toward more education among the lay ministers is clear.[18]

A recent study shows that 63.7 percent of the lay full-time parish ministers with advanced degrees have them in a pastoral field (liturgy, theology, pastoral ministry, or religious education).[19] However, an older study notes that the highest degree has often been in areas other than theology or pastoral ministry. Education (23 percent), business and administration (7 percent), and counseling or social work (5 percent) are some examples.[20]

However, degrees do not give the full picture of ministry preparation. The majority of the lay ministers (two-thirds) have taken part in non-degree programs, focused on Church topics, half of which were sponsored by dioceses, leading to some type of a certificate.[21]

Perhaps as important as a credential is the perception of the ministers, and their pastors, of the adequacy of their preparation. In theological areas, more than two-thirds of both ministers and pastors judge preparation in Scripture, doctrine, liturgy, and spirituality to be adequate. Fewer say the same regarding moral theology and justice concerns. In specific pastoral ministry areas (family life, social services, youth development, elderly concerns) significant numbers of those who say that these areas are important to their work do not feel sufficiently prepared.[22] Similarly, in regard to specific activities, such as managing conflict, counseling, and motivating people, many feel their preparation was not adequate.[23]

One interesting group to examine is youth ministers; their ministry is somewhat newer than that of DRE's, they are younger and the great majority (88 percent) are lay. What is their educational background? First, one notes that a third of the youth ministers had been students before their employment, most studying explicitly in preparation for church work. In the past very few new ministers had followed this student-to-minister path. Second, one finds that at the undergraduate level only 9 percent and the graduate level 7 percent of the youth ministers completed degrees in theology or religious studies. Furthermore, only about half of the youth ministers attended Catholic high schools, and less than half Catholic colleges, so a certain immersion in Catholic culture did not characterize the preparation of many. Youth ministers, who are handing on the tradition to the next generation, and often preparing volunteers for that task as well, do not have the religious and theological education usual for priests and religious or even DRE's. Furthermore, lay youth ministers do not consider such education that important for effective work with youth; they rank youth ministry education as more important.[24]

It is worthwhile contrasting these general statistics with those presented by Louise Bond in her report on participants' evaluations of ministry training programs, degree and non-degree. She found that 97 percent are satisfied with their abilities. Participants did identify areas in which they need more training (managing conflict ranked highest), but their overall assessment of their preparation for ministry was positive.[25]

Although no longitudinal studies have been completed, we can compare the results of a national study of lay ministers completed in 1986, with the laypeople in the 1992 and 1997 studies from which the statistics about education, given above, were taken. The proportion of those holding a master's degree has been increasing: 37 percent in 1997, 33 percent in 1992, and 26 percent in 1986. Similarly, doctorates were held by 2½ percent in 1997, 2 percent in 1992, and less than 1 percent in 1986. And in 1997, high school (or less) was the highest level of education for 6 percent, compared to 22 percent in 1986. The number holding certificates is about the same in both studies.[26] Add to this data the fact that younger lay ministers are better educated,[27] and one can say that the trend is toward a more educated group of lay ministers, although their educational level is not equal to that of vowed religious.

Finally, it is worth considering how the education of new ministers is funded. Traditionally, dioceses have borne most if not all of the cost of educating diocesan clergy; religious communities have financed education of their members. However, an older study shows that the lay ministers self-report that almost half their education was funded by themselves or their families. The parish underwrote the education of 28 percent, and paid part of the cost (with the individuals) for another 17 percent; the diocese funded the education of 1 percent. Whereas parishes funded undergraduate, graduate, and certificate study, they were more likely to pay for the latter.[28] Recognizing the importance of this issue, the Subcommittee on Lay Ministry of the USCCB surveyed graduate institutions and dioceses regarding financial assistance for laypersons. Graduate schools listed in the 1999 CARA Ministry Formation Directory who enroll laypersons preparing for ecclesial ministry were sent surveys; there was a 69 percent rate of return. Seventy-nine percent of the schools provided some type of financial aid to Catholic lay students, totaling $7,717,766. The dioceses had an 81 percent completion rate; they reported that 56 percent provided financial assistance to laypersons enrolled in graduate programs in preparation for ecclesial ministry, distributing a total of $1,598,025. Dioceses were also asked whether the topic of educational financial assistance for laypersons had been considered by diocesan leadership in the last few years. Sixty-two percent said yes, 38 percent, no.[29]

We can see significant shifts occurring in the funding of ministry education. Individual ministers are paying for their own education to an extent not done before in the Church. Graduate institutions are making a major contribution toward financing students preparing for church ministry. In 2001, compared to 1986, dioceses are taking more of a role in funding graduate education for their lay ministers. These shifts need further study, especially relative to the preparation for ministry of those from poorer parishes.

FORMATION

The Church has always understood that it is not just what a minister knows and does that is important but that who the person is requires attention. Programs of formation in recent centuries have been worked out according to varied models, in seminaries and novitiates.[30] Over the course of the past fifteen years a growing awareness of the importance of formation, and increasing consensus about what it should include, can be traced.

In lay ministry training programs, degree and non-degree, an early study found that most offer a combination of academic study, ministerial skills development, spiritual formation, and supervised field experience. Furthermore, "twice as much time is given to spiritual formation of participants in non-degree programs as in degree programs." Formation opportunities included Eucharistic liturgies, prayer/reflection groups, prayer services, retreats or days of recollection, and spiritual advisors.[31]

Among youth ministers two-thirds reported that they had formation opportunities in their preparation programs. Of these, 85 percent indicated their formation was good to excellent. Another 21 percent said they had received spiritual formation in a setting other than their preparation program.[32] Perhaps the various groups and movements within church life today were envisioned here.

A broad range of formation opportunities are offered through preparation programs. One study of degree and non-degree programs found that of the many possibilities, 50-80 percent of participants highly rated opportunities for Eucharistic liturgies, faith-sharing, Scripture sharing, spiritual direction, and spiritual reading. Other formation offerings included retreats, journaling, methods of discernment, theological reflection, and Liturgy of the Hours.[33]

Some years ago, a survey of graduate programs indicated that not all directors thought that spiritual formation should be a component. Ten percent strongly disagreed, and 17.5 percent tended to disagree with the idea of graduate programs being actively involved in this area. And, while 70 percent agreed that graduate programs should be actively involved, only 36 percent required students to participate in some form of spiritual formation as a part of their graduate program. As one director said, "We oppose the concept. As adults, our students have their faith communities in which we encourage them to participate."[34]

More recently, considerable attention has been given to the spiritual formation of lay ministers. At their yearly meeting, AGPIM (the Association of Graduate Programs in Ministry) has had an ongoing focused discussion on the topic, and a committee has continued conversations, probing models and components. In 2001, NALM (the National Association for Lay Ministry) sponsored an institute on the spiritual formation of the minister. The anticipated audience of 50 swelled to over 120; many seasoned leaders, confident of their efforts, shared perspectives and sought ways to further improve their programs. While the majority of those present represented diocesan programs, college and seminary formation leaders also attended.

A recent survey, done for the Subcommittee on Lay Ministry, demonstrates that the sense of the importance of spiritual formation for lay ministry has matured. Of all the programs (diocesan, college, seminary, clinical, pastoral education, or CPE and independent), 71 percent have a spiritual formation component. The group most likely to have this is the seminaries: 87 percent include spiritual formation, whereas 57 percent of colleges have formation for ministry candidates. The survey was helpful for identifying the general consensus that exists about components of such a program. Theological reflection is required by 78 percent, and faith sharing, shared prayer, and academic courses on spirituality are required by 60 percent or more. Higher percentages still offer these elements, than require them.[35] A follow-up consultation with a select group of ministry formation directors reflected on the report, and raised a significant question: "Is it time to start towards a document similar to the *Program for Priestly Formation* that focuses on lay ecclesial ministers?[36]

An additional dimension of spiritual formation is assessment of the suitability and readiness of persons for ministry. Many programs report a screening process to assess a candidate's spiritual readiness for the program (53 percent). Mechanisms for this process include letters of recommendation, a personal statement, an interview, and a self assessment process; each is used by more than 50 percent of the programs. (Though not reported in the survey results, some schools do use psychological testing, a process widely used with prospective seminarians.) Less frequent is a formal spiritual formation assessment process, reported by only 28 percent of the programs. Programs sponsored by seminaries are at least twice as likely to have such a process than those sponsored by dioceses, colleges, or independent groups.[37]

The data suggest that formation of laity for ministry sometimes includes intentional efforts focused on the development of ministerial leaders, and sometimes flows from the formation of Christians within the general life of the Church. The question of whether laity called into ecclesial ministry should be required to take part in a formation program is now clearer. The further questions of who should offer it, what should be included, and what duration is needed continue to require reflection. There are many questions that have not yet been explored by the official Church, but which individual program leaders are struggling with continuously. As the official Church engages these issues, consultation with such experienced leaders will be important.

SOCIALIZATION

There has been limited critical reflection on the processes of socialization which play a part in the formation of ministers. Religious educators have explored the role of religious socialization in faith formation, and their work provides a helpful context for examination of this issue. A definition offered by Westerhoff provides an outline of the concept:

> Religious socialization is a process consisting of life long formal and informal mechanisms, through which persons sustain and transmit their faith (world view, value system) and life-style. This is accomplished through participation in the life of a tradition-bearing community with its rites, rituals, myths, symbols, expressions of beliefs, attitudes and values, organizational patterns, and activities.[38]

Central to the concept is the idea of participation in the life of a community. Within this community, there are things that are explicitly taught, and others that are implicitly communicated. "The implicit curriculum . . . is what gets said in what is suggested, what is 'taught' by such things as organizational structure, forms of direct address (for example, the use of titles in contrast to first names) and patterns of decision-making."[39] Realization of the effects of socializing processes in the Church has led to increased awareness of issues such as the importance of which Marian feasts are celebrated in a community, what part of the parish budget is allocated to works of service and justice, and who stands within the altar rail (whether it is literally or symbolically present).

Just as persons are socialized into a faith community, so too they are socialized into particular roles within a community. Lay ministers have recently begun pondering the implications of their professional socialization into ministry. Central to the conversation are the following concepts. The "initial professional education must be in part initiation into a role, the inculcation of an attitudinal as well as a cognitive scaffolding upon which professional behavior is built."[40] Second, "this process of initiation takes place within a social matrix and results in deepening insertion in that matrix."[41] Third, the scope of professional socialization is wide, "a somewhat special language, an ideology. . . shared standards of relevance. . . models for social etiquette and demeanor, certain customs and rituals suggestive of how members are to relate to colleagues, subordinates, superiors, and outsiders. . . " Finally, an aspect of professional socialization is "the shared ordeal" which elicits solidarity among those involved.[42]

Examination of each of these aspects of socialization is warranted. Since the attitudes, knowledge, and behavior central to the professional socialization process is focused toward initiation to a role, a central question is, what is the role that programs preparing laity for ministry envision? What do the individuals who enroll in these programs themselves envision? As has been noted above, there is not clarity about roles, education, functions to be performed, and so on, when we ponder the emerging new ministers. How can people be socialized into a role when the parameters are not defined?

The second aspect of the socialization process is the social matrix in which it takes place. For physicians and police officers, for example, the social group is clearly delineated. In training, one begins to be part of the community; when training is completed, and one takes the Hippocratic oath or is inducted into the police force, one is defined as a member of that community, and is received as such by older members. What community is the lay minister part of? The Christian community, of course, but as a minister within that community, how can the professional community be named? And, if we can name the community, when does the lay minister become part of it? In light of the various paths to ministry noted above (volunteer first; hired first, then educated; religious first, then lay minister; DRE today, pastoral associate tomorrow) designating a "when" becomes very difficult, especially since there is no formal initiatory event.

The diversity of educational backgrounds of lay ministers easily highlights the difficulty in developing a common special language, ideology, standard of relevance, and models of social etiquette. Furthermore, because of this diversity, there is not a common experience of a shared ordeal. Yunker notes that "the length, intensity and close collaboration of this shared ordeal forges the collegial ties so characteristic of the medical profession."[43] Strong collegial ties among lay ministers *per se* are not prevalent; in fact, often tensions exist between subgroups such as DRE's and youth ministers.

But is the idea of professional socialization even relevant? Some people say that ministry is not a profession. Therefore it is worth considering the ways the concept of "profession" has been used regarding ministry. By way of definition, the Oxford English Dictionary (OED) states that the word applies especially "to the learned professions of divinity, law and medicine."[44] Similarly, Yunker says, "the term 'profession' in its earlier and more restricted usage referred to the fields of medicine, law, ministry and university teaching."[45] When one examines the use of the term regarding lay ministers, diverse patterns emerge. For instance, quite early in the development of the role of director of religious education many individuals involved in the work and others describing their role designated DRE's as a distinct group of professionals.[46] On the other hand, at the same time the USCC was gathering information about DRE's, viewing them simply as the people responsible for a parish religious education program. Priests, volunteers, those with masters and those without bachelor's degrees were all equally called "DRE."[47] More recently, youth ministers and pastoral associates have been concerned about professionalization, as efforts put into the development of competency standards demonstrate.[48] However, hiring patterns that sometimes bear no relation to academic background or credentials show that their standards are not, in practice, the norm. One can conclude that whereas ministry has traditionally been considered a profession, lay ministers may or may not be considered professionals.

Further light can be shed on this issue by reflecting on another OED definition. "Profession: A vocation in which a professed knowledge of some department of learning or science is used in its application to the affairs of others."[49] A vocation—most most lay ministers say that they feel called to their work[50] (even though the official Church has no way of naming this calling)—and the work they say they feel called to they name as "ministry." Great numbers of them participate in degree and certificate programs (not to mention workshops and conferences) seeking the knowledge needed for their work. They act like professionals.

And so we encounter an ambivalent situation within the Church in regard to the professionalism of these new ministers, while at the same time the professionalism of the clergy is accepted. The difference between priest ministers and lay ministers is particularly evident when one contrasts the socialization of priests with that of lay ministers. Whereas the role of the lay minister is not clear, that of the priest is so sharply defined that theologically we say ordination changes a person ontologically, and legally state that only by special dispensation can the role be abrogated. The role itself embraces several functions and may be exercised in diverse ways and settings (for example, teacher in a school, administrator in a diocesan office, or spiritual director at a retreat center), but the centrally defining role of priest, to which he has been socialized, remains. The clerical community is clearly delineated—each year the precise number of U.S. priests is published—and quite close knit. Events like a chrism Mass or the funeral of a priest (or his mother) give expression to the community esprit, and numerous "priest only" events are held in the Church. The ideology of priesthood gives rise to papal pronouncements, theologies of priesthood, and books supporting the spirituality of priesthood. The models for social etiquette, especially in ritual contexts, are an important aspect of education for priesthood. And priests throughout the world can share stories of their time in the seminary, a shared ordeal.

One concrete way of examining an aspect of these differing socializations is to think about how individuals come to a first ministry position. Think first of a new priest. The young man began discerning a call to ministry several years before. He was assisted and supported by many in the process: the whole Church that prayed often for priestly vocations; a vocations director, perhaps his pastor, seminary teachers, and formators; his fellow seminarians with whom he shared daily life for several years; the bishop, as he called the man to the orders of acolyte, lector, and deacon, each step marking a gradual entrance into his eventual role as a priest. Throughout these years, the importance of the call and his response is much emphasized; this contributes to the shaping of his identity. This process has a very public dimension. Eventually, the man is ordained, and then is assigned by the bishop to a parish.

Think now of a lay minister. Most lay ministers say they feel called to their work. They are often influenced in their choice of parish ministry by a parish priest and helped by spouses, family, and/or friends. There is no public dimension to their discernment, no ritual markers. The individual begins ministry when she/he is hired in a parish as a lay minister.

Assigned. Hired. Some corollaries of these two words could be: assigned—missioned, called, sent; hired—got a job, signed a contract, achieved a salary. And the "reversal" of the process is interesting, too: those who were assigned are reassigned, those who were hired may be fired. All of the dynamics of a socialization process are inherent in this example: an ideology, a community, social expectations, and so on.[51]

In the Church today, collaboration is much emphasized. But the differences in the socialization processes for priests and lay ministers often make collaboration very difficult. And both the priest and the lay minister may be at best only partially aware of what has shaped the attitudes, thinking, and behavior manifested in any particular situation. Until these issues are more systematically examined, understanding of the dynamics will continue to be, precisely, unexamined. Problems of collaboration will continue to be aggravated by the differences built into the structure. And any progress toward devising socialization processes focused on the ideals for ministry proposed in today's Church will be impeded.

EDUCATIONAL PROFILES: SOME VARIATIONS

Ministry training other than that offered for priests and religious through seminaries and novitiates is still quite new. Of the 156 programs identified in 1986, 80 percent were then ten years old or less. Only 4 percent of the programs had begun before 1965, the year the Council ended.[52] In light of this newness, what can we observe about the educational path of particular ministers?

One glimpse of the diversity is provided by reflecting on the experience of a single suburban community in 1969. That year, of the eight parishes in the town, five had DRE's, four employed and one volunteer. Two of these were single women who came to the community from out of state to assume their positions. One woman held a master's degree in education, the other a master's in religious education, from a program begun in 1964. One of the group was a sister, also from out of state, who held a master's in theology, from a program begun in 1962. The two married women did not have a ministry credential. One of them would eventually obtain a diocesan certificate from a program begun in 1985; the other would receive a master's in religious education from a program dating from 1964. All of the women had prior working experience in Catholic schools.

In the twenty-five years since then, these kinds of patterns have been frequently repeated. For example, Louise began working in the parish as a volunteer catechist. After some years, when the DRE was leaving, the pastor asked her to assume the responsibilities of the role. Louise had not completed her bachelor's degree because of her marriage and the birth of her children, but when she decided to take the job as

DRE, she was determined to return to school as well. Eventually, she would also complete a master's in pastoral ministry, continuing in the same position in her parish. Her role provided the motivation to seek academic credentials for her work. Pat, on the other hand, had been working in the business world for ten years when her company closed. She decided to use the opportunity to do some Scripture study, which had long fascinated her. Although her original intention was simply her own enrichment, she eventually would complete a master's in theology. During her studies, she started some Scripture sharing groups. Her success with them led to an invitation from an area pastor that she become their DRE. Her studies and moving into a ministry position both evolved over time in unplanned ways.

Jack had been involved in youth and campus ministry during his own school years. As a result of his experience, he was offered a position as youth minister in his parish community. He pursued a certificate in youth ministry at the local university, and then continued on in a pastoral ministry degree program. During this time, he also moved to another youth ministry position in a nearby diocese. Often certificates represent an initial credential for parish ministers, with master's level work later.

Jean was a religious studies major in school, primarily because religion interested her. She also was involved in leadership roles in her college's campus ministry programs. In her senior year, she decided to pursue a master's in pastoral ministry, although she was not certain about what kinds of positions would be available. Jean would eventually become a campus minister herself. Her path of study for ministry as a young adult did not exist in 1969. Even today, it is a minority of ministers who decide on a ministry education and work direction in their college years.

Finally, it is worth reflecting on couples who work in ministry. Mike and Sally met in graduate school while pursuing ministry related degrees; both had prior ministry work experience, and both resumed parish positions after their studies. Lucy and Jack were recent college graduates when they met in a certificate training program. Each of them worked in a ministry setting after completing their studies. On the other hand, Katherine and Ben decided in their 40's to move into church-related work; they each pursued a degree and then sought ministry positions. As young adults, Lil and Tim worked together as volunteers in ministry; they later pursued degrees together, and eventually began new ministry work, again together. For couples like these, issues surrounding the cost of their education are particularly important, because neither partner earns sufficient money to truly offset expenses.

TWO FORMATION MODELS

In reflecting on the formation of the lay faithful, John Paul II has placed this task within the context of "the call to growth and a continual process of maturation, of always bearing much fruit" of each Christian. The fundamental objective is "an ever-clearer discovery of one's vocation and the ever-greater willingness to live it so as to fulfill one's mission."[53] These words apply, of course, to every Christian, lay, clerical, vowed religious. So too, the rich resources of the Church's tradition for the formation of its members are the legacy of every Christian. Nonetheless, we have recognized that a certain kind of formation is needed for clergy and members of religious communities (and that for the latter, different formation is needed for the contemplative or the apostolic life).

What kind of formation is needed for the new ministers in the Church? Persons responsible for the education of laity for service in the Church have pondered this question. Many training programs have evolved, each with a unique combination of requirements, recommendations, and invitations. Two models will be described here; they have in common the kind of focus John Paul II recommends: opportunities for growth, maturation, ever-clearer discovery of vocation, and focus toward mission.

In the first model, assessment of the suitability of the candidates begins before admission to the program. Letters of recommendation from persons in ministry, interviews, and psychological testing are required. During the course of their studies, participants are required to have a spiritual director (of their own choosing) and to make a retreat of several days duration. Opportunities for communal liturgical celebration and evenings of reflection are provided. A ministerial mentor is assigned to each student. Field education is required, but is considered part of the educational rather than the formational program.

In addition, each student is required to take part in two offerings designed to assist growth and a fuller discovery of vocation. The first is a year long, one-evening-a-month gathering whose focus is community building (a shared meal and Eucharistic liturgy), shared prayer, and an experientially focused exploration of the spiritual life. The latter is rooted in Ignatian spirituality, and seeks to deepen the capacity for discerning God's movement within the individual's life, community, social setting, and world. The second offering is a course, part of which examines issues central to the leadership role of lay ministers.

In the second model, while there is also pre-acceptance screening, an in-depth ongoing formal evaluation process involving the student and faculty continually assesses suitability and capability. (The process is similar to that used with seminarians.) Spiritual direction, individual mentoring, and opportunities for retreats are also available.

In this model, personal and ministerial formation are particularly focused through several courses. These include field education and courses designed to assist students in exploring their ministerial identity. The informing spirituality is Vincentian. A focus on the charism of Vincent de Paul and Louise deMarillac permeates the formation program. A commitment to the poor as part of their ministry is encouraged. Lay graduates speak of serving in the spirit of Vincent and Louise.

What both of these models particularly seek to foster is growth in realization of the vocation to ministry that has impelled the students to enroll in the programs.

SOCIALIZATION AND ITS CONSEQUENCES

The differing socialization of priests and lay ministers was examined above. The consequence of these two patterns of socialization, one of which is defined, one diffuse, is that many unexpected difficulties arise as priests and lay ministers strive to work together in the collegial fashion the Church today expects. Consider the similarities and differences between the working together of doctors and nurses, in the medical field, with that of lay ministers and priests in the Church. Doctors and nurses belong to different, and defined, professions; they perform different functions, for which different education has prepared them; they identify with different groups both in their settings and in professional networking. Each group has specific expectations of themselves and of their counterparts in the other group.

Do lay ministers and priests belong to the same profession? Some lay ministers have the same education as priests, perform many of the same functions, and use the term *ministry* to name the professional group to which they belong. Most priests use the term *ministry* to describe their role (although they also use the term *priest*). Many priests invite lay ministers to be part of their professional group in the parish (through staff meetings, for example) and in professional networking (being part of vicariate meetings or an ecumenical Fellowship of Clergy, for example). At the same time, many lay ministers speak of being made to feel unwelcome by some staff members and area professionals when they do attend meetings which some view as ministry, and others as priest, gatherings.

Lay ministers also report various instances of their failure to follow models of social etiquette that priests knew well but of which they were unaware. One group described a process of working out standards of ethical behavior and just treatment for lay ministers. The group included diocesan personnel, priests and lay, and parish pastors and lay ministers. After much work and broad consultation, the finished guidelines were presented to the bishop, who said he did not see a need for them. However, he was willing to meet with the group to discuss the question. At the meeting, there was lively dialogue—between the lay members and the bishop. To the surprise of the laity, the clergy present spoke only when first addressed by the bishop. The priests' sense of obedience to the bishop was such that they did not align themselves with the work group and its product, despite the fact that they had been fully active members of the group and had contributed significantly to its work. Their socialization contributed to the dynamic of identification with the bishop and of speaking in this public forum only when spoken to.

A university group had planned a small invitational conference; participants included professional lay ministers, priests, and bishops. For the closing liturgy, the conference coordinator announced that a pastor from a local parish would be the presider, and asked that there be no concelebrants. This was done because the planners thought that with so many clergy present, many concelebrants would accentuate the clerical-lay divide in the group. The priests and bishops were angered by this, because it did not honor the bishop's requirement to preside—a norm the lay planners were unfamiliar with. In discussing the situation afterward a priest commented that everyone knew about the expected practice—but a more precise comment would be that everyone socialized to clerical etiquette knows that. The embarrassed and chagrined lay planner did not.

A more subtle example is noted when observing the dynamic when a group of seminarians and lay ministers are present in class together. Generally, the laity are much more likely to question, to challenge, to disagree than are the seminarians. For the latter, the social etiquette they are being socialized into affects their behavior; the laity are not similarly socialized. Furthermore, at times, seminarians judge lay students to be disruptive, and lay students judge seminarians to be passive—because they are using differing norms of acceptable behavior. Long after their years in school, the differing emphases arising from these socialization processes will still affect behavior of lay ministers and priests; the former may emphasize the need for critical reflection and honest dialogue, the latter the importance of adherence to the mind of the bishop and loyalty.

NOTES

1. Walters (1983), pp. 34–36.
2. Fox (1986), pp. 216–217. Murnion found that the pastor's personal invitation was a reason that almost half the laypersons gave for entering church ministry (p. 37).
3. Murnion, p. 27.
4. Murnion and DeLambo, p. 39.
5. It is worthwhile to reflect on the parallel here with findings regarding vocations to priesthood. Encouragement from others (especially vocation directors, religious sisters or brothers, and priests) is the most important single factor in influencing men in their interest in vocations. "Attitudes of Catholic College Students Toward Vocations and Lay Ministries," Dean Hoge (unpublished paper, 1985, p. 20).
6. Fox (1986), p. 166.
7. Murnion, p. 37.
8. Murnion and DeLambo, p. 38.
9. Zeni Fox, "Youth Ministers and Their Ministry: A Profile," unpublished report, Center for Youth Ministry Development, 1993, p. 12.
10. Fox (1986), p. 166.
11. Murnion, p. 40.
12. Ibid., pp. 36–39, and Murnion and DeLambo, p. 40.
13. Murnion, p. 41.
14. Murnion and DeLambo, p. 65.
15. Fox (1993), p. 38.
16. Murnion and DeLambo, pp. 39–40.
17. Fox (1986), pp. 217–218.
18. Murnion and DeLambo, p. 27.
19. Murnion and DeLambo, p. 27.
20. Murnion, pp. 33–34.
21. Murnion and DeLambo, p. 29.
22. Ibid., p. 30.
23. Ibid.
24. Fox (1993), pp. 12–13.
25. "An Evaluation of the Effectiveness of Lay Ministry Training in the Roman Catholic Church of the United States," unpublished D.Min. thesis, Catholic University of America, 1988.

26. Fox (1986), pp. 158–159, Murnion, p. 31, and Murnion and DeLambo, pp. 27–28.
27. Murnion, p. 32.
28. Fox (1986), pp. 161–162.
29. Report submitted to the Subcommittee on Lay Ministry by Dean R. Hoge and Ding, Kounian Life Cycle Institute, Catholic University, October 2001.
30. The issue of the formation of the laity in general is not what is being explored here. However, it is worth noting the link made between education and formation in *The Formation of the Laity* (Vatican City: Pontifical Council for the Laity, 1987): ". . . basic doctrinal knowledge should be completed by spiritual formation and if possible by a form of specialization with a view to a specific apostolate in certain fields" (p. 37).
31. Elsesser and Hemrick, pp. 1 and 9.
32. Fox (1993), p. 14.
33. Bond, p. 4. A very helpful analysis of ways to integrate findings from psychological testing into a formation program, focused toward both personal growth and assessment of candidates is developed by Paul N. Duckro, et. al, "Psychological Assessment in Lay Formation," *Human Development*, vol. 22, no. 4, Winter 2001, pp. 44–48.
34. Charles Topper, Geri Telepak, Thomas Walters, Rita Tyson Walters, *A Survey of Graduate Programs in Ministry 1992–1993* (West Hartford, CT: Association of Graduate Programs in Ministry, 1993), pp. 63, 65.
35. Mary E. Bendyna and Mary L. Gautier, *Spiritual Formation of Lay Ecclesial Ministers: A CARA Report for the Secretariat for Family, Laity, Women and Youth* (Washington, D.C.: CARA, 2001), pp. 7–10.
36. Unpublished report to the Subcommittee on Lay Ministry, "Spiritual Formation Study-Follow-up Consultation," October 2001.
37. *Spiritual Formation of Lay Ecclesial Ministers*, pp. 5, 7.
38. "What Is Religious Socialization?" in *Generation to Generation*, John H. Westerhoff III and Gwen Kennedy Neville (Philadelphia: United Church Press, 1974), p. 41.
39. Maria Harris, *Teaching and Religious Imagination: An Essay in the Theology of Teaching* (San Francisco: Harper and Row, 1987), p. 100. Harris also explores the null curriculum, the areas of study left out, and their effect.

40. Rose Yunker, "Professional Socialization Programs: Texts and Sub Texts," in *Ministry Educators in Conversation: What Kinds of Future* (Proceedings of the Invitational Conference, Association of Graduate Programs in Ministry, 1993), pp. 22–23.
41. Ibid.
42. Ibid., p. 28.
43. Ibid.., p. 29.
44. *Oxford English Dictionary*, vol. II (Oxford: Oxford University Press, 1987), p. 1427.
45. Yunker, p. 22.
46. See, for example, Maria Harsis, *The DRE Book* (New York: Paulist, 1976) and Gabriel Moran, "Professionalizing Religious Education" in *Interplay* (Winona: St. Mary's Press, 1981), pp. 91–105.
47. *A National Inventory of Parish Catechetical Programs* (Washington, D.C.: United States Catholic Conference), 1978.
48. Unpublished paper, "Current Challenge of Professionalization in Ministry," Joseph Merkt, Association of Graduate Programs in Ministry, February 1995.
49. *Oxford English Dictionary*, p. 1427.
50. Unpublished data from survey of persons employed in parish ministry; other data from survey in Fox (1986).
51. For a fuller discussion of the implications of the process of socialization for the identity of the lay minister, see Zeni Fox, *Forging a Ministerial Identity* (Chicago: National Association for Lay Ministry, 1999).
52. Elsesser and Hemrick, op. cit., p. 11.
53. *Christifideles Laici* (*Origins*, February 9, 1989), p. 589.

CHAPTER THREE

SUPPORT, SUPERVISION, AND EVALUATION

SUPPORT

INTRODUCTION

For any organization, support is an important issue in regard to its workers. For the Church, committed to creating community and to bearing one another's burdens, it should be a central concern in respect to its ministers.

The issue of support of persons in their work has several dimensions. These include the work itself (is the work valued? do others think these people should be doing the work?) and the persons as individuals (do they receive emotional/psychological support? financial support? supervision and evaluation?). An additional, though indirect way of inquiring about the adequacy of the support offered is to ask whether people are happy, are satisfied in their work. These are the issues we will turn to now.

SUPPORT FOR THE WORK THEY DO

The Notre Dame Study of Catholic Parish Life, the most comprehensive study of the parish ever undertaken, asked their sample of "core" Catholics the question: "Given limited resources within your parish, toward which of the following activities should the parish direct much of its attention?" Of ten possible choices, the five highest ranked were enhancing the religious education of teenagers, enhancing the religious education of preteens, helping poor people within the parish, making converts and/or reclaiming church dropouts, and enhancing religious education of adults.[1] Not surprisingly, then, when noting what programs parishes offer (other than Sunday Mass) the two most frequently cited were grade school level and high school level religious education. In sixth to ninth places are adult religious education, youth ministry programs, ministry to the aged, and social service programs.[2] Finally, respondents were asked about personal needs or family problems they would turn to the parish for; the religious education of children and of themselves are the two primary areas in which they would seek help from the parish.[3] For the most part these are precisely the functions for which the majority of the new ministers often have responsibility. Clearly, the community thinks this work is an important aspect of its life.

But do Catholics think that laity should have these responsibilities? Several studies help to shed light on this question. The oldest, undertaken by CARA for the Archdiocese of Baltimore, examined the attitudes of pastors, parish council members, and parish ministers toward career lay ministers. Of the pastors, 78 percent expressed clearly positive attitudes toward lay ministers; the kinds of functions they saw as appropriate for lay ministers to perform included work with youth, with planning and coordinating music for liturgies, with sacrament preparation programs, and with the elderly.[4] Similarly, parish council members thought work with youth, the elderly and the sick appropriate; their most highly rated categories were dealing with material and social needs, and coordinating training of parish volunteers.[5] Parish ministers (the majority of these were priests and deacons) also saw planning of music and work with youth, families, seniors, and the sick as central, adding oversight of the maintenance of parish facilities to their list.[6] Clearly, this early study indicates that the Catholic community is supportive of laity performing the functions that are, indeed, now being done by lay ministers.

Another study asked student campus ministry leaders about fourteen tasks that according to church law may be done by persons other than priests. Marriage preparation work, responsibility for CCD programs, and adult religious discussion groups are some of the items.

> A vast majority of the students said that only priests should do two things—officiate at marriages (84 percent said this) and officiate at baptisms (75 percent said this). Also 45 percent said that only priests should preach at Masses. Besides these three functions, the students thought that priestly tasks could be done as

well by other persons. If priests have too much work to do now, about half of the students said that two tasks should be done only by a lay person—supervising work on buildings and grounds (45 percent said this) and maintaining the financial books of the parish (44 percent said this).[7]

The essential openness to a broad range of functions being performed by lay ministers is clear from the study.

In another study, the attitudes of priests, adults, and campus ministry student leaders in relation to possible changes in the Catholic Church also indicates an openness to new roles for laity. Two of the questions were, Would it help, hurt, or have no effect on the Church to "hire full-time lay parish administrators in parishes," and "hire full-time lay religious educators and liturgical experts in parishes." Hiring parish administrators was judged potentially helpful by 63 percent of the priests, 55 percent of the adults, and 72 percent of the students; religious educators and liturgists were judged potentially helpful by 75 percent of the priests, 67 percent of the adults, and 75 percent of the students. Furthermore, in each instance the "no effect" response outnumbered the "hurt" response.[8] Again, the profile that emerges is of an essential readiness on the part of representative groups of Catholics to support the new ministers in their work.

These studies were in the nature of "what if" regarding new ministers; however, some indication of response to the actual ministry of laity can be discerned in some other statistics. When asked whether they had sufficient authority for their ministry, 92.7 percent of the new ministers agreed.[9]

These are, of course, the self-reports of the lay ministers. However, parish leaders and members are also very positive in their assessment of their functioning. When presented with a list of twenty-five areas of parish life and asked whether lay/religious ministers had made a contribution in those areas, in every category 50 to 90 percent of respondents (pastors and parishioners) said they had "added considerably" or made "some improvement."[10] Murnion concludes:

> The most important general message is that the parish ministers have a very beneficial impact on parish life, by everyone's measure. As we will see, they themselves derive enormous satisfaction

from what they are doing, but even more importantly, the pastors and parishioners judge that they are improving the life of the parish.[11]

Within this context of an overview of the positive valuing of the work lay ministers do, it is worth considering their response to a request to rank ways their work situations could be improved. "That my efforts are valued" ranked first by a significant margin. "That my role or function be clarified" and "that people thought more highly of my role" ranked second and third, respectively. The lack of role clarity is in accord with much of the data presented earlier in this book. But it would appear that the lack of appreciation of the work and role implied in this assessment by the lay ministers sounds a cautionary note in regard to the support they receive. While persons may respond positively to the lay ministers and their work in a survey, they may not be communicating their response to the ministers. That the ministers feel that these issues are very important can be seen when one notes that items regarding more money, security, success, and autonomy were all ranked considerably lower than those regarding appreciation of their work and role.[12]

Their response is given particular weight when considered in the context of cultural norms that associate the worth of a position with money, success, and independence. The question of why issues of appreciation are such intense concerns for the new ministers needs further investigation.

Who needs to express appreciation for the work of the new ministers? By their self-report, their most important "audience" is those they directly serve. Whether asked whose praise of their work is most valued, whose critique most painful, whose evaluation they most seek, or who most values what they are doing, the answer was the same, and by a significant margin. Generally, the second most important group is the pastors, and the third the parishioners. Staff, professional peers, and parish lay leaders are also important. However, diocesan personnel and the bishop ranked very low.[13] Perhaps part of the struggle for appreciation can be explained by noting this locus of attention on the people. Those served are always diverse, with varied expectations and understandings of ministry and the minister. As the maxim says, it is not possible to please all of the people all of the time.

SUPPORT FOR THE MINISTERS, PERSONALLY AND PROFESSIONALLY

When asked to whom they turn for personal, and emotional support when they experience difficulty in their work, the response was, primarily to spouses, family, and/or friends. Fellow staff members and other professionals ranked second and third, and pastors fourth. More than half the respondents did not rank the pastor at all in their listings. However, when asked to whom they turn for technical help when they experience difficulty in their work, they named the staff, pastor, and other professionals, in that order, with little difference between the rank given each group.[14] While the support of the pastor is not primary, it is important. "Among the full-time ministers, all but about 15 percent say that the pastor's support is adequate and even fewer feel somewhat distant from their pastors." In fact, the majority of the ministers characterize their relationship to the pastor as team member, colleague, or staff member and the minority as employee.[15]

Another way to measure support is by assessing the structures for interaction and cooperation for members of the parish staff. In 1992 and 1997 the survey results show that the great majority have staff meetings and pray together; more than 80 percent of the parish ministers also report socializing together. (But only 37 percent of the pastors say this, a seeming discrepancy.) The majority of the parish ministers would like more work retreats, days of recollection, and faith sharing than are held; pastors, on the other hand, would like significantly fewer than are held. "All of this shows the continuing need both to discuss such possible ways for pastors and staffs to relate to one another and to recognize that people's interests and needs vary."[16]

For professionals, one source of support is other professionals; professional memberships and informal networking with colleagues provide contexts for sharing ideas and stories of ministry. Many of the new ministers belong to professional organizations, although these are much more likely to be diocesan or area groups than to be national, professional ones. The majority of the new ministers meet at least once a month with fellow professionals; they also frequently confer informally by phone.[17] It could be argued that these meetings are important not only for the professional and personal support they offer, but also for developing, however informally, a sense of who these new ministers are in the Church, a sense of their ecclesial identity.

SALARY AND BENEFITS

Census bureau statistics have shown that of ten professions, persons involved in church ministry are paid the least. As with all non-profit organizations, the issue of how to sufficiently compensate people is a problematic one. The most recent study concludes that "the area that parish ministers think needs the greatest improvement is the salary situation, far outstripping other factors like their interaction with the clergy, their own spiritual development, diocesan support systems, working conditions, and the security they need." On the other hand, the majority (two-thirds) of the full-time ministers report that their salaries are adequate to their needs, and even more say they are satisfied with their salary relative to others with a comparable position. It is important to realize, however, that about one-third do not find their salaries adequate for their needs.[18]

The salaries of lay parish ministers have been increasing. The median salary in 1997 was $23,000; when compared with the 1992 salaries and measured in "real" dollars (adjusted for inflation) there was a 20 percent increase. Some positions command a greater salary (liturgists average $27,966) and some less (general pastoral ministers average $21,975). Men earn more, $26,000, than women, $22,000.[19] It is clear that, given the educational level of the individuals in the sample, their compensation is considerably less than what they probably could command in the marketplace. But as this study, and others, indicate, ministers do not put primary emphasis on salary; indeed, they "regard the privilege of ministry as far more important than the income they receive."[20]

A telling aspect of the salary issue emerges when one asks the ministers about the use of their income. For married women, their salary represents 38 percent of the family income (41 percent if she is working full time). On the other hand, for the average married man their salary is 59 percent of the household income, 68 percent if they are full time.[21] In an older study, one person said, "Men are forced to leave ministry if they intend to marry and have a family. Women stay, if it's a second income."[22] The data suggest this may be the case. Perhaps the salary issue is the primary one for explaining why 82 percent of the new ministers are women.

In addition to salary, benefits such as health care coverage and a pension plan are very important in today's society. The more recent Murnion and DeLambo study does not report on benefits; the older Murnion study gives a dollar value to the benefits the new ministers receive, but it is not clear what benefits are included. Furthermore, the study does not indicate what percentage of the sample receive benefits. A NACPA study found that 9 percent of the employees receive no health care/insurance benefits, and 20 percent no disability insurance.[23]

Another aspect of the question of pensions is their portability. Presently, each diocesan plan is separate; a minister who moves from one diocese to another generally loses the benefits accrued from membership in that retirement plan. In a highly mobile society like ours, this is problematic.[24]

SATISFACTION IN MINISTRY

An indirect way of assessing the support ministers receive is by exploring satisfaction with their work. The data demonstrate that the level of satisfaction is very high. In Murnion's first study he asked if their ministry were satisfying; 94 percent said yes. Asked whether it gave a sense of accomplishment, 92 percent said yes. And, asked if it were spiritually rewarding, 92 percent said yes.[25] Murnion has said that these findings were the most challenged in his study. However, they are consistent with measures of satisfaction from an earlier study. There, when asked why they would continue in church work, the highest ranked response was that they enjoy the work. Not only were they happy in their jobs, 72 percent said they would continue as volunteers in the Church if they left ministry work, while only 3 percent said they would not![26] And in the most recent study, the following summary is offered:

> Parish ministry can clearly be called a wonderful experience for parish ministers . . . (I)n their own lives they have grown closer to God, to the Church, and to the parish . . . More than 90 percent agreed . . . [that] ministry has been affirming . . .

Furthermore, over 80 percent agreed that they would encourage others to enter parish ministry.[27]

Many people have expressed surprise at these positive findings. However, two sub-sets of information and a hypothesis may shed light on this. When identifying characteristics of their working situations, over 85 percent of respondents chose these descriptives: satisfying, good, creative, respected, challenging. And 59 percent chose frustrating.[28]

When asked why they might leave church work, given sixteen possible choices, burnout and frustrations in the work ranked second and fourth.[29] Perhaps, when ministers get together they emote about the frustrations in their work, and do not as often share the joys they experience. But when formally assessing their ministry, while completing a survey, they strongly affirm the positive dimensions.

A final way of reflecting on satisfaction in ministry is to look at the long-term intentions of these ministers. In terms of commitment to a particular place of ministry, we note that there is a pattern of parish ministers moving from parish to parish, or another place of ministry. In the most recent study, two-thirds of the laypersons had worked in another parish or school. They moved for "career" reasons (change, growth), personal and family reasons, and employment conditions in the previous parish.[30] A more telling question is how long they plan to stay in church ministry. In an older study, dated but indicative of an emerging pattern, 38 percent said they planned to continue indefinitely, the same number were unsure, and a sixth planned to leave in three years or less. There was a positive correlation between those planning to continue indefinitely in ministry and those who said they were very happy in their work. A study done about ten years later reports that almost two-thirds of the laypersons, 70.1 percent of the full timers, plan to pursue a lifetime of ministry in the Church. Murnion and DeLambo observed, "There appear to be emerging not only new positions of ministry but also new commitments to ministry . . ."[31] This is precisely what the Church needs to examine more and respond to more fully.

CONCLUSION

The picture of the support given by the community to the new ministers is essentially a positive one. The work they do addresses concerns that are central to the Church's ministry, in the minds of laity and clergy alike. Priests and parishioners generally think that it is appropriate for laypersons to be performing the functions involved in their ministry. They also judge that the work of these new ministers has made a considerable contribution to the life of their parishes. And yet, the new ministers express the strong desire that their efforts be valued and that people thought more highly of their role. Somehow, they do not feel sufficient support. By their own report, they are very happy in their work, and yet many are unsure that they will continue indefinitely. There are some paradoxes involved here that existing studies do not help elucidate. Further investigation is needed in order to better understand how the community can more fully support its new ministers.

SUPERVISION AND PERFORMANCE EVALUATION

THE DATA

As we have seen, the roles held by lay ministers are still relatively new, and many of those fulfilling these roles also are quite new to their work. Especially in light of this information, it is helpful to inquire about their supervision and evaluation.

Murnion considers the issues of performance evaluation and affirmation. He notes that performance evaluations are infrequent; about one in three report this. He places this in the context of church culture, where there is not a tradition of evaluation. Furthermore, some pastors seem reluctant to engage in the very personal and direct communication required by evaluation. He also reports that pastors do not often give "affirmation," that assurance that the work of the parish ministers is valuable and appreciated, which they do look for.[32]

An older study, using the language of supervision ("ongoing oversight and evaluation of their work") also found that only about one-third of lay ministers received this. Significantly fewer indicated that criteria for the evaluation of their work are known and agreed to beforehand.[33] In light of the lack of clarity about their roles that has already been noted, questions about criteria become even more pressing. One wonders, on what basis are they evaluated?

Some further perspectives on how parish ministers view assessment of their work can be gained by exploring additional dimensions of how it functions in the parish. When evaluation is given it is generally the pastor who conducts it; his assessment is understood by the ministers to be most important for their continued employment. However, when asked whose evaluation *should* be most important fewer said the pastor, and a significant number said a committee of parishioners.[34] Similarly, when asked who they most often seek evaluation from, the most frequent response was those they serve.[35] They affirm this despite their acknowledgment that they are directly responsible to the pastor, and that he has the authority to hire and fire them.[36]

This focus on those they serve is apparent in some other data. When asked what gives general guidance as they plan their work for any given day or week, the needs of the people was clearly ranked first. Their own faith and their job description ranked second and third, and direction from the pastor or pastoral team fourth. Several other items were ranked much lower.[37] And, as noted above, those they directly serve are the most valued source of praise, the locus of the most painful critique, the ones they most often seek evaluation from, and those they estimate as most valuing the work they do. Cross tabulation of the responses to each of the praise and critique questions offers an interesting note. About 20 percent name the people they serve in both instances; about 10 percent name the pastor both times and 5 percent the staff both times. Clearly, within the total sample, there are different perspectives on who is the primary locus of attention as they evaluate their work.[38]

The picture that emerges from the data indicates that supervision and evaluation are infrequent. Perhaps this should not be surprising, given the lack of a tradition of evaluation in the Church. However, with new roles and new workers it certainly would be valuable. Further, the data indicate that when there is evaluation, the pastor usually gives it. However, many of the ministers think that parishioners should have a role in evaluating them, and, in fact, they often informally seek that evaluation. Implicit in this view is an understanding of the Church as the people of God. Ministers serve the people, and seek evaluation of their service from the people. Clearly, the pastor is seen as important, but for most of the new ministers his evaluation of their work is not the primary concern.

In this context, it is worth reflecting on the new ministers' assessment of the role of priests. They were asked how important the role of the ordained clergy is in the life of the Church today, compared to the recent past. Sixty percent said it is different today—but not in importance. Fourteen percent see it as more important today, and 18 percent as less important.[39] So, despite their affirmation of their own leadership role and the authority granted to them, the great majority of the lay ministers do not see a diminishment in the role of priests. Their focus on the people they serve is not anticlerical in its origin.

With or without evaluation, at times ministers are fired, and at times they think that this is unfair. What recourse do they have? Asked whether there is a grievance procedure in their parish or diocese (and given yes or no as their choices), 51 percent said yes, 38 percent no, and 11 percent did not respond. Probably they did not know.[40] A sobering finding in a NACPA study is that "only 40 percent of employees and 42 percent of administrators felt that employees would be treated justly in a grievance." In a Church with a primary commitment to justice, this is indeed a disturbing perception. NACPA concludes:

> Much effort needs to be made by church employers to improve the perception of workers about grievance handling in church workplaces. Also much room exists for improvement of church grievance procedures.[41]

A SUPERVISORY PROCESS

In the early 1980s, the Center for Youth Ministry Development (now the Center for Ministry Development) devised a program for training and placing interning youth ministers in parishes and, at times, other youth serving organizations. Recruitment and placement was administered jointly by the Center and participating dioceses. Training was accredited through a local university. A supervision and evaluation process was devised that involved the Center, the diocese, and the placement site. Most of the youth ministers were recent college graduates, with little or no work or youth ministry experience. Furthermore, the great majority of the parishes did not have youth ministry programs in place, and had never had a youth minister. The youth ministers, mostly in their first job, were role and program initiators. They were asked to make a two year commitment. The training program was addressed to developing them as persons and ministers, and giving them knowledge and skills for youth ministry. For eight weeks they lived together, building community, praying, and studying. In class, the emphasis was on the needs of youth and various strategies for meeting those needs in a parish. Twice during the year they would convene again for residential weeks to explore themes of leadership and religious education. A second year provided additional youth ministry study and personal and professional growth opportunities.

When they began their work in a parish, they were assigned a "contact person," usually a staff member, sometimes the pastor himself, with whom they were to meet weekly. The contact person's role was partially that of mentor, helping the new minister learn about the parish and its ways, and partially supervisor, giving support and, eventually, evaluation. An early task of the youth minister, hopefully done with the assistance of the contact person, was to formulate priorities for the year's work.

Late in the fall, the first evaluation visit would be held; late in the spring a second visit was made. The same schedule was repeated the second year. The outside evaluation team consisted of one or more members from the diocesan office and a staff member from the center. The parish evaluation team included the youth minister and a small group designated by the pastor for the task. This group always included the contact person and the pastor. Other staff members were usually part of the team, and occasionally one or more parishioners with knowledge of the youth ministry effort also served.

Before the evaluation visit, parish participants individually filled out questionnaires, which would form the basis of the evaluation dialogues. The youth minister listed his/her priorities, and described how they were being implemented. There were also questions about various aspects of their youth ministry. Some were programmatic (how much time is spent on each dimension of youth ministry), some personal (how were they feeling about their ministry, how were personal strengths/weaknesses affecting their ministry, were they taking sufficient time for prayer, reflection, recreation), some contractual (were living and working arrangements satisfactory, were needed resources available), some focused on staff (were relationships supportive, was communication satisfactory), some structural (were meetings with the contact person satisfactory). Staff members also listed the youth minister's priorities, and assessed progress toward the goals. They rated level of satisfaction with the youth minister and the youth ministry, as well as with the training program, and responded to various specific questions about the youth minister's personal and professional performance. They were asked to offer recommendations for the minister's personal growth, as well as for the youth ministry effort.

At the time of the evaluation visit, the outside team first interviewed the youth minister, for about forty-five minutes. Then they met with the staff as a group for approximately the same length of time. The outside evaluators conferred to identify strong and weak points to high-light and any recommendations they wished to make that had emerged from the interviews. Then they met with the youth minister and staff together for about thirty minutes, to communicate their findings and clarify any issues that arose.

After the visit, a summary of the principal points was sent to the youth minister. If particular recommendations warranted it, needed information was also forwarded to the pastor. Issues that affected several youth ministers were identified by both the diocese and the Center, so that ongoing education opportunities could be tailored to the concrete needs.

SUPERVISION/EVALUATION BENEFITS

A process like this has many benefits. Some are specific to the individual minister and ministry. Others apply more generally. Some of what individuals learned through this process may eventually have been learned through the life processes of growth and maturity. But because of the process, the learning was probably more focused, more communally enriched, and more quickly gained. What kinds of things were learned?

Intentionality: By making a primary focus of the evaluation process discussion of the priorities being addressed in the ministry, and ways they were being implemented, both the minister and the parish were encouraged to be intentional about what they were doing. At the beginning of the ministry, sometimes there was not clarity about the priorities. Expectations needed to be examined. The youth minister needed to learn more about the history and hopes of the parish; the staff needed to learn more about youth ministry strategies. The evaluation process helped the necessary dialogue occur. Many ministers today say that their role needs to be clarified; that was one of the outcomes of this process.

Realistic self-appraisal: Caroline offers a good example of this. Highly motivated, and with very high expectations of herself, she worked with troubled teens. Initially she was very discouraged, feeling that her efforts had little impact. Over time, she began to trust the staff's perception of the importance of the gentleness, love, and patience she brought to the young people, and to believe the staff person who said: "The children here are very damaged. Almost anything you accomplish here is a real achievement." Caroline began to understand her own gifts better, but also to recognize how limited our ability to help really is.

Identifying specific strategies to help ministry: Courses deal in generalities; evaluation visits provided many opportunities for addressing specific issues and strategies. A few examples will easily illustrate this. Kay's relational abilities were strong. As a result, teens often came to her, individually or with a friend, to talk over problems. But that did not augment the numbers at her programs, a keen interest of the parish council. The evaluators suggested that Kay keep a record of how often teens met with her, and present that account as part of her report to the council. Marian was having difficulty with the organization of her time and programming. The evaluators recommended some resources and strategies to both Marian and her contact person. Marge and her pastor had worked out a realistic and comprehensive job description. They were encouraged to share their work with others at a diocesan workshop. As these examples show, the evaluation process offered an excellent teaching opportunity because concrete and specific problems were surfaced for which help could be offered. And the youth ministers and staff were motivated to learn.

Identifying areas of personal growth: Reflection on the individuals as persons and ministers often surfaced areas of needed growth. Roseanne said, "The pastor tells me about things he expects and I get this rising feeling of rebellion. I know he's not my father, but I react as if he were. I really need to work on that." Her self-identified difficulty presented an area of growth. A pastor observed, "If only he wouldn't personalize issues." That led to a helpful conversation which located a conflict with the youth minister's performance, not his person. A parent suggested, "I think that the parents wouldn't think of her as just a kid if she didn't dress so much like one. They have a certain expectation of how a youth leader should look." Marge was allowing her ministry to absorb all of her time. The evaluators addressed the need for a day off, for recreation and renewal. In each of these cases, it is unlikely that the issues would have arisen without the framework of the evaluation process.

Identifying situational factors that affect performance: Persons who have not worked before have not developed their skills for "reading" situations.

Evaluators were often able to bring some perspective. Fox example, Ken recently graduated from college; he had grown up in a sophisticated New York City suburb. He was ministering in a rural, blue-collar community. He was discouraged by his minimum success in drawing youth into the program. The staff's assessment was that Ken was hard-working and well-intentioned, but that he did not relate well with the youth. They decided they needed someone experienced, not a beginner, but were concerned about Ken's feeling of failure. The evaluators were able to help Ken and the staff see the impact of the class difference between Ken and the youth in the parish. The pastor said, "Yes, that's true. Our people are very simple people." And Ken could say, "It wasn't all my fault."

Facilitating communication: Sometimes a third party can provide a helpful bridge for communication. Several examples illustrate this. Maureen said, "I would like to have more regular and frequent meetings with my contact person." The evaluators were able to address the importance of weekly meetings with him. Robin said, "Sometimes I would like more feedback from the pastor." A strategy for eliciting feedback by giving short reports to the pastor with questions about her performance at the end was suggested. Mary expressed her dismay at feeling odd-person-out with a close-knit team. The visitors were able to point out to the team that when a new member joins a group a new group exists and needs community building to include the new members. The evaluation process itself facilitated conversation, both during it and, according to reports of participants, afterward.

Assisting termination: Even when a youth minister's contract was not to be renewed, evaluation served a helpful role. In one instance, the pastor had concluded, "I think she doesn't have the psychological maturity to handle a leadership position. Somebody has to tell her the truth." The evaluation process helped Cathy reflect on what she did well, and assisted her in naming her gifts. It provided a context for her expressing her pain and sorrow at her termination and beginning the process of planning the next step.

CONCLUSION

The data demonstrate that supervision and evaluation of new ministers is minimal. Experience with supervisory and evaluation processes show that they have potential for assisting ministers with their professional and personal growth, and that they provide a context for support of ministers in their work, even at its termination. The process described here drew on people beyond the parish to assist in the task. There are many helpful aspects of that strategy. However, the basic ingredients—an instrument to assist reflection and a structured time to dialogue—can be adapted for use in any parish. One of the youth ministers described her experience of the evaluation process this way, "I have learned what I should be doing, what I'm good at doing, what those books all talked about, and I've seen it happen. I've learned to humbly acknowledge my God-given talents." And a pastor concluded, "This process is very helpful. I wish we had something like this for ourselves."

NOTES

1. Report no. 4 (Notre Dame: University of Notre Dame, June 1985), p. 6.
2. Report no. 8 (July 1986), p. 7.
3. Report no. 14 (March 1989), p. 4.
4. *Career Lay Ministers in the Archdiocese of Baltimore: An Assessment of Future Roles and Functions*, Ann Patrick Conrad and Joseph J. Shields (Washington, D.C.: Center for Applied Research in the Apostolate, 1982), pp. 16 and 20.
5. Ibid., p. 30.
6. Ibid., p. 46.
7. Dean Hoge, *The Future of Catholic Leadership* (Kansas City: Sheed & Ward, 1987), p. 184. A more conservative response is seen in response to the question, what ought lay ministers be able to do. Murnion, p. 90.
8. Dean Hoge, "Attitudes of Priests, Adults and College Students on Catholic Parish Life and Leadership," unpublished paper, January 1986, pp. 7–8 and 25.
9. Murnion and DeLambo, p. 58. A valuable portrait of the acceptance of several "lay pastors" is provided by Peter Gilmour, *The Emerging Pastor* (Kansas City: Sheed & Ward, 1986). See also Gary Burkart, *The Parish Life Coordinator* (Kansas City: Sheed & Ward, 1992).
10. Murnion and DeLambo, p. 52.
11. Ibid., p. 54.
12. Fox (1986), pp. 202–203.
13. Ibid., pp. 204–205.
14. Ibid., p. 188. The very same pattern is repeated in the study of youth ministers, Fox (1994), pp. 32–33.
15. Murnion, p. 56. Murnion found that youth ministers were less likely to feel support than many others in the sample. Similarly, Fox (1994) found that in giving reasons why they might leave church work, 20 percent of youth ministers ranked lack of support by the pastor among their first three choices, and 46 percent among their first eight (of sixteen). And, when saying why they might stay 61 percent did not rank "receive personal support from the pastor and/or colleagues" among their first eight choices (p. 33).

16. Murnion and DeLambo, p. 57.
17. Fox (1986), p. 189 and Fox (1994), pp. 18–19.
18. Murnion and De Lambo, p. 60. Fox (1986) found there was a somewhat predictive pattern of fair/not fair responses according to salary level (p. 194). Furthermore, Fox found a correlation between salary level and educational level, as a pattern, but found significant variations. Some people with masters' degrees earned significantly less than those with high school diplomas. This, too, affects a sense of fairness.
19. Murnion and DeLambo, p. 59.
20. Murnion, pp. 92–93. Focus group sessions with lay ministers also found that while acceptance was a primary issue, financial compensation is a major concern. *NALM Listening Sessions*, David DeLambo (Chicago: National Association for Lay Ministry, 1995), pp. 21–22. Although the population studied is more specific (professional DRE's), in 1992 43 percent of DRE's had salaries of $21,000 or more, and 16 percent $27,000 or more. Furthermore, half of the vowed religious were earning $21,000 or more. Walters, Smith and Marotta, pp. 16, 18.
21. Murnion and DeLambo, p. 60.
22. Murnion, p. 92.
23. Murnion, p. 93; NACPA, p. 12.
24. The focus groups cited in endnote 20 also brought up the portability of pensions issue, p. 22. An earlier study found that only 41 percent of the full-time workers were part of a retirement plan. Since only 23 percent of the sample had worked in ministry less than three years (some diocesan plans have a three-year employment eligibility norm), about one-third of the ministers lack a benefit considered standard by most. Furthermore, some full-time workers had no health care coverage. Because these particular statistics are more time-sensitive than other parts of this study, they are not a reliable measure of what might be found today. Fox (1986), p. 182.
25. Murnion, p. 98.
26. Fox (1986), pp. 198 and 195. Even among youth ministers, who Murnion found to be more dissatisfied in their ministry, 79 percent said they would volunteer, and only 2 percent said they would not (Fox, 1994), p. 23.
27. Murnion and DeLambo, p. 61.

28. Murnion, p. 98.
29. Fox (1986), p. 198.
30. Murnion and DeLambo, pp. iii and 42.
31. Murnion and DeLambo, pp. 39 and 69.
32. Murnion, p. 72.
33. Fox (1986), p. 211. On the other hand, almost half of the youth ministers receive supervision. NACPA found that about 60 percent of parish employees in their survey (this included professional and support staff) had a job description. See *Attitudinal Survey on Working in the Catholic Church*, Ann Margaret O'Hara, ed. (Cincinnati: National Association of Church Personnel Administrators, 1991), p. 6. Without clear job expectations, evaluation is not possible. In fact, NACPA found that 48 percent of employees said they received annual performance appraisal (p. 7).
34. Fox (1986), p. 212 and Fox (1994), p. 36.
35. Fox (1986), pp. 204, 211; Fox (1994), p. 31.
36. Fox (1986), pp. 207–208.
37. Fox (1986), p. 187. The same pattern is found with the youth ministers; they even more strongly place the needs of youth first. See Fox (1994), p. 31.
38. Fox (1986), pp. 204–205.
39. Fox (1986), p. 210.
40. Murnion, p. 109. Fox (1986) found that many said they did not know whether their diocese had a procedure. Furthermore, in the same diocese some said yes and some no. And many judged the process as ineffective when it was used (pp. 213–214).
41. *Attitudinal Survey on Working in the Catholic Church*, pp. 14 and 19.

CHAPTER FOUR

THEOLOGICAL SELF-UNDERSTANDING: PRACTICAL AND CONCEPTUAL

WORK PRACTICES AND RELATIONSHIPS

FOCUS ON THOSE THEY SERVE

Ministers are part of an organization, which is an aspect of the Church. People who work in organizations can direct their attention in various ways—toward their "boss," toward fellow workers or fellow professionals, or toward those who are served by the organization. What is the pattern with the new ministers? When parish ministers were asked what guides their decisions as they plan their work for any given day or week, the needs of the people emerged strongly as the highest ranked. As has been noted above, when asked whose praise is most valued, whose criticism hurts most, to whom they turn to know whether they have done well and who they think most values their work, each time the highest ranked response, significantly more so than the next ranked, was those they directly serve. The only exception was in response to the question, in making decisions in work, whose voice is most important; the response here was, the pastor's. Those served was not offered as a choice; parishioners were ranked second. A second pattern that emerges from this data is that fellow workers, both staff and other professionals, are somewhat important to the lay ministers, and that the bishop and pope are significantly less so.[1] This ranking of the bishop and pope may be influenced by the lack of formal relationship of many of these ministers to the diocese.

COLLEGIAL PATTERNS OF MINISTRY

At both the theoretical and the practical levels, it is clear that the new ministers espouse collegiality. This pattern was evident in the older studies of parish ministers. Ninety percent endorsed the idea of collegiality as a goal for the universal Church, and almost the same percent as a goal for the local church. Furthermore, their practice reflected their theology. Asked how they make important decisions in their work, only 7 percent replied "alone." However, the dominant pattern of collegiality was of shared decision making with the staff (the pastor and/or other staff) rather than the people. Only about 20 percent included parishioners in their decision-making processes. Among youth ministers, on the other hand, this number doubles.[2]

The more recent Murnion and DeLambo study examined the preferences and practices of parish staffs regarding structures for interaction and cooperation. The data indicate that staffs have certain working styles. "A fifth report that they essentially work on their own; 8.8 percent said that they generally worked with the pastors and others; 69.8 percent report that sometimes they work together, but mostly on their own." In the area of decision making, "in 41.6 percent of the situations, parish ministers report that decisions are made by all the staff with the pastor, and half the time with the parish council as well. For 40.3 percent each makes decisions with the pastor or in a few instances on her/his own." In regard to structures of collaboration, lay ministers were much more likely to view them as important than were pastors. With both groups, about 75 percent think staff meetings are important, but regarding work retreats and days of recollection about twice as many lay ministers as pastors consider them as important. Also telling is the term the parish ministers chose to describe their relationship with their pastors: 30 percent said team and 35 percent staff, suggesting a collaborative working style, and only 12 percent and 2 percent, respectively, employee and helper.[3]

The new ministers invite parishioners to be involved in many different ministerial roles. And, both the ministers and the parishioners report that usually or always the people say yes. (Two-thirds of the parishioners and 57 percent of the ministers say this.)[4] The new ministers have also worked with various decision-making groups, including committees, planning teams, and advisory boards. Only 13 percent say they do not work with such a group, and 75 percent have personally formed one.[5] More people are involved ministerially and collegially in shaping the direction of ministry, because of the work of the new ministers.

RELATIONSHIP WITH THE DIOCESE

Both theologically and organizationally, the parish and other institutional ministries are organically related with the diocese. This structured relationship is very clear in the case of diocesan priests, who are assigned to their place and role in ministry by their bishop. And, should a priest have occasion to serve in a diocese other than his own, he must seek the permission of the local bishop. Deacons, too, are individually assigned by the bishop. With vowed religious, the relationship is much less structured. However, the process initiated by the major superiors years ago which requires that a contract be signed by the pastor and the major superior and sent to an appropriate diocesan office, provides some standard formalization of relationship. With laypersons, there is not standard practice.

Some dioceses have initiated a diversity of services related to the new parish ministers. Certification standards and processes, recruitment, screening of applicants for positions, guidelines for ministry positions and salaries, and sample contracts are some examples. Diocesan convening of ministers (for example, meetings of DRE's) provides a way of developing support groups. At other times, lay ministers form these groups themselves.[6] Between 1992 and 1997, diocesan services for parish ministers increased, relative to their placement and training, as well as in establishing personnel policies, providing continuing education, and including parish ministers in diocesan life. Furthermore, this is a trend that both pastors and parish ministers wish to see furthered.[7]

THEOLOGICAL SELF-UNDERSTANDING

MINISTRY

The word *ministry* has re-appeared in Catholic circles in recent decades. *The New Catholic Encyclopedia*, published in 1966, does not have an article on ministry; under that heading it simply says "see Protestant minister." In the 1970s, as the *Catholic Guide to Periodical Literature* demonstrates, many articles began to appear addressing the issue of "lay ministry." It was not until the 1980s that "presbyteral ministry" would be discussed. In this context, it is instructive to realize that in 1986 the word that 60 percent of salaried, professional church employees chose to describe their work was ministry. An additional 13 percent chose other words associated with church mission: vocation, discipleship, apostolate. Ten percent chose profession, and 9 percent other words associated with secular work: position, job, role. Furthermore, participants in the survey indicated that though some originally used another word, they had later adopted ministry to describe their work.[8] Today, the word appears to be universally used by salaried, professional church employees in ministerial roles.

The sociologist John Coleman has pointed out the significance of the prevalence of this word as a "pervasive catch phrase in Catholic circles of religious professionals," not only because of its quick adaptation, but also because those who use it "rarely bother to define the term, so sure are they that everyone knows what ministry means." When a word is "taken for granted, undefined and unreflected on" it "defines our world and charts our view of reality." In this way, it maps expectations, it represents an ideology, it serves as a motivational symbol.[9]

Statistical data demonstrates that the new ministers work longer hours than they have contracted for, at salaries often significantly lower than their educational background would usually command, with little security and a fair level of frustration in the work. And yet, they report that they are very happy. Conversations with them reveal the motivational power that engagement in ministry holds for them. I would contend that calling their work ministry does not add status to what they do, but rather, meaning.

CHARISMS

Traditionally, the Church associates ministry and charism. Almost three-fourths of lay ministers affirm that they have received charisms or special gifts of grace for service in the Church; 6 percent said they have not.[10] While sometimes charism is seen as over-against "order," the official hierarchical organization of ministry, this could not explain why some lay ministers, whose role is unofficial, are unsure about or deny that they have a charism. Perhaps theological understanding of the term is lacking.

AUTHORITY

As shown above, the new ministers think that the authority they need to exercise their roles is delegated to them, and accepted by the parishioners. The ministers also state that they function as leaders in their settings.

When asked to rank in order what gives them their authority for their work in the Church, they responded Baptism and Confirmation, with a strong preference for this response. Professional training and competence was ranked second, and a vocation from God third. The other possibilities were ranked significantly lower, in this order: being hired for the role, a mandate from the community, a mandate from parish priest(s), and a commissioning or investiture. Theologically, the majority of new ministers do not see their authority as derived from the clergy. (However, 25 percent of those surveyed did place this among their first three choices.) On the other hand, the majority do not see it as derived from the community either.[11]

It is interesting to contrast their response about the derivation of their authority and their view of what gives a priest the authority for his work in the Church. A vocation from God was ranked first, with Holy Orders ranked second, and baptism and confirmation, third. While the lay ministers ranked their own professional training and competence very high, the priest's seminary training was not given significant status.

An interesting perspective arises from a cross tabulation of responses to these questions. Two patterns of thought among the lay ministers are then discernable. Thirty-four percent place baptism and confirmation first for both themselves and priests, and 65 percent within their first three choices in both instances. Therefore, one-third of the sample see the sacraments of initiation as the primary authorization for all ministry, and two-thirds see them as very important. The second pattern concerns "a special vocation from God." Twenty-one percent rank vocation first for both themselves and priests; 50 percent rank it first or second. Another significant portion of the sample see vocation as the primary authorization for ministry, and half the group see it as very important. Within the group of ministers, therefore, there are differences in self-understanding.[12]

NATURE OF COMMITMENT

As has been noted earlier, when asked how long they intend to continue in ministry about 40 percent of the lay ministers said indefinitely. They were also asked whether their type of work in the Church implies a permanent commitment, perhaps analogous to that of a permanent deacon. Forty-five percent said yes, and 40 percent no. A cross tabulation shows that the majority who say it is a permanent commitment plan to stay indefinitely (and vice versa), but there are several variations in response.[13] Furthermore, three-fourths of the group said that leaving church work is not like leaving other fields of work. Forty-four percent said they would experience something close to guilt, very much or somewhat; 34 percent said they would feel no guilt. Ninety percent said they would feel a sense of pain or loss, 46 percent very much so. In light of their emphasis on vocation, the responses about guilt and sense of loss are not surprising.[14] What is surprising, especially when one reflects on how happy the ministers are in their work, is that 40 percent are unsure of how long they will continue in ministry. The factors contributing to this need further examination.

In light of the rich ritual life of the Church, respondents were asked whether they would choose a rite of installation for their role, if there were one. In 1986, 40 percent said yes, and 34 percent perhaps. Only 14 percent said no. (A cross tabulation indicates that 24 percent of the total sample both plan to stay indefinitely *and* view ministry as a permanent commitment.[15]) On the other hand, in 1992, 5.7 percent said they were commissioned by the diocese; this number increased to 19.9 percent in 1997. Furthermore, almost all parish ministers indicate that they want to see the diocese so involved.[16] The ritual tradition of the Church does not yet take account of the new ministers, either formally or informally. Especially in light of the questions about the relationship between the diminishment in the numbers of clergy and the increase in laity in ministry, it is worth considering the following.

The statistics indicate that the commitment the ministers envision is generally as laypersons. Only 4 percent say they are not yet finally decided about seeking ordination or entering religious life. Forty percent had never considered these options; others had seriously considered them (17 percent), or had begun to prepare and not continued (13 percent), or left after ordination or vows (12 percent).[17] In all likelihood, the latter two categories would have significantly lessened over the years.

WHY THEY ARE EMPLOYED

The new ministers do not think that the primary reason they are employed is that there is a shortage of priests, nor because of a shortage of sisters. Those reasons ranked third and fourth. Rather, they believe that the community recognizes the need for the areas of specialization they are trained for, and recognizes that a variety of gifts are given to various members of the community. These reasons ranked first and second, by a strong margin. That priests or sisters are not interested in particular areas of ministry were each negligibly ranked.[18]

CONCLUSION

The self-understanding of the new ministers is, surely, influenced by theological discussions in the Church today. They are, as their educational profile shows, well educated theologically, whether through academic or diocesan ministry formation programs. The surveys utilized here, however, asked direct, personal questions—how do you name your work, what gives you authority, how long will you continue in your work in the Church, and so forth. In a sense, what emerges is their personal statement about who they are, theologically. In summary, the majority present this picture: they are engaged in ministry; they have received charisms, or special gifts of grace, for service in the Church; their authority is given in baptism and confirmation, or by a special vocation from God; they are employed because the community needs specially trained ministers and recognizes that a variety of gifts are granted various members. However, while the great majority say they would feel a sense of pain or loss if they were to leave church work, a minority plan to continue indefinitely. And, while a large majority are open to a rite of installation for the role, less than 20 percent have been commissioned. The ambivalence they feel about continuing is mirrored in the ambivalence the community shows about formally ritualizing their ministry.

NOTES

1. Fox (1986), pp. 185–186, 204–205. Although this study is dated, these issues have not been surveyed more recently. As an indication of the locus of attention of a group not socialized into a hierarchical structure, it has descriptive value, even if it is no longer predictive of the present group of parish ministers.

2. Ibid., pp. 237–238; Fox (1994), p. 17. The Murnion study gave very similar results, although the focus of the questions were slightly different (pp. 74–75).

3. Murnion and DeLambo, pp. 57–58.

4. Murnion, pp. 104–108.

5. Fox (1986), p. 239. With youth ministers, the commitment is even stronger; only 13 percent have not helped to form a decision-sharing group (Fox, 1994, p. 18).

6. Murnion, pp. 104–108.

7. Murnion and DeLambo, pp. 65–66.

8. Fox (1986), pp. 220–221.

9. "The Future of Ministry," *America*, March 28, 1981, p. 243.

10. Fox (1986), p. 222.

11. Ibid., pp. 222–223.

12. Ibid., pp. 224–225.

13. Ibid., pp. 228–229. The NACPA study found a higher percentage (60 percent) who expected to work always for the Church. Interestingly, 95 percent of deacons in their study expect to do so (p. 8).

14. Ibid., p. 204.

15. Ibid., p. 229.

16. Murnion and DeLambo, p. 65.

17. Ibid., p. 242.

18. Ibid., p. 236.

✛

Section Two

Responses by the Church
to the New Ministers

INTRODUCTION

Many and varied individuals and groups have contributed to the developments in the Church associated with the roles and functions of the new ministers. The ministers themselves, whose personal experience is of their call to ministry—from God, from the community—represent an initial response. Those who encouraged them including priests, spiritual directors, spouses, teachers, families, and friends also represent a response of the Church. Pastors and others who saw a pastoral need and recognized that the new ministers could help fulfill it played an important role. Clergy colleagues and parishioners who accepted the new ministers, by that acceptance, responded. Bishops, individually through diocesan initiatives, and collectively through the United States Conference of Catholic Bishops, have begun to respond. And all those in universities, colleges, and dioceses who helped design education and formation programs, developing preparation criteria for not-yet-defined ministries, added an important dimension. Especially in the late 1960s and early 1970s, many individual and discrete actions by all of these people began to create the scenario that today has a national profile. Over time various groups have begun to focus collective attention on this new phenomena: they raise questions, identify issues, advocate for particular responses. In this section, a brief overview of some of these groups and their efforts will be given. Obviously, those considered are not all who have contributed. Individually, the work these groups are doing is important. Collectively, in many ways, their efforts are part of a great discernment process by the Church, as we strive to respond to this new development in our midst.

CHAPTER FIVE

CANONISTS

EARLY WORK: THE PERMANENT SEMINAR

Law is indeed a conservative dimension of the Church. It attempts to order the life of the community at a particular time in history. But the work of canonists, a work of examining precedent and the law, and making interpretation in the face of pastoral need, necessarily moves forward in time, seeking ways of adapting to the contemporary pastoral situation, in light of our history. Perhaps it is because of this task that the Permanent Seminar of the Canon Law Society so early recognized that "ministry . . . after centuries of stable canonical ordering was showing signs of developing new forms and structures." In setting ten year goals in 1974, the society had determined that this was one of three foundational issues in canon law and theology that it would research. Major changes they noted included:

> Non-ordained persons are assuming functions previously limited to the ordained. The traditional distribution of functions among ordained ministers is being questioned. The concept of "official ministry" in the name of the Church and specially mandated by church authorities, has been called into question and demands at least a re-examination in light of renewed understanding of the Church itself.

The results of their research was published in *The Jurist* in 1981.[1]

One value of the Canon Law Society's work is that it places the issues raised regarding the new ministers in a broader context of official ministry in general. Papers on the episcopacy, the language of ordination rites, and the "fullness of orders," for example, begin with existing structures and understandings of official ministry in order to better understand the new developments today. Here, however, only some of the points raised in this volume that are most directly applicable to our study will be mentioned. The authors raise many questions; as they indicate, answers have often not evolved.

Osiek explores the relationship between charism and rights and responsibilities in the New Testament Church. She draws a definition of charism from its description in Scripture: "a gift of the Holy Spirit bestowed upon an individual Christian for the sake of building up the community." In the Pauline churches, there is not tension between charism and ministry or charism and office. ". . . (S)ome charisms are expressed in leadership and governance while others are expressed in other ways . . . A charism by its very nature brings with it a certain authority, but of many different kinds." In the later New Testament period, "the primary locus for the manifestation of a charism is that of delegated and authoritative leadership, a view not totally alien to the earlier Pauline ecclesiology but certainly one which represents only a small portion of it." From the Pauline theology can be derived the *duty* to give expression to charisms as a response to the grace received; the *right* is to have the gift recognized and discerned by the community, so as not to extinguish the Spirit. While the *Decree on Apostolate of the Laity*, leaves it to pastors to make a judgment about charisms, in Paul the whole community has a role. The issue is the faithful working of the Body, with its various functions—flowing from charisms.[2] Implicit in this discussion is a basic question: who discerns the gifts of official ministers in the Church today, especially the new parish ministers, and what process is used? Osiek would argue that pastors alone cannot do this—but, that we do not have structures to involve the community in this task.

Power moves one step beyond the discernment process, to the legitimation of lay ministry. He explores the various forms of appointment now being used: designation by official appointment, liturgical installations, special blessings of various kinds, and the practical recognition of leaders by a community without formal ceremony. The context of the discussion is an examination of the evolution of the episcopacy and presbyterate in the early church; the role of the community in the recognizing of legitimate leadership is stressed. However, some offices not part of the sacrament of order are also considered, such as reader/teacher and almoner. "The question then is whether some ministries do, according to their nature or to the circumstances of time and place, need the authority of official appointment, and whether this can be given without yielding to the temptation of clericalization." Power sees ambiguity in special commissioning ceremonies for acolytes, readers, and ministers of communion, because if these ministries belong of their nature to all the baptized, a special appointment serves to clericalize the persons. On the other hand, Power thinks that "new structures of leadership and new ways of promoting people to this responsibility have in fact emerged" in basic Christian communities. In addition, the possibility of non-clerical offices, for different pastoral or teaching roles, could give formal recognition and authority to those whose ministry is directly related to their baptism.[3] Although the new parish ministers are not named by Power, his analysis is valuable in trying to resolve the question of what legitimization, what ritual, does the fact of lay ministers serving in diverse roles call for.

Kilmartin explores the participation of laity in the apostolate of the hierarchy, specifically an exercise of the power of jurisdiction. Traditionally reserved to the hierarchy, Kilmartin examines the question in light of the roles laity have assumed, as assistant pastors, as primary leaders in parishes, as vicars for religious, all roles involving the exercise of both teaching and decision-making functions. Does this mean that they share in the pastoral authority of the hierarchy? On the one hand, Vatican II grounds the pastoral power of teaching and governing on the sacrament of order; on the other hand it does see the possibility of laity being appointed to some ecclesiastical offices. How can this be? To develop theological understanding of what is emerging in church life, Kilmartin suggests that the varying ecclesiologies of Vatican II must be analyzed. In the "juridical" and "christomonistic communion" models, the exclusion of laity from the power of jurisdiction is shown to have a theological basis. However, a trinitarian ecclesiology opens the possibility to acknowledge "the spiritual capacity of the laity, based on their charisms, for . . . exercise of pastoral leadership" when called by the Church. In this ecclesiology, a canonical mission may be given to the laity to exercise the power of jurisdiction; the source of the power "must be baptism." The prudent judgment of the local bishop should be a sufficient basis for the awarding of the exercise of this power to the gifted layperson for his or her pastoral ministry.

> It does not involve the bestowal of the spiritual gifts on which the spiritual authority of the lay minister rests. As in the case of the

canonical mission given to the ordained, it provides the juridical basis for the free exercise of these gifts in the public forum and so contributes to the acceptance of this ministry by the community.[4]

Kilmartin's study identifies the many complexities, historically, theologically, in regard to the issue of laity and jurisdiction. It is apparent in his presentation that varied opinions exist, among theologians and canonists. What is happening in the life of the Church is ahead of our capacity to explain it; the effort to connect present reality with the tradition is a work-in-progress. The need for this theological work, by theologians and pastoral ministers, and for patience as it unfolds, is evident.

Provost is one of only two canonists contributing to this early discussion; his topic is "official ministry" in the United States. His study focuses on priests, but does provide some valuable insights for our concerns. He notes that according to the 1917 Code, only clergy can obtain the power of either orders or jurisdiction, thus limiting official ministry to clergy. The code also indicated that to be ordained to Holy Orders, a cleric must have an assured source of income; in the United States this was provided by the diocese, through its network of parishes. However, Vatican II broadened the meaning of official ministry: "'From now on [an ecclesiastical office] should be understood as any function which has been permanently assigned and is to be exercised for a spiritual purpose' (*Presbyterorum Ordinis*, 20). Not only clerics but also lay persons can participate in this official ministry." Furthermore, the funding for ministry received a new emphasis: the recompense for clergy should be standardized. He says that the way these changes will be enfleshed in the Church will depend in part on the revised Code, but even more on "the underlying understanding of official ministry which is put into operation." One stance is that ministry is the prerogative of a separate class or caste in the Church (a "status"); another sees it as the performance of a function a minister provides that brings about the special standing of an official minister (an "ordo"). Historical and theological arguments for each position can be offered.

The significance of the issue is the understanding it represents of official ministry—service as the primary focus, or special status. One cannot deny that ordained ministers—and even non-ordained ones—have a special social status. The canonical question is whether this role is essential to ministry and must be expressed and protected by a separate legal structure apart from the rest of the community.

Provost indicates that the issue in the United States has an additional dimension, the tension between being a bureaucrat and a professional. "As official ministers, are they professionals, serving the needs of the people? Or, are they agents of the organization, serving the needs of the church institution?" "Priests find themselves peculiarly faced with the contrasting and even opposed principles of bureaucratic and professional modes of organization, without a ready escape from the resulting tension by transfer, change of firm, or the option of private practice." Nonetheless, Provost thinks that the reality of the Church as both a communion and a mission means that official ministers cannot be only professionals, nor only bureaucrats. And that laypeople who will be official ministers will face these same tensions. His analysis, drawing on social science research, maps the tensions lay ministers must anticipate in the future.[5] The research indicates that at the present time, the new ministers see themselves as serving the needs of the people, rather than the institution. This is certainly an issue that must be evaluated.

REFLECTIONS ON THE NEW CODE

In 1983, the Canon Law Society published a slim volume that explored the pastoral implications and opportunities of the revised code. Of importance for the present study is the following judgment:

> It would seem the intent of the Code to maintain a basic connection between the power of orders and the power of jurisdiction. Therefore, the exercise of formal lay ministry and, to a great extent, the ministry of the deacon, is ordered to those activities which do not require those powers intimately connected with priestly ordination. In practice, deacons and lay persons may certainly be considered collaborators in ministry and even carry out significant pastoral responsibilities in partnership with members of the presbyterate.

Therefore, while some diocesan personnel offices have begun to function as clearinghouses for laypersons seeking a pastoral position, "the appointment of non-clerical persons is not a canonical appointment." Nonetheless, in light of the decline in the number of priests, "It will become increasingly necessary to promote lay ministries and new pastoral structures . . ."[6] Central to the development of these new structures will be a full realization of the new way of thinking embodied in the code. Whereas the 1917 Code viewed the Church as a monarchy, "the revised Code attempts to take seriously the sense of Church as a communion, a bonding together of people in the Lord and with one another . . ." Furthermore, the expansion of ministry to include laypeople leads to a stress on empowerment.[7] For the first time rights and freedoms of the laity are named in the new code, and the many ways that they may share in official ministry are enumerated.[8] What is apparent in the commentary is that while limits are placed on lay ministry, "the Code has at least opened the door toward a more creative approach to pastoral ministry."[9] For lay ministers in particular, it is important to realize both the limitations, and the open door, and to note the significant historical development the revised code embodies.

Focus on Lay Ministry

Once again in 1985 the Canon Law Society set its priorities, "attempting to determine those areas in church life. . . which will need to be addressed by canon lawyers during the coming decade." One of the three areas identified was "parish life, and especially the rapid increase of lay persons in parish ministry." A committee developed an approach to this, proposing "a study of theoretical issues relating to the laity in church law in order to set a foundation for more practical efforts to address the canon law needs of lay persons actually involved in ministry, as well as the canon law which should be included in formation and continuing education programs for such lay ministers." When the Society's Board of Governors reviewed this, they directed that, in light of the upcoming Synod on the Laity, the topic be broadened to include the spirituality of laypersons and their involvement in the secular mission of the Church. A symposium was held, with this focus; at the symposium, a consensus statement was developed.[10] One result of the broadened purpose is that attention to the topic of our concern here is more limited in the symposium papers, and the final statement, than originally envisioned.

The consensus statement does, however, offer several perspectives that are of interest. Observing that the code has a narrower use of "ministry" and "service" than Vatican II, the need to balance this by the broader use of these terms in the magisterium is asserted. Pastors are encouraged to recognize and foster charisms, and provide adequate preparation and support, as required by church law. Lay involvement in what was formerly done only by clergy is judged "not always an exceptional service, but actually an example of the proper collaboration and cooperation of clergy and laity." Therefore, "it is important that this be given official recognition." To assist ongoing collaboration, common preparation of clergy and laity for ministry is recommended. The admission of laywomen to installation in lay ministries is also recommended. The need for research and practical proposals concerning the appointment, qualifications, evaluation, and removal of persons in official ministry, including laypersons, is affirmed. This would involve procedures, structures and criteria, and must include "the special situation of professional lay ministers." Similarly, the collaboration and cooperation of clergy and laypersons involved in ministry and the laity in general needs practical models. Inclusion of these matters in ministry preparation also requires new models.[11]

In addition to these perspectives, much work at the symposium was devoted to the secular condition of the laity, and the relationship of laity, Church, world, spirituality. A summary of this point of emphasis is given by Normand Provencher: for laypersons "their relationship to the world constitutes what is most specific, although not most fundamental" about them.[12] As will be explored later, this point, so well founded in Vatican II teaching, is problematic in relation to the new parish ministers.

An important issue, addressed by John Beal, is "Protecting the Rights of Lay Catholics." Naturally, this applies to all laity, however, it is a special concern of lay ministers. Beal observes: "judicial procedures are simply not available to resolve most intra-ecclesial conflicts of rights." While voluntary conciliation and arbitration are possible, they depend on "an existing foundation of good will and mutual respect." If commitments to submit to such processes as needed were written into contracts, funding, staffing, training, and standards would be needed for the mediators. At the present time, there seems to be resistance by church officials to such processes, seeing them as "unwanted and unneeded intrusion by outside meddlers into ecclesiastical administration."

> The style of administration prevalent in the Church until recent times has been highly paternalistic. Authorities have grown accustomed to having their decisions go unquestioned while "subjects" have grown accustomed to being unquestioning in the face of authority. If this assessment is correct, protection of rights in the Church will require not just improved procedures but a profound change of heart.

Furthermore, "the sharp diversity in power between the parties that is typical of conflicts between lay people and church officials biases the process against the complainant." Beal thinks that while such processes can be helpful, at times a "definition of rules governing people's relationships" is needed, and so sees the need for judicial processes for vindicating rights; he presents various options. He concludes by noting that one of the most serious problems is lack of awareness of these possibilities, and insufficient experience with them.[13] The research demonstrates that many lay ministers are not aware of procedures for resolving conflicts of rights, and that when aware they often do not judge them as effective.

Elissa Rinere analyzes the ministry of the laity by referring to the priestly, prophetic, and royal munera of Jesus. She describes the differences between the laity and the hierarchy in each of these areas as presented in Vatican II documents, concluding:

> The munera of the people of God include the activities of life. They are fulfilled in the sphere of activity which the council saw as proper to the laity, the world. The munera of the hierarchy, on the other hand, are fulfilled in the Church, the sphere of activity which the council saw as proper to them. Provision was made for a degree of interchange between these spheres of activity; for instance, the possibility of laity holding church offices which are part of the munus of governing (LG 33), or the possibility of the hierarchy entrusting laity with pastoral duties which fulfill the munera of teaching or of sanctifying (AA 24). Although

the acceptability of this interchange was articulated, no clear boundaries were set for it.

Several examples are given including liturgical ministers, diocesan curia members, and teachers of doctrine to non-Catholic school students. Rinere judges that these encompass a sharing in the hierarchical munus of sanctifying, governing, and teaching. On the other hand, ministry is also applied to activities that are a fulfillment of the munera of the people of God, for example, a ministry of the Word described as witness of life. Especially in the *Church in the Modern World*, ministry is applied clearly to the ordinary activities of human life. This represents a distinct development in thinking about the ministry of the laity. Rinere then analyzes the understandings of a ministry of the laity in the revised code, examining each of the relevant canons. She concludes:

> In the code, "ministry" is a fulfillment of the hierarchical munera only. Laity may be brought into it by hierarchical invitation, but there is no ministry which belongs to the laity through baptism. There is no ministry which is fulfilled in the secular sphere, and there is no ministry which laity carry out on their own initiative. This limiting of "ministry" was deliberate on the part of the code commission.

So, ministries such as that of catechist, teacher, and missionary are no longer, in canonical terms, lay ministries. Rather, they are exercises of the hierarchical munera. Furthermore, "the code is neither clear nor consistent in explaining the means through which laity are authorized and thereby permitted to act in the name of the Church. This ambiguity *could* open the door to wide possibilities for action and interpretation.[14] But, at the present time, it is clear that there is in the Code a real ambivalence about a basic acceptance of lay ministers *qua* ministers in the Church.

The final issue examined is that of "Laity and the Inner Working of the Church." The issues examined are the possibility of laity holding an office, cooperating in the exercise of *potestas regiminis* (the power of governance), being employed by the institution, and acting as agents of the institution for civil law considerations. In each case, McDonough's exploration of these topics unfolds the diverse schools of thought among canonists. She concludes that, while "there is certainly provision in the new code for a greater presence and visibility of lay persons in the so-called 'inner-working of the Church' it is also true that there is almost no position, role, function, office or status in the Church that is open to laity which is *not* either heavily conditioned (cc. 204,1; 208; 210; 216), carefully qualified (cc. 212,3; 218), institutionally circumscribed (cc. 226,2; 229,1; 230), or hierarchically controlled (cc. 223,2; 228)." Furthermore, insofar as laypeople hold office in the Church, certain canons apply to them, for example, that they be in communion with the Church, and, for certain ministries that they fulfill specific requirements (for example, catechists: proper preparation; missionaries: sent by competent ecclesiastical authority; teachers of sacred sciences: have a mandate). Proper preparation and competence and honest remuneration are some of the other requirements of canon law. McDonough admits that her assessment is quite negative. But she hopes "that the presence of some talented, qualified, professional lay persons in some of these places and positions formerly reserved to clerics—whether these lay persons hold offices and whether they cooperate in *potestas*—will eventually change the landscape and alter the horizon of the institutional Church."[15]

Since the 1987 work of the Canon Law Society, there has been a significant increase in the number of "talented, qualified, professional lay persons" in places and positions formerly reserved to clerics. Individual canonists continue to address questions relevant to the new developments in ministry. John Beal's article, discussed more fully in chapter 9, looks at the ways in which laypeople today are, *de facto*, exercising power and governance, though in a subordinate and dependent way by virtue of delegation from the diocesan bishop or the pastor. He gives as examples "lay principals of Catholic schools, superintendents of schools, directors of religious education, business managers, and numerous other diocesan officials and parish ministers."[16]

Michael Joyce examines the issue of the collaboration of laity and clergy in the parish. He takes as his starting place the actual changes occurring in parishes, and focuses the discussion within a canonical and liturgical framework. An important consideration is the shift between the codes of 1917 and 1983, from an emphasis on the parish as a territory to that of a people. This relational view is, of course, theological: the Church is the people of God, the pastor is a member of the parish. The Eucharist is "a paradigm for the relationship between the common priesthood and the ministerial priesthood. Likewise, the reformed celebration of the Eucharist serves as a model of the collaboration of lay and ordained ministers in the parish."[17]

The Missal of Paul VI gives offices and ministries to various members of the assembly. The priest, the assembly, and other members all play their part.

> Among the members of the assembly there are special ministries: the acolyte, the reader, the cantor, special ministers of communion, bearers of elements for the celebration, greeters and collectors ... According to the liturgical law expressed in the General Instruction of the Roman Missal, it appears that a legitimate Eucharist requires a diversity of ministries.

So too in the life of the parish. Members of the community place "their proper gifts at the service of the other members." In addition,

> Some of the duties in the parish are borne primarily by members of the pastoral staff. Their tasks reflect the celebration of the Eucharist in which some members of the assembly fulfill very visible and singular offices and ministries.[18]

An implication of this Eucharistic focus is a recognition of the common bond of the ordained and the rest of the people. "Mutuality lies in pastors ministering to the faithful with the faithful in turn collaborating with ordained ministers." This is true at the Eucharistic celebration and in the priest's collaboration with those who also provide pastoral ministry in the parish. For this, several things are needed: "An understanding of the Church as communion, the fundamental equality of all the faithful, and the desirability of collaboration . . ."[19]

To strengthen such collaboration, Joyce offers various suggestions. One is that priests develop skills for working effectively with lay ministers. The pastoral and liturgical formation programs, for seminarians and workshops for continuing formation are mentioned. Another is that the collaboration in pastoral care in the parish be mirrored at the Eucharistic celebration.

> Members of the parish who lead these activities perform ministries in the parish similar to the various ministries of the

eucharistic liturgy. It might be appropriate at special celebrations to have these people exercise their parochial ministries liturgically within the context of the Eucharist. Thus, the leaders in Christian formation would serve as readers while those coordinating service programs of the parish would assist at the altar and serve as special ministers of communion.[20]

WOMEN AND THE PERMANENT DIACONATE

In October of 1995, the Canon Law Society received the report of an ad hoc committee, "The Canonical Implications of Ordaining Women to the Permanent Diaconate." The committee had been charged with the task by the Board of Governors, to implement a resolution adopted by the membership in 1992. The resolution gave two reasons for the study. First, the 1976 Declaration *Inter insigniores* and its commentary published by the Congregation for the Doctrine of the Faith spoke of the need to study the ordination of women to the diaconate. Second, this need is evident in the United States, since the earlier NCCB drafts of the pastoral letter on women's concerns recommended a study of its possibility. The report states:

> Women have been ordained permanent deacons in the past, and it would be possible for the Church to determine to do so again. Cultural factors were a major element in the decision, in various local areas of the Church in the past, to ordain women as permanent deacons; cultural factors continue to be a major consideration in the decision to ordain men as permanent deacons today, and would be a major element in any decision to ordain women as permanent deacons in a local area of the Church.

The committee judged that the canonical restrictions on such an action are rather limited. They said that a bishops' conference could petition the needed derogations, and adopt needed revised guidelines for the permanent diaconate. They view the implications as considerable, when seen from the perspective of the ministry of women in the Church: "It would provide the grace of the sacrament for women who are already doing important service in the Church, would open the way for women to exercise diaconal service in the teaching, sanctifying and governing functions of the Church, and would make them capable of holding ecclesiastical offices now open to deacons but closed to lay persons." The committee notes that this would mean that ordained ministry was opened up to women, and that they would be enabled to receive all seven sacraments. The committee hoped that its own report would stimulate further studies, perhaps involving other disciplines, so that dialogue on this topic could continue.[21] As with other work by the CLSA, initiation of the study of the issue of ordaining women to the diaconate was the result of observing the "signs of the times" within the life of the Church. Part of the reality observed was that of significant numbers of women, lay and vowed religious, engaged in many forms of ministry. Certainly, actions by the Church in the United States on this topic would significantly affect the existing patterns in lay ministry.

CONCLUSION

The Canon Law Society had begun their 1985 work on the issue of laity and ministry in part with the question, what canon law study should be included in the formation and continuing education of lay ministers? The perspectives they offered through their studies, especially the reflections on the revised code, are certainly essential ones, so that lay ministers may understand the institutional limitations at this point in time, even as they present, through their ministry, a pastoral reality that requires a fuller response in law.

NOTES

1. Vol. 41, no. 2, subsequently published as a book; James H. Provost, "Introduction," in *Official Ministry in a New Age*, ed. James H. Provost (Washington, D.C.: Canon Law Society of America, 1981), pp. 1–2. A helpful unpublished dissertation is "The Term 'Ministry' as Applied to the Laity in the Documents of Vatican II, Post Conciliar Documents of the Apostolic See and the Code of Canon Law" by Elissa Rinere (Washington, D.C.: The Catholic University of America, Canon Law Studies, n. 518, 1986).

2. Carolyn Osiek, "Relation of Charism to Rights and Duties in the New Testament Church," in Provost, ed., pp. 44, 47–48, 51, 57–59.

3. David Power, "The Basis for Official Ministry in the Church" in Provost, ed., pp. 60, 63–77, 78–79, 81, 86. James H. Provost, in "Ministry: Some Canonical Issues" further develops the question of authorization. He says: "There is a double 'sending' involved in ministry. On one hand, there must be the call by God. . . On the other hand, there must be a sending by the Church. Ministry. . . is acting in the name of, on behalf of, the Church. . . [it] requires the authorization from one who himself acts in apostolic succession." He explores the relative limitations and values of giving an office, delegating and mandating laity.

4. Edward J. Kilmartin, "Lay Participation in the Apostolate of the Hierarchy," in Provost, ed., pp. 89–90, 92, 95–106, 107, 112, 114, 115. Very significantly, Kilmartin observes: "As is well known, Vatican II never made the attempt to show how the ministries of the laity and ordained derive from the mystery of the Spirit-filled Church and are ordered to one another without the one simply being under the control of the other." (p. 107).

5. James H. Provost, "Toward a Renewed Canonical Understanding of Official Ministry," in Provost, ed., pp. 197, 198, 199, 200, 201, 211, 220, 225.

6. Kenneth E. Lasch "Personnel Issues" in *Code, Community, Ministry*, James H. Provost, ed. (Washington, D.C.: Canon Law Society, 1983), pp. 69–70.

7. James H. Provost, "Approaching the Revised Code" in *Code, Community, Ministry*, op. cit., pp. 15–16.

8.   Bertram F. Griffin, "A Bill of Rights and Freedom," pp. 28–31 and "The Laity in the Revised Code," pp. 32–37, in *Code, Community, Ministry,* op. cit.

9.   Lasch, p. 70.

10. James A. Coriden and James H. Provost, "Introduction" in "Studies in Church Law and Ministry," *The Jurist,* 47, no. 1, 1987, pp. 1–2.

11. "Laity in the Renewing Church: Vision and Opportunities. Statement from the Symposium on Laity in Church Law, Canon Law Society of America." *The Jurist,* 47, no. 1, 1987, pp. 5–9.

12. "The Church in the World," p. 32. For example, see also, "Who is a Lay Person," Ann Prew-Winters: "Lay persons have a secular quality," p. 51. *The Jurist,* 47, no. 1, 1987.

13. *The Jurist,* 47, no. 1, 1987, pp. 131, 143, 144, 145, 146, 151, 152, 163. John Beal, *The Jurist,* 47, no. 1, 1987, pp. 131, 143–146, 151–152, 163. See also Beal's article in *Together in God's Service,* as described in chapter 9 of this book.

14. "Conciliar and Canonical Applications of 'Ministry' to the Laity." *The Jurist,* 47, no. 1, 1987, pp. 205, 207, 208–210, 214, 219, 220, 221, 222. Rinere also compares the use of "service" in conciliar documents and the code. She concludes: "'Service', along with 'ministry,' had been applied by the council to both laity and clergy. In the code, however, both are rendered to the Church primarily by the ordained. Laity may offer special service or engage in certain ministries, but only by invitation of the hierarchy" (p. 226).

15. Elizabeth McDonough. *The Jurist,* 47, no. 1, 1987, pp. 229, 238, 240–242. Sharon Euart also points out the difficulty for ecclesial ministers: "On a practical level the code does not take into account the increasing number of lay persons entering into specific forms of ministry in the Church. As a result a general legal framework for lay people engaged in service to the Church is lacking. At the same time, it is not at all clear what is meant by church service, ecclesial ministry or lay ministry. Various understandings and interpretations lead to inconsistent application of the law, and, in some cases, to the exclusion of lay persons from rightful roles in the common mission of the Church." She holds that these issues will be worked out first at the practical level, in the local church, and only later in theory, and law. "Council, Code and Laity: Implications for Lay Ministry." *The Jurist,* 47, no. 2, 1987, p. 449.

16. John Beal, "Lay People and Church Governance: Oxymoron or Opportunity?" in *Together in God's Service: Toward a Theology of Ecclesial Lay Ministry*, National Conference of Catholic Bishops (Washington, D.C.: United States Catholic Conference, 1998), p. 120.

17. Michael Joyce, "Laity and Clergy Collaborating in Parishes," *The Jurist* 59, no. 1, 1999, pp. 78–83.

18. Ibid., pp. 83–89.

19. Ibid., pp. 90–92. Joyce offers a very helpful analysis of the relational aspects of the role of the priest supervisor in places with a parish coordinator as their primary pastoral caregiver, and of priests who are sacramental ministers only, pp. 91–93.

20. Ibid., pp. 93–94. Joyce says that pastoral ministers need a sound liturgical formation consisting of both theory and practice so that they will be able to work effectively at the connection between the pastoral care of the parish and the liturgy.

21. "The Canonical Implications of Ordaining Women to the Permanent Diaconate, Report of an ad hoc committee of the Canon Law Society of America" (Washington, D.C.: Canon Law Society of America, 1995), pp. 1–2, and pp. 50–51. The Catholic Theological Society of America had also reflected on this issue, in 1978. They noted that in the early church, and in the Greek Orthodox Church today, women have been ordained as deaconnesses. They concluded: "Actual services being performed by women, both secular and religious, could often be rendered more effectively if they were performed from within the office of deacon" (pp. 195–197). "Restoration of the Office of Deacon as a Lifetime State: A Report to the U.S. Bishops," *Worship*, vol. 45, no. 4, April 1971.

CHAPTER SIX

PROFESSIONAL ORGANIZATIONS OF MINISTERS

INTRODUCTION

In the Church in the United States today, there are many organizations of ministers. Some originally had only clergy as members but now include laity; others were founded as laypeople became involved in ministry, and have always included vowed religious, laity, and clergy. Some have a national membership; others a diocesan or area base. They have different histories, including longevity, and different points of emphasis. All are responding to the reality of lay ministers in the Church. By their existence, they offer opportunities for mutual support, and evolution of a sense of ministerial identity. Sometimes, they are proactive in addressing concerns of lay ministers, and advocating for change. In order to highlight some of these varied aspects, a somewhat random sampling of such organizations and their work will be presented. In many ways this brief overview will show only "the tip of the iceberg," both in terms of diversity of groups and of activities. Furthermore, the activities highlighted will be only snapshots of a particular point in time.

ORGANIZATIONS OF PARISH MINISTERS

Religious educators/catechetical ministers may belong to the National Catholic Educational Association/Forum, the National Conference of Catechetical Leaders (NCCL), and a myriad of local groups. One ongoing concern of these groups has been the definition of the role of the DRE (other titles are also used), and the appropriate qualifications for someone who will fill the role. Hiring procedures, salary scales, and contracts have been an aspect of this focus. Recently, NCCL published national certification standards for professional DRE's. In addition efforts have focused on the development of competencies common to various ministries, drawn from the standards developed by individual groups. A joint publication presents the common formation goals.[1] Another concern has been the ministry of religious education and cate- chesis itself, how it is most effectively performed, and the ways in which various individuals and groups share in the functions of catechesis.[2] These two broad delineations are shaped by a sense of professionalism on the part of the DRE's, a sense that looks both to self-definition and remuneration, and effective service of others.

Similar concerns are the focus of the work of the National Feder- ation for Catholic Youth Ministry (NFCYM).[3] Pastoral associates do not have a parallel national organization, although the National Pastoral Life Center includes as one of its functions being a membership association for pastoral ministers, and the National Association for Lay Ministry has developed competencies for pastoral associates, pastoral ministers, and parish life coordinators, and has participated in the development of the common competencies (see endnote 1).[4] The National Association of Pastoral Musicians (NPM) has various divisions of membership, includ- ing one for full-time diocesan and parish ministers who have responsi- bility for managing the overall liturgical music program. The organization has developed standards for pastoral musicians, hiring guidelines and samples of job descriptions, contracts, and salary scales. NPM also con- ducts various national training programs for pastoral musicians, such as the Choir Director Institute and School for Organists.[5]

ASSOCIATIONS OF MINISTERS IN OTHER SETTINGS

Memberships in various national associations help to show both the growing numbers of laypeople in ministry, and the diversity of roles which they fill. Some examples will illustrate this. The National Associa- tion of Catholic Chaplains, founded in 1965 with a membership entirely of priests, now includes members who are lay, vowed religious, and ordained. They work in many settings, including hospitals, nursing homes, academic institutions, hospices, and parishes. The institutions they are affiliated with are often Catholic, but Protestant, Jewish, federal, and state affiliations are also noted. Laymen compose 7 percent of the membership, laywomen 25 percent, sisters 45 percent, and brothers 2 percent. The association was the first to develop standards for certification, through the USCC Commission on Certification and Accreditation (now USCCB); it certifies both chaplains and supervisors.[6]

The Catholic Network of Volunteer Services (formerly the International Liaison of Lay Volunteers in Mission) is a network of lay mission programs, which coordinates and facilitates the efforts of lay volunteer mission organizations. Its 233 member programs have 9,642 (almost double the number serving in 1997) laity in full-time service, for a time span of a summer to three or more years, in missionary work both in the United States and internationally. Most of the lay missionaries are 21-35 years old, though several hundred are over 55.[7] The Catholic Campus Ministry Association reports that there are approximately 1,700 Catholic campus ministers in the United States, serving Catholic and non-Catholic college and university campuses. CCMA has approximately 1,100 members, including 430 priests and 150 sisters. Nearly 1,000 campus ministry centers serve about 2,300 higher education institutions in the United States.[8] Spiritual Directors International has over 4,000 members, about a third of whom are laypeople.[9]

These "snapshots" of individual organizations are interesting, but the collective picture of laypeople involved in so many aspects of pastoral care, in so many settings, is striking. Certainly, chaplaincy, missionary work, campus ministry, and spiritual direction are not areas in which laypeople were involved in the recent past, but now here, too, there is an explosion of lay ministry.

THE ASSOCIATION OF GRADUATE PROGRAMS IN MINISTRY

This group first convened in 1987; it is an organization of Roman Catholic graduate programs whose focus is the education of individuals for ministry. It has conducted research on graduate programs in ministry and graduate ministry students[10] and sponsored a symposium for ministry educators.[11] The latter effort brought together leaders from a variety of formation programs—including staffs of diocesan and free-standing programs in ministerial education, seminary personnel, leaders in deacon education, and formation coordinators for religious congregations, along with AGPIM members.

From the standpoint of this book, what is particularly interesting is the kind of issues being addressed and questions being raised by AGPIM. For example, part of the mission statement is an affirmation of the centrality of practical/pastoral theology that is seen as "a new theological paradigm in graduate education for ministry." So, while the *Program of Priestly Formation* of the United States Bishops has increased the philosophy requirements for seminarians, and deemphasized pastoral theology, the organization of graduate programs for ministry has as a central part of its mission statement a description of practical pastoral theology. It stresses "a mutually interpretative, critical and transforming conversation between the Christian tradition and contemporary experience." One can anticipate that this educational approach will develop outlooks different from what a traditional seminary program would develop, with implications for the collaborative working of ministers. Another illustration of their approach is the choice of principle topics to address at the symposium: the history of ministry formation, presented by a theologian; the nature of professional socialization, addressed by an educator; and an overview of current lay ministry formation, reflected on by a sociologist. These are topics central both to the development of an understanding of what is happening in the Church today, theologically speaking, and how we should be responding educationally, formationally, pastorally. Of course, a symposium only begins a conversation; those who prepare laity, deacons, and priests for ministry need to continue such dialogue, especially with an eye toward the future working together of these ministers.

THE NATIONAL ASSOCIATION FOR LAY MINISTRY

The early history of NALM was as a gathering of diocesan coordinators of lay training/formation programs. Membership now includes those who are professionally committed to and involved in the development of laity in ministry. The focus is on coordinators of programs for laity in ministry and career and volunteer lay ministers, especially pastoral ministers, pastoral associates, and parish life coordinators. NALM pursues its educational and enrichment goal primarily through an annual conference that is open to all who are interested. A second ongoing task is collaboration; efforts have included both work with other organizations concerned about lay ministry and the development of a published model for fostering collaborative working. A newsletter and directory assist networking. Some local chapters have begun, furthering these goals at the grassroots level.

NALM developed competency-based certification standards for pastoral ministers, pastoral associates, and parish life coordinators, which have been approved by the USCC Commission on Certification and Accreditation. An extensive collaborative effort, including the involvement of ministers "in the field," contributed to their development. The intent is to serve the ministers and the Church:

> By providing professional, national certification standards for pastoral ministers, pastoral associates and parish life coordinators, NALM is giving direction to the future of these evolving ministries, confirming the work of ministers in the field, encouraging a continuing supply of parish ministers rooted in the tradition and faith of the Church and ensuring the quality of the profession.[12]

This earlier work has been furthered through NALM's collaboration with NCCL and NFCYM in the development and publication of the common formation goals, described above.

The professionalizing focus is evident in the very definition of a "standard," drawn from the USCC/CCA: "the criteria established by a professional organization or an accrediting agency by which competency and quality of service are assessed."[13] At the same time, the mission of NALM also emphasizes volunteer lay ministry. The issue faced by the larger Church, of the relationship between volunteer and (here, even the name varies) professional, employed, career, lay ecclesial ministers is part of the tension experienced by the association. The efforts to define roles functionally by delineating the knowledge and skills essential for their performance is one way of engaging this issue. It may be that it will prove a way of engaging a second issue, the relationship between those ministers who are ordained and those who are not.

Because NALM wanted both to gain the wisdom of laity active in church ministry at the grassroots level for the formulation of its own action agenda, and to assist in the dialogue about the shape of ministry for the next millennium, the Board planned a series of focus group meetings. These were held in different parts of the country; some groups were composed of career ministers, others of volunteers in ministry. The researchers summarized the main themes which emerged; some are of particular interest in the context of this book:

> . . . The shortage of priests will precipitate an ever-increasing sharing of essential ministry functions, and will cause a blurring of the roles of priest and lay minister . . . Lay ministry is flourishing, but will not continue to flourish if the individual ministers do not feel accepted and recognized in their various capacities-especially by the clergy. Beyond recognition, career ministers are vitally concerned about adequate compensation and benefit packages . . . There was consensus among participants that women in the church do not receive recognition or acknowledgement commensurate with their contribution to parish ministry . . . It was recognized that multi-culturalism was a challenge facing the church . . .[14]

NALM published a study, "No Turning Back," in which many of the issues identified through statistical studies of lay ministers are addressed, such as recognition for ministry performed, and issues of just compensation. NALM placed a new emphasis on the fact of "ministry from a lay perspective," underlining the importance of our social locations in affecting our experience of reality. For example, they point out that commitment in marriage to a spouse, parenting, and economic responsibility for oneself and one's family provide distinctive social locations, and therefore perspective. The authors conclude, "Lay ministers who are spouses, parents and providers are in the right social location to minister effectively to the vast majority of people whose major life concerns are centered on being loving and faithful spouses, responsible parents and just and competent workers who earn enough to provide adequate resources for themselves and their dependents."[15]

Most recently, NALM has focused in a special way on spiritual formation for ministry. In 1997 they initiated a study of the documents of the Church related to the formation of seminarians, deacons, vowed religious, and laity, seeking to identify key formation factors. An outcome of the work was the publication of a monograph that summarizes four official documents and identifies key findings relative to formation of the laity.[16] In 2001, NALM convened leaders of programs to share their experiences, models, questions, and concerns at an institute. A second institute is planned for 2002. Participants, over 120 (there are 295 lay ministry formation programs, as identified by CARA, so a substantial proportion were represented), were primarily laypeople; but there were also a large number of vowed religious and a few priests. Many were seasoned directors who had begun the program they lead. The participants were people who have reflected deeply on how we grow spiritually, and were able to articulate the processes, dynamics, and methodologies for furthering growth. They represent a maturing of lay ministry formation, a consensus regarding what is helpful, and an affirmation that the work has been well begun, and needs to continue.

THE NATIONAL ASSOCIATION OF CHURCH PERSONNEL ADMINISTRATORS

NACPA was formed because of a resolution by the National Federation of Priests' Councils. When it began in 1970, all participants were priests, though women religious were invited to its first meeting, as observers. The choice of its name, Church Personnel Administrators, rather than Clergy Personnel, was deliberate, and significant. By the 1978 convocation, half the membership was priests, half vowed religious men and women. In 1981, specific objectives directing the association to be proactive for the just treatment of lay personnel were adopted.[17] In some ways, NACPA's story echoes the developments in the larger Church in the United States, with this inclusion of vowed religious and laity in central aspects of ministry.

In 1986, NACPA's *Just Treatment for Those Who Work for the Church* advocated for a comprehensive approach to church personnel administration that would include laypeople, sisters, brothers, deacons, and priests. The range of functions they described included recruitment, selection, training, formation, policy development, salary administration, benefits, due process, termination, and retirement. Their document invited each category of ministers to examine whatever advantages they receive because of their status as clergy, religious, or lay and stressed that "justice urges all to recognize that the treatment of one category of persons has direct implications for the treatment of others." The entire reflection was rooted in relevant church documents.[18]

In 1991, a NACPA study examined attitudes of administrators and employees regarding the church environment as a place of employment, focusing on job satisfaction and working conditions. Concerns surfaced by the research centered in five areas. Training and development was shown to be highly valued, and the need for attracting and keeping workers recognized as a great challenge. The issue of promotion in an institution in which most of the top positions are open only to the ordained was seen as a significant aspect of the development question. Salary and benefit packages, employment security concerns, expanded opportunities for women, and increased support for training and development were all seen as needing attention. Efforts to improve both the perception of workers about grievance handling and the procedures themselves were called for, and developing ways to enhance workplace communication to minimize the need for formal grievances recommended. Finally, increased efforts to improve the employment and promotion of ethnic and other minorities was stressed.[19]

NACPA has produced two position papers, "The Individual and the Institution: Strengthening Working Relationships in the Church" and "Workplace Justice: Guidance for Church Leaders." These seminal documents present a vision, rooted in Catholic social justice principles. The writers define church workers as all those who labor for the Church, from bishops to volunteers. They point out, however, that clergy and religious have special canonical relationships with their bishops or religious communities, whereas civil law governs the institution's relationship with laypeople. They examine the employer-employee relationship which some priests, many religious, and most laity experience. Principles and norms for developing comprehensive personnel policies and procedures are presented, with the Church's social teaching and canon law as their context. Especially important are the intrinsic value and dignity of the human person, a focus on the common good, justice in the workplace, and participation and an appropriate level of influence. Careful attention to legal protection for the institution, justice for the workers, and the focus of both on the mission informs the paper.[20]

In order to adequately address these concerns, the association recommends that each diocese have a personnel/human resource director and a coordinator for parish personnel. If the diocese is too small, they suggest that ways of getting the needed functions performed be addressed. They point out that in human resource development, the usual ratio is 100 employees per director. Issues relative to human resources are significant at both the diocesan and the parish levels.[21] If it is understood that human resources are most important for the mission of the Church, the professional analysis provided by NACPA surely calls for response by dioceses, individually and collectively.

FOUNDATIONS AND DONORS INTERESTED IN CATHOLIC ACTIVITIES

Although not an association of ministers, it is worth considering the contribution FADICA is making to the development of lay ministry. Since 1976, this organization of private foundations and donors has existed in order to facilitate mutual exchange of information. It also serves as a forum, by discussing grant requests and programs; it works to coordinate joint efforts; and it helps members keep abreast of recent developments in the Church. The members are themselves all lay. Dr. Frank Butler, the director said, "These are people who have a strong sense of their own Baptism, and a sense of responsibility for the Church. They are trying to live their Christian lives conscientiously, by putting their financial resources to bringing Christ's kindness to people."[22]

In 1987, FADICA convened to discuss "laity in Catholic ministry." From the NCBB study of programs preparing laity for ministry they knew of the 14,000 individuals in those programs who would be serving in many roles in the Church. They asked: "Are laity sufficiently prepared for and supported in these roles? How does their ministry change that of priests? Are dioceses allocating theological and financial resources for laity proportionate to their larger role in the ministry of the Church of the future?"[23]

Participants heard Richard Rohr reflect on the fact that today there are fewer priests, and yet ministry has increased. He posited the possible separation of the charisms of pastoring and sacramental ministry, and suggested that this "is what the Lord is forcing upon us—to discriminate the charisms." A youth minister and a pastoral associate addressed the group, speaking of their conviction of a call to their work, and naming some of the difficulties they face, in areas such as acceptance, adequacy of salary, and evaluation procedures. The need for collaboration of clergy and laity and good communication skills was stressed. The president of the Dominican School of Philosophy and Theology at Berkeley spoke about issues of preparation and education of lay ministers, stressing that "lay students need to develop the skills and the habits and the discipline that they will use in the ministry." Two lay diocesan administrators discussed the implications of the hiring of "career lay ministers," both financially and administratively. Points raised ranged from the need to expand vocation awareness to include career lay ministry to the role of a personnel office, from the need for internships and networking to the implications of employer-employee relationships.[24]

What was the result of hearing these presentations? One way of knowing this is by reviewing the discussions, which highlight the kinds of concerns FADICA members had. Many issues were raised: clergy/lay relationships, salaries, the role and identity of priests in light of the emergence of lay ministers, personnel policies, financial assistance for education, collaborative structure, the education of parishioners and of pastors, the institutional cost of educating ministers (both clergy and lay), the differing needs of seminarians and laypersons in theological studies, spiritual formation of laity, preparation of Hispanics and Asians, holistic evaluation procedures for ministry students, longevity, the title "minister," and more![25] The evident interest and high level of concern of the participants was abundantly clear.

A second national symposium for FADICA members was held in 1999, with a particular focus on the question of the formation of lay leaders in church service. Their concern was framed by their realization that, "Waves of lay persons are stepping forward as parish council members, teachers, ministers, principles, presidents and administrators." Therefore, "The Catholic foundation community was eager to know more about this massive transition from a church led and managed principally by clergy and religious, to one in which the leadership of laity is ever more evident."[26]

The exploration of the issue began with a presentation by Bishop Gerald Kicanas, "Do We Really Have a Theology of Lay Ministry?" He answered the question by saying that much can be said theologically, and more needs to be done. Building on his outline of theological perspectives, he presented areas that need further development. These included clarifying language, such as "ministry," and exploring the difference in essence between laity and the ordained; seeking to understand the proper relationship of those ministers who have significant pastoral responsibility in the Church with the bishop; finding ways to delegate and depute such lay ministers; and how to develop a more multicultural ministerial leadership.[27]

Dolores Leckey was the first respondent. She noted the parallel between the formation of lay ministers, by "inserting them in scripture and in the sacramental life of the church" and the formation of priests and religious, and said, "It has always worked, most of the time." The second respondent was Philip Murnion. He stressed the need for appropriate recognition of the new ministers, including that recognition "must be part also of the training of priests so that they begin to see as they become priests their sharing of this ministry with others within the life of the church." Second, he noted the importance of education, and the financial constraints attendant on that, and, finally, the importance of inclusion—of men as well as women, of varied ethnic groups and of the poor.[28]

Cardinal Mahony also stated his conviction that the involvement of lay leadership is not a stopgap measure, and the particular need "to promote, cultivate and sustain ecclesial lay ministries . . . in full-time pastoral ministry." However, Mahoney continued, there is also a need to educate the larger community to the legitimacy of their ministry, and to provide adequate education and formation of the lay ministers. In addition, formation of laity for their work in the world is a central concern.[29]

Also treated at the symposium was the task for higher education relative to the formation of lay leaders. Dolores Leckey gave the final presentation, inviting FADICA members to use the theological reflection method rooted in the spirituality of St. Ignatius and the philosophical and theological insights of the Jesuit, Bernard Lonergan. As the steps in the method were outlined, she focused on the new reality of lay ecclesial ministers and suggested that FADICA ponder how to respond.[30]

FADICA members considered the possibility of establishing "a national fund with a sizeable corpus with an allocation of interest for the support of lay ministers," to be resourced by numerous foundations. Another option was for individual foundations to focus on leadership development for church initiatives. Whether to fund higher education and diocesan initiatives, or individuals preparing programs, or the wisdom figures who could be the mentors for future leadership was asked. The symposium did not draw such questioning to a close.[31] In order to discern a next step, FADICA commissioned a study of laity in leadership roles.[32]

These symposia are of significance for two reasons. First, the very fact of this—that FADICA examined the issues of lay ministry and lay leadership twice in just over a decade. Second, the evidence that many of these foundations are, indeed, supporting both research and various efforts in the field of lay ministry. For example, the Lilly Foundation has funded initiatives such as the convocation on "The Role of Educational Divinity Schools in Catholic Theological Education," sponsored by the Catholic Task Force of Yale Divinity School (1992), *The New Parish Ministers* study sponsored by the National Council of Catholic Bishops (1992), and the *Just Wages and Benefits for Lay and Religious Church Employees* sponsored by the National Conference of Diocesan Directors of Religious Education (1990). More recently Lilly has funded a broad range of initiatives at a number of Catholic seminaries, focused on the lay students. These have ranged from improved recruitment and student services to the development of formation programs to expanding a multicultural focus. The Raskob Foundation also has funded various efforts, such as the National Association for Lay Ministry study of the longevity of lay ministers. The work of the Subcommittee on Lay Ministry, of the Bishops Conference, has been significantly funded by the Lilly Endowment, with additional help from an anonymous foundation.

Foundations and donors have recognized that the new developments in the life of the Church require new initiatives, and therefore financial support. The new ministers are not integrated into the institution in such a way that there are established ways of dealing with the issues that arise in relation to them. Therefore, the actions by FADICA and individual members of the group are important, in that they serve both as a recognition of the new reality and a way of supporting development, growth, and, perhaps "establishment."

CONCLUSION

When looked at collectively, the professional organizations offer a profile of priests, vowed religious, and laity working together collaboratively to name and respond to the myriad practical issues raised by the changing picture in ministry today. The particular focus of their work is influenced by their areas of expertise. So, for example, professional organizations of ministers have developed competency standards, out of reflection on what is needed to do their ministry, and personnel administrators have reflected on the implications of the Church, an institution committed to certain principles, being an employer. Perhaps the weakness in the endeavor is that too often the larger Church is not sufficiently aware of what these groups are addressing, and at times the groups are insufficiently aware of work being done by other groups and by canonists, liturgists, and theologians.

NOTES

1. See, for example, *The Emerging Role of a Director of Religious Education*, Dolores I. Gerken (Rockford, IL: Community of Religious Education Directors, 1970); *DRE: Issues and Concerns for the 80's*, Thomas P. Walters (Washington, D.C.: National Conference of Diocesan Directors of Religious Education, 1983). A very extensive study, of value to all lay ministers, is NCCL's *Just Wages and Benefits for Lay and Religious Church Employees* (1990). Both the "Final Report" and "A Summary Report" are helpful. The standards were approved by the USCC Commission on Certification and Accreditation: *National Certification Standards for Professional Parish Directors of Religious Education* (Washington, D.C.: National Conference of Catechetical Leadership, 1996). *Common Formation Goals for Ministry*, Joseph T. Merkt, ed. (National Association for Lay Ministry, National Federation of Catholic Youth Ministry, Inc., and National Conference for Catechetical Leadership, 2000).

2. Illustrative of this are the National Conference of Diocesan Directors of Religious Education (now renamed and reconfigured as the National Conference of Catechetical Leaders) titles such as *Religious Education and Catechesis: A Shift in Focus*, Robert J. Hater (1982); *The Role of a Diocesan Religious Education/Catechetical Office*, Robert J. Hater (1981); *Priestly Formation and Catechetics* (1978/1986) and NCEA works such as *Collaborators in Catechesis: Bishops, Publishers, Diocesan Directors* (1990); *Toward Effective Parish Religious Education for Children and Young People*, Francis D. Kelly, Peter L. Benson, and Michael J. Donahue (1986).

3. See, for example, their delineation of competencies needed by youth ministers (1990) and *The Challenge of Adolescent Catechesis* (1986).

4. *Competency-Based Certification Standards for Pastoral Ministers, Pastoral Associates and Parish Life Coordinators*, 1994; *Common Formation Goals for Ministry*.

5. *Qualifications for a Director of Music Ministries: A Statement and Bibliography*; *Hiring A Director of Music: A Handbook and Guide*; *NPM Workbook: Job Descriptions, Contracts, Salaries*.

6. Conversation with Rev. Joseph Discoll, Executive Director (National Association of Catholic Chaplains), February 18, 2002.

7. Conversation with James Lindsay (Executive Director, Catholic Network of Volunteer Service), February 13, 2002.

8. E-mail communication with Edmund Franchi (Executive Director, Catholic Campus Ministry Association), February 27, 2002.

9. E-mail communication with Jeffrey Gaines (Director, Spiritual Directors International), January 31, 2002.

10. *A Survey of Graduate Programs in Ministry 1992–1993*, Charles Topper, et al (1993); *Ministers of the Future*, Barbara J. Fleischer (1993).

11. *Ministry Educators in Conversation: What Kind of Future?: Proceedings of the Invitational Conference* (1993).

12. Competency-Based Certification Standards for Pastoral Ministers, Pastoral Associates, Parish Life Coordinators (National Association for Lay Ministry, Inc.: 1994), p. v.

13. Ibid., p. iv.

14. *NALM Listening Sessions*, prepared by David DeLambo (Chicago: National Association for Lay Ministry, 1995), pp. 2–3, 51–52.

15. Graziano Marcheschi, ed. (Chicago: National Association for Lay Ministry, 1998), pp. 19–34.

16. Carol Weber, *Formation of Laity for Ecclesial Ministry: Significant Findings from a Select Review of Related Literature* (Chicago: National Association for Lay Ministry, 1997).

17. *Just Treatment for those Who Work for the Church* (Cincinnati: National Association of Church Personnel Administrators, 1986), p. 14.

18. Ibid., pp. 5 and 15–20. Further development of these themes is found in *Pathfinder for Just Compensation: A NACPA Working Paper* (1989).

19. *Attitudinal Survey on Working in the Catholic Church: An Executive Summary*, Ann Margaret O'Hara, ed. (Cincinnati: National Association of Church Personnel Administrators, 1991), pp. 3, 18–19.

20. "The Individual and the Institution"(Cincinnati: National Association of Church Personnel Administrators, 1994), especially pp. 2, 6–9, and 13–15.

21. Conversations with William Daley and Sr. Ellen Doyle, National Association of Church Personnel Administrators, November 9, 1996, and January 31, 2002, respectively. Information about services and resources is available at *www.nacpa.org*.

22. Conversation with Dr. Francis J. Butler, President, FADICA, January 10, 1997.

23. *Laity in Catholic Ministry: Moving Into the Future*, edited proceedings of a symposium (Washington, D.C.: FADICA, Inc., 1987), pp. 2, 4.

24. Ibid., pp. 10, 22–32, 48.

25. Ibid., pp. 58–66.

26. *Forming Lay Leaders: Church Service in the Twenty First Century* (Washington, D.C.: FADICA, 1999), p.i, "Executive Summary."

27. Ibid., pp. 4–11.

28. Ibid., pp. 11–17.

29. Ibid., pp. 19–25.

30. Ibid., pp. 27–43 and 51–57.

31. Ibid., pp. 58–60, further.

32. Zeni Fox, *Laity in Leadership Roles in the Church in the United States Today: A Theological and Pastoral Overview* (Washington, D.C.: FADICA, 2000).

CHAPTER SEVEN

LITURGISTS

INTRODUCTION

The topic of ministry is an aspect of the study of liturgy, and so liturgists, too, have responded to the phenomenon of the new parish ministers. *Worship*, the publication of the North American Academy of the Liturgy, gives an indication of what is considered topical by liturgists, though some other sources are also used in this chapter. While a systematic consideration such as that undertaken by the Canon Law Society has not been done, several issues have been addressed. Whereas many of the studies of "ministry" focus only on ordination and attendant questions, some do have a particular emphasis on the new ministers. A brief overview, developed chronologically, will give a picture of what liturgists are contributing to the conversation about the new ministers.

TOWARD A VARIETY OF MINISTERS

Nathan Mitchell framed the question by defining ministry as the "genus" in which particular "species" of ministries may be found. He posits that one may have a valid ministerial vocation in the Church that does not involve reception into a body of ordained ministers. Mitchell argues that greater clarity about the distinction of roles in the community is needed, because the roles define the relationships, and without role-maintenance an amorphous condition results. The problem he sees is the way in which the presbyterate has been "a kind of ministerial Moloch which has gobbled up and ingested virtually all other expressions of Church service." Perhaps, he says, we have too many priests.

What we have too few of are bishops, deacons, teachers, evangelists, healers, prophets, cantors, preachers, and so forth. We will find it impossible to take the current felt need for diversification in ministry seriously until we are willing to admit that the presbyteral role is a good deal more modest than we once thought.[1]

The lack of role-clarity Mitchell identifies is also a significant problem for the new ministers, as their survey responses indicate. The variety of their ministries and their own evaluation of why they were hired conforms to his analysis of a felt need for diversification in ministry.

The current diversification of ministry is approached in a different way by Leland White. He names as one of the three unique contributions America has made to Catholicism the professionalization of the work of members of religious communities. An aspect of this is professional ministers, of which "our American Sisters. . . (are) preeminent examples." His analysis of ministry is based on this professional model, rather than on vocation. Because the whole People of God is called to mission, "all members of the Church have specialized but integrated ministries." He thinks that to say some have a special vocation undercuts the vocation of all. "Individual responses to this common call may be functionally distinct, but they must be part of an integrated effort to work out the implications of the common call." Ministries are professional services—rather than a special vocation.

Those who serve are in fact "ministers of the Church" not as we have been wont to express it, "ministers of Christ" or "other Christs." They are "other Christ's" and "ministers of Christ" in common with all the baptized. Specialized ministries provide the Church professional services that contribute to the common task.

White says that the functional specialization of tasks among the people to carry out the Church's mission and vocation will vary from time to time, but that this is a secondary concern. The Church as a whole would need to discern the individual call to ministry to specific functions in the community. Finally, White asks whether commitment is permanent or revocable. He concludes that the commitment to our common vocation is permanent. Commitment to specialized tasks involves a relationship to those one is called to serve; therefore it implies a commitment greater than personal inclination or satisfaction. Nonetheless, there could be situations in which the commitment was revocable.[2]

White's starting point is precisely the new ministers, especially vowed religious women. His analysis stressing our common vocation as the broader context for specialized, professional services suggests a way of avoiding inappropriate "clericalization" of ministers, yet recognizing that some Christians serve in distinct ways.

John Grabner is also concerned with the tendency "to subsume all ministry under the omnivorous priesthood. . . and to define all other ministries lay, diaconal, or episcopal, in essentially presbyteral terms." He thinks that what is needed is a communitarian understanding of ministry "concerned less with preserving the traditional offices than it is with providing the actual variety of ministerial functions needed to meet the diverse needs of given local congregations of the Church." He thinks that the original functions gave rise to particular offices, and their theological interpretation. But over time the original job descriptions have not been significantly altered to suit changing needs and circumstances, nor have they always been respected in their actual variety. Furthermore, we are sometimes reluctant to recognize that the same and new responsibilities are being exercised in ways that have departed from the traditional threefold ministry. "Attempts to revise ministerial job descriptions which do not take seriously the varieties of ministry actually being performed by all the members of the community—clerical and lay—can lead to the perpetuation of 'them-us' distinctions and outmoded structures in different guise."

In keeping with his functional approach, Grabner concludes, "It has been said that the primary difference between the ordained and the unordained has primarily to do with *liturgical* function. Whatever other functions ministers are to perform, they are ordained to function *liturgically*."[3] Survey data from the study of the new ministers indicates that there is an effort to define themselves as functionally distinct from priests, and a strong tendency to make presidency at the Eucharistic celebration a particular point of demarcation.

MINISTRIES: ESTABLISHED AND UNESTABLISHED

The most extensive treatment by a liturgist affecting our topics is that of David Power in his book, *Gifts That Differ: Lay Ministries Established and Unestablished.* The origin of the volume is itself significant. The publisher printed each of the new rites of the Church, and a series of books to explain them. Power was asked to write about the rite for the two offices of acolyte and reader, proclaimed by Paul VI in *Ministeria Quaedam* as official lay ministries. Power replied that any such treatment would have to take into account "the wide spectrum of lay activity in the Church . . . especially as it has developed since the council." He had in mind the fact that while "one seldom seems to meet a person who has been installed as either acolyte or reader, yet lay ministries, liturgical and other, thrive, and installation ceremonies of one kind or another are common." Power used the term *established ministries* to refer to the official ministries of lector and acolyte, and *unestablished* to refer to all the other lay ministries which have evolved in the Church, especially since Vatican II.[4]

Central to understanding the significance of *Ministeria Quaedam* is realizing that Paul VI's action deliberately separated the ministries of lector and acolyte from the sacrament of order, and from the clerical state. The pope also decreed that other ministries could be established, according to the needs of the local church. In fact, in 1973 *Immensae Caritatis* provided for extraordinary ministers of the Eucharist, who could be commissioned by a special church blessing. Power concludes that, theologically speaking, "these ministries are a way of realizing the share in Christ's priestly office which the people receive through the sacraments of initiation." And, because the document makes clear that the lay minister's responsibilities extend beyond the liturgical assembly, this "may have the implication that a share in one of Christ's three offices involves some particular share in the others."[5]

To situate his analysis of these actions, Power traces the history of ministry in the first five centuries of the Church's life. He concludes that "official appointment, personal choice and the grace of the spirit, manifested either in personal witness or in charismatic gifts, are the grounds on which persons serve the Church and acquire rank in the community." And second, this period of the Church shows "a development which gradually institutionalized all liturgical ministries and even in the spiritual life set up a hierarchy of orders in the churches." Therefore he sees in Paul VI's reforms a dilemma. On the one hand, they "harken back beyond the age of clericalization." On the other hand:

> . . . there is in the case of non-clerical roles a tendency to formalize and order services which had probably been more indebted to the graces of the Spirit and an informal recognition thereof in earlier times. This goes along with a tendency to limit to the few certain offices which had, at least to some extent, belonged to the many . . . we are forced to ask how the recognition of the service of the laity can be advanced by the institution of special ministries, or by their liturgical installation, especially when they touch on matters which are common to all rather than peculiar to the few.[6]

Power's consideration of ministry in the New Testament leads him to conclude that "the needs of the church and of its mission are what determine ministry;" ministry comes from the spirit, as a participation in the *diakonia* of Jesus. Therefore ministries are plural and charismatic; there is a diversity because of the sense of mission of local communities.[7]

For the Church today, Power concludes that it is necessary "to leave behind the theological and canonical system which had its point of departure in the hierarchy, and look instead to the reality of the unit which is the people of God in Christ." Both discipleship and apostolate derive from Baptism; grace and charism are "organically interrelated efforts." Gifts of service (all gifts, including institutional authority) "are for the church, belong to the church and have to be discerned by the church."[8]

Power concludes with the topic of the recognition of ministries. He does not think the present canonical rites for the commissioning of acolytes and readers are needed. His reason is that, "Many of the actions which they require can be done by one and all, and simply need care and supervision to be done well." On the other hand, he recognizes that some ministries require special skills and training. "Music direction, teaching, prayer in public, prophecy, involve the careful and well prepared use of special gifts and special skills." For these he suggests that a blessing could be a way of recognizing the ministries, used as a means of bringing a process of discernment to a close.[9]

It may be that many of the new ministers have never read Power. Nonetheless, they share his perspectives. The theological vision that roots their specialized ministries (as well as the general ministry of the laity) in baptism informs their thinking, as the survey results show. And many of them desire some liturgical recognition of their ministries.

LEADERSHIP AND MINISTRY

Power's reflections on the recognition of ministries are continued in a later volume, this time in a "dialogue" between sacramental/liturgical theology and the human sciences, focused on the topic of leadership. Essays include review of the historical shifts in envisioning and structuring leadership in the Christian community, and understandings of leadership and power derived from contemporary social science research. The reflection is rooted in the diverse experiences of leadership in parishes today, outlined in a series of vignettes focused on several people such as a financial manager of a parish, a pastoral administrator, and the leaders of a base community.[10]

The analysis begins with an overview by James Whitehead of the shift that has occurred in the Church since Vatican II, from an emphasis on hierarchy and power over, to an emphasis on mutuality and power for and with. He contends that both may be traced in our early tradition. Today, the conviction of the community as active and the rediscovery of collegiality have led to new emphasis on the role of official ministers as supporting and guiding the various ministries of the community. However, "our rhetoric has raced ahead of our structures and of our ability to implement change." This, of course, gives rise to differing expectations and to a painful transition.[11]

Approaching the same issue from a social-science perspective, Evelyn Whitehead outlines a central dynamic of religious groups: their originating experience is spoken of as a personal encounter with power, transcendent power. This leads to a unique orientation to organizational power: "religious groups foster patterns of social power that tend toward ever greater centralization, even as they foster movements of social power that necessarily tend toward radical decentralization." The centralized structures that emerge serve to preserve the truth of the group's original transforming encounter with God; the decentralized aspects of group life are needed in order to continue to invite persons into such a transforming personal encounter with God. At times these two movements will be experienced as working against each other. She states that today as the Church we are attempting to reestablish organizational patterns that respect the religious power of believers and of the local church; we are emphasizing decentralized aspects of church life. This has implications for the style of leadership that will be most helpful, one that will serve to empower groups. Research suggests that such a style will need to recognize the importance of the relations within the group, and not only between the group and the formal leader.[12]

As the reflection continues, James Whitehead suggests an image for a style of leadership faithful to the example of Jesus, and to our understandings of the tasks of leadership. Wanting to stress the idea of a community of mutuality, and also of a leader able to powerfully initiate, confront, heal, and endure, he proposes stewardship as an image which "blends power with service and authority with dependence," because a steward serves another. The spirituality implicit in such a style is drawn out by reflection on the gospel and the social sciences. Part of this spirituality is an awareness of responsibility for the Church itself, not only the individuals within the Church. This includes responsibility for the Church even in its failings.[13]

Out of this context, David Power, as a liturgical theologian, reflects on present experience and our tradition and suggests some themes important for our exploration of the Church's response to the new ministers. His particular focus is the liturgical assembly, and the way power is exercised and envisioned in that context. Here, the question is not simply the way the president relates with the people, but more the ways in which individuals affect one another and in which they affect the corporate reality. Power sees this as one of the new awarenesses emerging from Vatican II.[14]

The images of power in the Christian tradition "speak not only of a power to which Christians are subject, but of a power that is given to them." The Lordship of Christ, the Indwelling Spirit, the Cross of Jesus, God's Word, these signal both total dependence on God and power in the community, as well as power in the midst of suffering, and the compassionate power of God's love.

This is a new wisdom, a power that is hidden in powerlessness, the strength and testimony of suffering undertaken for others. It is the power of judgment pronounced against other wisdoms and powers. A radical sharing in this power is given through the sacraments of initiation.

Because of this sharing in power, he sees a problem in restricting certain activities of the faithful in the liturgy to some of its members. This risks "denying the expression of that power which comes to all the baptized." Power states once again that some of the canonical rulings on the offices of acolyte and reader "actually take away from the full participation of the faithful in the liturgy." He also questions seeing laity who minister the cup or bread as substitutes for a priest or deacon, rather than "as a normal part of their presence in the assembly."[15]

Power's concern is that we may not take seriously enough the role in liturgy and ministry of all baptized Christians. Special acts or rituals of empowerment for some may prevent a fuller discovery of our empowerment of each other. A central focus of his article is the relation of ordination to these themes. Again, a concern is that the role of the community not be overshadowed. "The apostolic and evangelical renewal of the Church, however, is not well served by a revival of images of the sacred that sharpen distinctions between members of the community, or that negate the sense of the power that all Christians share by attributing a greater and more holy power to officeholders."[16]

Finally, Power turns to "the power of the weak," reflecting on the role of the materially and socially weak or marginal in the renewal of both Church and society. He states that, "The cultural models that have affected the Church's own conception and exercise of authority have normally prevented it from giving much recognition to the socially weak, or from allowing the socially weak to have power in the Church's life." The exclusion of the poor from ordination is a concern for him. Out of a rethinking of our structures of officially recognized authority, Power believes that new understandings of Eucharistic precedence and other kinds of structural leadership will emerge. He concludes,

The ultimate ground of an appeal to be accepted as a leader, in whatever post of ministry, lies not in official recognition or appointment, but in the integration of one's witness and service into the life of the community in such a way that it serves and develops mutual empowerment among all and a common sense of life and shared task. A rediscovery of the significance of ordination and other forms of social appointment to ministry depends on this integration.

Power's reflections place the questions faced in the American mainstream culture regarding ecclesial ministers in the context of both the poor of the world Church (including those in the United States), and our scriptural tradition.[17]

The final chapter in this volume is by John Shea, who examines the question of theological assumptions and ministerial style. Building on James Whitehead's constructs, he says that many ministers today "are moving from a hierarchical to a mutual image of Church and from a discipleship to a steward image of themselves within the Church." He sees this as an imaginal shift, which still needs to effect changes in theological understandings and actual ministerial forms. But for such growth to occur, "educational contact with scholars, participation in the sacramental life of the church and personal prayer, and disciplined reflection on significant experiences" are necessary. What is needed is a discovery of the grounding of ministry in "a conviction about divine activity in human life and an understanding of what that activity is trying to accomplish." The life of ministry itself provides the "material" for reflection; attention to the depth experiences within ministry is what will allow greater integration of faith and life and a deeper relationship with God.[18]

The authors of this volume bring their individual reflection and dialogue with each other about "leadership ministry in community" to a conclusion not with a discursive chapter, but rather with reflections about and examples of new rites which could serve the new forms of leadership that we see today. The importance of such action is that: "Attempts to ritualize the current experience of ministry in various communities do not simply follow upon theological consensus; they help generate such consensus by manifesting, at least in part, the sense of the faithful and by submitting all things to the discernment of faith in the Spirit that takes place in common prayer." The need to contextualize such new rites within a Church where the community is respected, where the charisms and ministries of all are recognized, is stressed. The tension that exists is that between "the sociological need to distinguish the leader sufficiently so that the role of guiding the community's power is clear and the evangelical need to keep the leader a minister and servant of the community." Because parishes and local communities are experiencing the emergence of many different kinds of leadership, experimentation with rites of commissioning and blessing is helpful.[19]

One of the difficulties in developing these new rites is finding the appropriate terminology. The term *lay ministry* refers both to the universal call to holiness which flows from baptism and the gift of the Spirit and to non-ordained persons who are serving in designated roles in ministry. Many of the latter have advanced training and professional competence, and serve in full-time and paid positions. The terms used for naming a rite celebrating the movement into ministry include graduation, acknowledgment, recognition, deputation, commissioning, installation, and ordination. Each reflects a theology of ministry. Communities have already been experimenting with various of these forms.[20]

In order to illustrate ways in which such rites may serve to celebrate both the empowerment of the entire baptized community and the designation of someone for a particular leadership role in that community, the authors developed several examples of rituals. Each strives to embody the principles developed in the total book. The first, the ordination of a presbyter in a church constituted by basic Christian communities, is not intended for use now because of existing church law. The others, however, could serve as models for immediate use. They include a blessing of provincial leaders in a religious community, celebration of the completion of a diocesan-based program of ministry training, and a celebration of the appointment of a director of religious education in a parish. The last could be adapted for the appointment of a music director, a director of social work, a director of youth ministry, and so on.[21]

What is particularly striking in the last ritual is the physical placement of the director of religious education within the group of catechists with whom she or he would serve, and the presence of the entire group within the assembled community. Clearly the blessing does not set the person apart from, and certainly not over, the community. This visible sign summarizes well the understanding of leadership in ministry, and official recognition in ritual, of these authors.

MINISTRY AND THE COMMUNITY

The concern about the need to develop a fuller realization of the empowerment of the whole People of God is shared by other liturgists. Richard Szafranski addresses this by analyzing the role of the minister in the early church. He notes that the focus of the role was not on the celebration of the Eucharist, but rather on the building up of the community with preaching and leadership. However, in the second and third centuries "the rich diversification of ministries of leadership shared by many in the community (e.g. prophet, elder, presider at Eucharist) gradually came together and was focused in fewer and fewer people." Gradually, too, the locus of a particular community as the basis of authority when ordaining someone was lost. Eucharistic presidency might not mean that the person had a leadership role in that community.[22]

The relationship of the leader and the community is developed further by Gordon Lathrop. He states: "At their origin, the symbolically formulated Christian leadership positions [bishops and preachers and pastors and ministers] were liturgical positions." Ordination designated individuals to act in the assembly, or in direct extension of the assembly. "By this conception, 'office' is nothing other than a place to stand and a task to do in the assembly." The rules governing moving to another local church are grounded in this understanding. Many important leaders may emerge in the Church (teachers, writers, organizers, trained counselors). However, since they do not have a particular role in the assembly, they need not be ordained. "Ordination would add nothing to the authority of these leaders. Competence and clarity, wisdom and communal responsibility should be authority enough. Nor can ordination make up for the absence of these qualities."[23]

Richard Gaillardetz takes as his starting point the great expansion of lay ministry, and asks how to integrate Christian ministry in all its forms, in light of our doctrinal and liturgical tradition. He suggests grounding the various manifestations of ministry in their service to communion. Each ministry—liturgy, evangelization, catechesis, reconciliation, peacemaking, family ministry, pastoral counseling—has its meaning "in the proclamation and/or restoration of the life of the communion." "The mystagogical task of Christian ministry, then, is first to recognize the basic events of communion which are woven into ordinary human existence, and second, to name those events of communion as graced events, as encounters with nothing less that the God of Jesus Christ." The context of ministry, then, is this relational ontology seen as a servant of communion. Such an image of ministry embraces every concrete ministry, ordained and non-ordained, professional and occasional.[24]

Each of these authors analyzes precisely the relationship of ministers and the community they serve. Ministry is not envisioned as power over, but rather is an action from within the very network of relationships which constitute the life of the community. In fact, for Gaillardetz, ministry finds its fullest meaning in an understanding of its essential role as relational service to communion.

THE DIACONATE

In 1971, *Worship* published a report prepared by members of the Catholic Theological Society for the United States Bishops, on the restoration of the permanent diaconate. The report bears both directly and indirectly on the issue of the new lay ministers. The writers stated that along with an emphasis on collegiality, the restoration of the diaconate as a permanent office in the Roman Catholic Church "is the most significant structural innovation instituted by the Council in regard to church office. In effect the latter move constituted the beginnings of a restructuring of all the ministries in the Catholic Church."[25]

The discussion is placed in the context of the rapid decline of the numbers of "church servants ordained and unordained" and the growing number of groups with special needs (for example, ethnic minorities, the isolated old, the disenchanted young) that cannot be met with existing ministries. The writers anticipated that those ordained as deacons would be people who had already been dedicated to serving the needs of the Church. They also said that since the role of the deacon had varied in the past, "we may expect a pluralism of diaconal function in the future," according to the needs of the people, priests, and bishops where he serves. While the functions deacons perform may well be what laypeople do, the deacon would function "in the name of the risen Christ and the community, as one who holds a stable office of service in the community." The authors noted that in the early church (and still today in the Greek Orthodox Church), women have been ordained as deacons, that women's roles in society have broadened in modern society, and that many women feel called to the diaconate. They conclude: "Actual services being performed by women, both secular and religious, could often be rendered more effectively if they were performed from within the office of deacon."[26]

Fifteen years later Edmond Cullinan explores the issue of women and the diaconate more fully. First, he states that the reasons put forth for excluding women from the priesthood do not apply, because there is a precedent for women deaconesses, and deacons do not consecrate the Eucharist. He traces the precedents in Scripture (Phoebe, and perhaps the women referred to in Timothy 3:11) and the patristic period. Cullinan then notes that in the Church today, many women are "carrying out a pastoral ministry which is very similar to that carried out by deaconesses in the patristic period. . . Ordination to the diaconate would situate this activity within the sacramental structure of the Church. It would give official recognition to their work and enable it to be extended."[27]

In both the report and the article outlined here, the idea of giving official recognition to those who are already ministering in the community is presented. In both cases, the precedents in our tradition are affirmed, as well as the fact that the Church is "free . . . to shape the structure of its various ministries."[28] And both indicate that the ordination of women to the diaconate would make their ministry more effective.

AN ORDERING OF MINISTRIES

John Grondelski examines present church practice by analyzing *Ministeria Quaedam* and how it is presently embodied in the life of the Church. The document states that ministries exist for the proper ordering of worship and the service of the people; historically various ones that had once been entrusted to laity over time came to be regarded as preparatory steps toward ordination. "It noted that this clericalization of various ministries was dominant but not entirely universal in the Church and that the 'functions' . . . were once again being exercised by laity . . . The replacement of the terms 'orders' and 'ordination' by 'ministries' and 'installation' was itself indicative of MQ's desire to declericalize these roles." Central to *Ministeria Quaedam* was the belief that "the dissociation of lector and acolyte from proximate priestly preparation and the reopening of those ministries to lay persons would permit '[t]he distinction between clergy and laity [to] emerge with greater clarity, the distinction between what belongs to the clergy and is reserved to them and what can be entrusted to the laity.'" Although laypeople could be installed as lectors and acolytes, seminarians were to be installed, and were to exercise these ministries, as stages in their formation.[29]

Grondelski then reviews current practice in the United States. He asserts that in fact today the ministries of lector and acolyte are minor orders in everything but name. He says there are two de facto categories of lectors and acolytes, "official" ones (usually seminarians who are few in number) and "unofficial" ones, "the vast majority that one encounters in the typical parish on Sunday morning . . ."[30]

Drawing on his personal experience working at a seminary and graduate school of theology, he notes "the destructive impact of separation of ministry from function," in that there is a tension between seminarians wanting to exercise ministries to which they have been installed and lay students who, seeking to form a worshipping community, want to exercise functions as they do in their home parishes. He questions whether the situation is not leading to a reclericalization of the ministries that were envisioned by *Ministeria Quaedam* as being properly lay.[31]

In conclusion, Grondelski calls on bishops to actively promote the ministries of lector and acolyte as lay ministries, with requisite preparation, and a change in practice regarding rituals now part of preparation for priesthood. He states:

> The old minor orders, however vestigial, did give the seminarian something new to do and, in each step, further separated him from the laity and initiated him into the clerical state. After MQ, however, we have seminarians being installed to lay ministries, laity not being installed in them, declining number of priests to provide example of priestly identity to seminarians, and the rich soil for identity-confusion.[32]

Most relevant for the purpose of this volume is Grondelski's reminder about the need for clarity regarding what belongs to the clergy and is reserved to them, and what can be exercised by the laity, and the place of ritual in helping to define that.

Also starting from *Ministeria Quaedam*, Winfried Haunerland presents a picture of developments in the world Church that call for official
acknowledgment of new ministers. He begins his analysis by repeating
three insights from Vatican II: "all the baptized are empowered members
within the one church...; the connection between being the presider at
the Eucharist and being ordained a priest is constitutive for the church
structured... in a sacramental way...; the priesthood of service handed
on in a sacramental way is... not an office containing in itself all possible ecclesial functions." This grounding opens his exploration of the new
pastoral ministries which he sees "as the possible result of a balanced rel-
ativizing of the ordained ministry resulting from conciliar renewal."[33]

In his review of the history of the minor orders, Haunerland traces
the story back to the third century *Traditio Apostolica* and its understanding of a number of ministries in addition to bishop, presbyter, and deacon. While originally the levels of order corresponded to different
offices actually present in the Church, over time there was less linkage to
real activities. "The more ancient insistence that everyone who was to be
ordained a presbyter had previously to prove himself through successful
effort in other ministries—this ultimately yielded to the formal demand
that the presbyter must go through all the levels of orders but without at
all showing experience and dedication by actually exercising any of those
ministries connected to the minor orders." Trent had wanted a reform of
this situation, but not until 1972 did Paul VI respond to the problem of
the offices connected with the minor orders no longer having any real
meaning for the life of the Church. His action demonstrates the Church's
"freedom in ordering its ecclesial life." However, like Grondelski, Haunerland notes that today seminarians are installed, while men and women who
read at Mass are not. "So the difference between the work and those
entrusted with that service—something Trent criticized—continues on
today." Furthermore, he says that those laity who read at Mass "have a
far greater impact on liturgical life than the few men ... solemnly
installed ... into official ministries of the church." Therefore:

[t]he reform of the minor orders is stuck along its track because
its point of departure was never the real needs of the church
today. It would be more realistic to develop a reform which
emerges from the permanent ministries which are actually being
given to men and women in the church today. Those active men

and women delineate the new *ministeria*, proceeding, as they do, from concrete profiles of what these ministers do.[34]

A further point emphasized by Haunerland is that in a world Church we will need "to live out a greater pluriformity of ecclesial structures, structures which are not essential to its very identity..." *Ministeria Quaedam* itself invited conferences of bishops to request offices other than those common to the Latin Church. He offers illustrations of diverse ministries that have emerged in Zaire, Taiwan, Honduras, and Germany, saying that such diverse ministries "depend on the ethos and educational possibilities as well as on the socio-economic presuppositions and spiritual approaches of each place."[35]

He concludes with a consideration of the liturgical commissioning of the new pastoral ministries.

> A theology seeking suitable ecclesial location for the new lay ecclesial ministries cannot neglect a suitable liturgical and sacramental expression for them. A commissioning, although it is not a sacrament, should not be understood as only a formal, juridical act. It is a participation in the sacramental, basic form of the church.

Central to this, he holds, is establishing differences, outlining how diverse ministries are an exercising of properly different services, even if the rite were similar to that for the institution of lector or acolyte. "The issue is basically the formal understanding of a specific ministry realized in the local church according to a certain analogy with the services of acolyte and lector as they exist in the church around the world." He argues that the ceremonies that evolve are significant because they are concerned with the ecclesial situation of ministries. They help raise unresolved questions and articulate a consensus "which has or has not been reached." Such ceremonies should have the approval of the bishop. Because the ministries have a local character, a single rite binding on the entire Church is not desirable. And, when lay ministries "have a clear identity and are analogous to the ministries of lectors and acolytes" bishops' conferences could request installation of these new ministers.[36]

Ritual is central to the Roman Catholic imagination; sacramentals and sacraments are at the heart of our tradition. The research shows that the new ministers increasingly desire a ritual that will celebrate their place in the ministry of the Church. Liturgists are exploring what such a ritual should be and what it would signify.

CONCLUSION

A common theme found in the reflection of the liturgists is an emphasis on the community, the assembly, the People of God. The need for various ministries, the multiple functions that must be performed, the many ministers who serve the community are all considered, but they are secondary. While the need to differentiate the leader is affirmed, the greater need is mutual empowerment. While the ways of ritualizing a new minister's acceptance of a role of leadership in a community are explored, care is taken not to overshadow the role of the community itself in ministry—a variety of ministries, certainly, but within a ministering community. The Church's tradition of minor orders, especially as reconfigured by *Ministeria Quaedam*, offers a fruitful source for identifying a way to ritually designate new ministers for a new role in this community.

An uncommon theme is sounded by Power: the place of the materially and socially weak or marginal in the life of the Church. In light of the fact that so few of the new ministers are from minority groups, it is of great importance that we ask about both how the needs of the poor and marginalized members of the Church will be adequately met, and how these members of our community will be empowered for ministry.

NOTES

1. Nathan Mitchell, "Ministry Today: Problems and Prospects," *Worship*, vol. 48, no. 6, June-July 1974, pp. 336–346.
2. Leland J. White, "Ministry Is Public Service," *Worship*, vol., 53, no. 6, November 1979, pp. 511–518.
3. John Grabner, "Ordained and Lay: Them—Us or We?," *Worship*, vol. 54, no. 4, July 1980, pp. 327, 330.
4. (New York: Pueblo Publishing Company, 1980), pp. vii–viii.
5. Ibid., pp. 4–9.
6. Ibid., pp. 59–84, especially 62, 75.
7. Ibid., pp. 88–107, especially 89, 96.
8. Ibid., pp. 127–131. For a fuller development of this theme, see David N. Power, "Church Order: The Need for Redress," *Worship*, vol. 71, no. 4, July 1997, pp. 286–308. In the conclusion he states, "Highlighting hierarchy can well result in a transfer of ecclesial priorities. These are, in brief, the transfer of authority from the canon of the Word to the canonical authority of the bishop, from the obedience to all the gifts of the Spirit to the control of the charism of episcopacy, and from a Eucharist focused on the common table of the one Body to a Eucharist enthralled with the ritual performance of the bishop, or the presbyter" (p. 308).
9. Ibid., pp. 157–158 and 133–147.
10. *Alternative Futures for Worship*, vol. 6., *Leadership Ministry in Community*, Michael A. Cowan, ed. (Collegeville, MN: The Liturgical Press, 1987), pp. 9–19.
11. James D. Whitehead, "Christian Images of Community: Power and Leadership," in *Alternative Futures*, pp. 24–37, especially pp. 24, 34.
12. Evelyn Eaton Whitehead, "Leadership and Power: A View from the Social Sciences," in *Alternative Futures*, pp. 39–68, especially pp. 42–43, 46.
13. James Whitehead, "Stewardship: The Disciple Becomes a Leader," in *Alternative Futures*, pp. 69–80, especially pp. 71, 78.
14. David N. Power, "Liturgy and Empowerment," in *Alternative Futures*, pp. 81–82.
15. Ibid., pp. 83–84.
16. Ibid., pp. 85–98, especially p. 97.

17. Ibid., pp. 97–107, especially p. 103.

18. John Shea, "Theological Assumptions and Ministerial Style," in *Alternative Futures*, pp. 105–128, especially pp. 106–107, 114, 116, 119, 121.

19. David N. Power, "Guidelines for the Development of Rites," in *Alternative Futures*, pp. 139–141.

20. Evelyn Eaton Whitehead, "Celebrating the Ministry of the Unordained," in *Alternative Futures*, pp. 153–154.

21. *Alternative Futures*, pp. 150–176.

22. Richard Szafranski, "The One Who Presides at Eucharist," *Worship*, vol. 63, no. 4, July 1989, pp. 307, 309, 310–311.

23. Gordon Lathrop, "Christian Leadership and Liturgical Community," *Worship*, vol. 66, no. 2, March 1992, pp. 102, 103, 106, 107.

24. Richard Gaillardetz, "In Service of Communion: A Trinitarian Foundation for Christian Ministry," *Worship*, vol. 67, no. 5, September 1993, pp. 418–419, 427, 428, 432, 433.

25. "Restoration of the Office of Deacon as a Lifetime State: A Report to the U.S. Bishops." Report prepared by members of the Catholic Theological Society of America at the request of the Bishops' Committee on the Permanent Diaconate. *Worship*, vol. 45, no. 4, April 1971, p. 186.

26. Ibid., pp. 187–197.

27. Edmond Cullinan, "Women and the Diaconate," *Worship*, vol. 70, no. 3, May 1976, pp. 261–265.

28. "Report: Catholic Theological Society," p. 188.

29. "Lay Ministries? A Quarter Century of *Ministeria Quaedam*," *Irish Theological Quarterly*, vol. 63, no. 3, 1998, pp. 272–277.

30. Ibid., pp. 278–279.

31. Ibid., pp. 280–281, 277.

32. Ibid., pp. 281–282.

33. "The Heirs of the Clergy? The New Pastoral Ministries and the Reform of the Minor Orders," *Worship*, vol. 75, no. 4, July 2001, pp. 305–307. The article first appeared in *Theologische-Praktische Quartalschrift*, 147 (1999), pp. 381–391; it was translated by Thomas O'Meara.

34. Ibid., pp. 308–310.

35. Ibid., pp. 311–316.

36. Ibid., pp. 317–320.

CHAPTER EIGHT

THEOLOGIANS

INTRODUCTION

The focus of this chapter is an exploration of evolving theological understandings of ministry which gradually include consideration of the meaning of laypeople involved in leadership in the Church. It begins with the larger context of theological reflection on ministry in general. The second half of the twentieth century had been very rich in studies of ministry. One reason for this is that the work done by scripture scholars and church historians, especially in the first half of the century, called for a rethinking of our understandings of ministry. Another reason is that ecumenical dialogue provided new ways of looking at our patterns and meanings of ministry. Finally, throughout the world the Church has experienced new developments in ministry at the grassroots, in parishes, within movements, and in base communities, and theologians have begun to ponder these realities. A full review of the vast literature that has appeared is not possible. However, a brief commentary on some of the influential works will highlight the way an expanded understanding of ministry is unfolding. Reflection on the emergence of the new ministers in the Church in the United States will conclude the chapter.

THE CONTEXT

A clearer understanding of the significant changes in understandings of ministry emerges when the pre-Vatican II period is compared with theologians' views today. Before the Council, the language "ministry" was not used in Catholic circles, and theological reflection on ministry as such was uncommon. There was much study of the theology of priesthood, but the exploration of the meaning of ministry as a concept wider than priesthood was not usually undertaken. In fact, Bernard Cooke pointed out that "the nature and exercise of Christian ministry has until quite recently been neglected in the theology of every Christian denomination." Cooke says that the most significant earlier work was done by Anglican scholars of the 1930s and 1940s, with *The Apostolic Ministry* edited by Kenneth Kirk as "the best known and probably most influential study."[1] A brief overview of this volume gives a summary, therefore, of pre-Vatican II understandings.

The subtitle captures the essence of the view of ministry it propounds: "Essays on the History and Doctrine of Episcopacy." The introduction gives the theme: "the ministry, as embodied in its highest exemplar, the episcopate, is 'from above,' endowed with grace and authority from on high." Kirk delineates function and office, concluding that in the New Testament although there are many functions, there are "only two orders of ministers in the Church, 'apostles' and 'elders.'" Furthermore, the order of apostle is "Essential," whereas the elder is "Dependent," insofar as the apostles appointed them, whereas "the apostle is appointed by God alone." In time, the duties of the apostle were handed on to the resident bishops. "Thus the retention of an apostolic ministry must be regarded as of the essence of early Christianity." The deacons and presbyters on the other hand were "the Dependent Ministry; it contributed nothing of real importance." The Essential Ministry was responsible for commissioning new members, presbyters, deacons, and bishops to the ministry. Therefore, "no one could be a member of that ministry unless he had been admitted to it by those who were already members of it themselves. This is, in brief, the Catholic thesis."[2] Other functions exercised in the New Testament church (for example, teacher and prophet) are not offices and have "nothing to do with Church order or government at all," being simply "so many kinds of partial service."[3]

In short, the view of ministry given in this volume is centered in the episcopacy: bishops have the fullness of ministry, most especially the power of admitting others to the ministry. Apostolic succession is wholly vested in the episcopacy; not even the presbyters share in this. Sacramental ministry, stewardship of the tradition, teaching, all these belong in their fullness to the bishop. As with the teachers and prophets of the New Testament, those in the Church who exercise other functions offer only "so many kinds of partial service." Ministry is primarily singular, and episcopal. Today's language and experience, "an explosion of ministries," is inexplicable in this context.

CHARISM AND ORDER: PROTESTANT PERSPECTIVES

In the 1960s, several theologians helped to refocus our attention on both the charismatic dimensions of the New Testament church, and on the multiplicity of orders discernible in the various communities in the earliest period of our history. A foundational article is "Ministry and Community in the New Testament" by Ernst Käsemann. He stresses the concept "charisma" found in the Pauline and sub-Pauline theology which,

> . . . describes in a theologically exact and comparative way the essence and scope of every ecclesiastical ministry and function. A charisma is the specific part which the individual has in the leadership and glory of Christ; and this specific part which the individual has in the Lord shows itself in a specific service and a specific vocation.[4]

For Käsemann, there is a multiplicity of gifts, and of ministries. These include the ministry of Kerygma (including the gifts of inspiration and ecstasy, and the functions of apostles, prophets, evangelists, teachers, and admonishers); the ministry of Diakonia (comprising deacons and deaconnesses, those who give alms and tend the sick, the widows, and those with the gifts of miraculous healing and exorcism); the charismata pertaining to governance (from the "first fruits" and "those who are over you" to the pastors and bishops); and the charism of Suffering. The unifying element is captured in the image of the Body of Christ. The conclusion Käsemann draws stands in strong contrast to the preconciliar views outlined above. He says that all Christians are members of the Body of Christ and all are endowed with charisma.

> . . . in His gifts and in the ministries which they express and indeed create, He Himself is present . . . Every ministry is grace received . . . and points to [Christ's], who is the first and proper apostle, prophet, deacon, teacher, pastor, evangelist . . .[5]

Fourteen years had elapsed between Kirk's and Käsemann's analyses of ministry. Much of the discussion in Catholic circles for the next two decades will be, in some way, a development from these two very different theologies of ministry. Käsemann's views of ministry rooted in charismata and shared by the whole Church, of a multiplicity of ministries, of a need for charism and order, of ministry transcending the realm of the sacred, will help to shape the continuing dialogue.

While Käsemann acknowledges that an ordering of ministries is found in the New Testament, he does not develop this idea. He states, though, that he held much in common with Schweizer's *Church Order in the New Testament,* an extensive analysis of the various communities whose lives are described in Scripture. Schweizer's conclusion is that, "There is no such thing as *the* New Testament church order. Even in New Testament times, circumstances were very varied." In his work, he is particularly interested in uncovering the theological concerns that caused the order to take the precise forms that it did, viewing the developments as one way in which the Church's witness is expressed.[6]

Schweizer holds that the historical Jesus did not found a new Church. Rather, he lived entirely within the national religious association of Israel. The Twelve were not leaders, not even teachers, but messengers. The emphasis is on the role of "the many;" "everyone is engaged in service, and there is no point in distinguishing between ordinary believers and those called to service." However, in the primitive Church in Jerusalem, a new communal life began to form, centered in the breaking of the bread, gradually shutting itself off from Judaism by opening itself to the nations. In this context, a new order begins to emerge: The Twelve, apostles, prophets, all with roles in the Church.[7]

Subsequently, the churches of Matthew, Luke, and the other subapostolic communities emerge, each with their own characteristics. For example, in the diaspora community of Matthew, the Church has a new self-consciousness of herself as Israel, obeying the law in a new way in its following of Jesus. The Matthean tradition traces itself in a special way to Peter. Scribes who held a central role in Jewish communities of the day are also important in Matthew's church. But as chapter 18 indicates, there are no office bearers, and no graduated titles; "the only hierarchy is the paradoxical one that the highest is the one who renders most service. . . and that the 'little ones' are the most important members of the Church."[8]

Schweizer points out that it is in Luke that the Church's conscious-ness of its own history first begins to emerge, its realization that there will be a history between the Resurrection and the Parousia. Because of this realization, Luke emphasizes the idea of apostleship as the role of eyewitnesses of Jesus' earthly life and work, for which there can be no successors. In this Church, there is an openness to "new and unaccus-tomed ways," and when new tasks arise "then individual church members must be separated for those special tasks."

> Again and again [Luke] refers to the Spirit as determining the Church's order. The greatness of Luke's view lies in his showing more impressively than anyone else that the Church can live only by evangelizing and by following whatever new paths the Spirit indicates.[9]

By contrast, in the Pastorals Schweizer perceives the Church experienc-ing its own existence "much more strongly as a static one . . . it has estab-lished itself firmly. . . [and wants] to remain what it is." Therefore, its essential feature is as a "guarantor of the 'truth'—that is, of right doc-trine." For Schweizer, the Spirit seems to hardly play a part in this Church.[10]

Again by contrast, Hebrews presents an image of the Church as a "people on the move." In light of that, the ministry of teaching is based both on tradition and on spiritual growth which is inspired by the Spirit. Ministering is the activity of all church members. A special insight of Hebrews is that all the Old Testament ministries are fulfilled in Jesus Christ. Schweizer sees Hebrews as combating the institutional Church. And in the Johannine epistles, these features are shown "in a more advanced stage."[11]

From his detailed study of the individual church communities, Schweizer draws several conclusions. The early church believed that the message, rooted in the historical Jesus, must be proclaimed *and* that they had met the Risen Lord and he was ongoingly present with them. There-fore, they emphasized both creedal formulae and the exaltation of Jesus. Hence, church order included both historicity, tradition, and the link with Israel (as found in Luke and the Pastorals) and newness and the role of the Holy Spirit (as found in John). He holds that there are dangers in both directions and that "the New Testament Church sustained these very sharply defined groups in the one Church."[12]

CHARISM AND ORDER: CATHOLIC PERSPECTIVES

Both Käsemann and Schweizer are Protestant. During this same period, in the Catholic community Schnackenburg addressed the idea of order in the New Testament. He, too, states, "It is difficult to make out the order that prevailed in the first Christian communities because it varied according to place and time." In Roman Catholic writing, this was a new assessment.[13] Compared to Schweizer, greater emphasis is given to a shaping of ministry "from above." He says: "the offices and ministries which appear from time to time, their number, the way they are named, and their nature, are not the decisive factor as long as the order willed and determined by God is maintained."[14]

Central to Schnackenburg's view is the idea that the primitive church, both as a whole and in its individual communities, "did not lack order and that this order was not one which had to be created each time by the Holy Spirit, and which had to be recognized and acknowledged by the community." This order was "a fundamental constitution of the Church determined by God and obligatory from the start, and followed from the 'mission from on high.'" The action that Schnackenburg views as central in the New Testament churches is that of the proclamation of the Word. Evangelists, apostles, prophets shared in this activity. However, Schnackenburg maintains that nonetheless, "there is no mention in the New Testament of their [the prophets] being in any way rivals to the official ministry."[15] Hence, in this view, ministry belongs to office, not to the function or activity of proclaiming the Word.

What Schnackenburg contributes to the developing theology of ministry is the fact that a Catholic has entered the dialogue and has accepted some of the fundamental insights of the decade, but has given a particularly Catholic valuation to the data examined. Hierarchy is emphasized—but not the way it was in Kirk. The God-givenness of the Church's order is maintained—but with a careful faithfulness to the complexity of the New Testament record. A marked difference is the minimalization of the role of the community as a whole, compared to that in the previous authors. For Schnackenburg, they are both the people of God, instructed by the Lord, and the flock of Christ, ruled and guided by pastors,[16] not a primary locus of the Spirit's activity.

Hans Küng, another Roman Catholic writing in this period, provides a complement to Schnackenburg's minimalist view of the role of the community in the Church's order. Küng takes as his starting point for an analysis of offices in the Church the priesthood of all believers. His intention is not to say that the community precedes or is higher than ecclesiastical office, only that it also is important. Jesus Christ is the highest authority, followed by His first witnesses and heralds. All believers are "a royal priesthood." All have direct access to God, all offer spiritual sacrifices of prayer and penitence; all are called to preach the Word, to share in the actions of Baptism, the Lord's supper and the forgiveness of sins; all mediate by their witness and their prayer for the world; all have a share in ministry.[17]

Küng roots his understandings of ecclesiastical office in the New Testament choice of the word *diakonia*. (A fuller treatment of this characteristic of ministry is given below, in chapter 12.) He links this concept to Jesus' commandment to love one's neighbor, and says that Christian office is not based on law, power, knowledge, or dignity, but service. Furthermore, the service one offers is rooted in charism. Therefore, "the variety of ministry in the Church is as unlimited as the variety of charisms in the Church." These gifts are of two types: private (for example,. those who exhort or give aid) and public (for example, apostles and elders); the latter must be exercised regularly and constantly. The "second type of especial charismatic ministry is what constitutes the diakonal structure, a particular side and aspect of the general and fundamental charismatic structure of the church."[18]

Küng notes that "the New Testament offers no fixed and exclusive catalogue of these permanent ministries within the community which would be valid for all communities." He types the public ministries as preaching (the apostles, evangelists, prophets, and teachers are grouped here) and welfare and guidance (these include the vaguely defined ones who are "over" the community, the "fellow-workers" of Paul, bishops, deacons, and elders). In analyzing the life of the Pauline communities, Küng, like Käsemann, concludes that what is central is the call from God, the charism of the Spirit. However, Küng also delineates the system of elders present in other New Testament communities. In them, ordination "is the giving of authority and commissioning of particular members for a particular service, effected by the laying-on of hands, which serves as a public legitimization of the minister and his endowing with the charism needed for his ministry."[19] In the latter concern, he is closer to Schnackenburg's perspectives.

A final aspect of Küng's theology that is relevant is his assessment of apostolic succession. Like Schweizer, he maintains that "the fundamental element is the apostolic succession of the Church as a whole and of each individual member of it." However, Küng also sees "within the apostolic succession of the Church as a whole. . . a particular apostolic succession in the various pastoral ministries." He sees these as including both presbyters, bishops, and deacons and "other gifts and ministries," especially "those who succeed the New Testament prophets and teachers."[20]

Küng's work adds new perspectives to the theology of ministry that are important today. He reflects on the New Testament data in a way similar to that of the Protestant scholars we have examined, but with Catholic sensitivities. His assessment of "public ministries" and "private ministries" indicates a place for both other official ecclesiastical ministries and the "priesthood of all believers." His balancing of the call by God and the place of ordination, of the apostolic succession of the community and of special pastoral ministers, of the threefold ministry of deacon, presbyter, and bishop and other special ministries, all reflect the situation of the Roman Catholic community. But within this community, his ideas represent a distinct widening of the concept of ministry.

To complete an assessment of ideas about ministry in the Roman Catholic period at this time, it is helpful to examine Raymond Brown's *Priest and Bishop: Biblical Reflections*. Although Brown focuses on priesthood, which is not central for this study, some of his perspectives have relevance for our topic. First, he argues that the sacramental powers were given to the Christian community in the persons of the Twelve. Therefore, while they "themselves may have baptized, presided at the Eucharist and forgiven sins, the Church may also have recognized the sacramental authority of others who were not ordained by the Twelve. In other words, if the sacramental power resided in the Church, it can be given to those whom the Church designates or acknowledges, without a lineal connection to the Twelve." The idea of the Church having control over its ministries is significant, as we ponder the emergence of new ministers in the Church today, and how to respond to them.[21]

Second, when he looks at the question of apostolic succession, he notes that the presbyter-bishops are "not in any traceable way the successors of the Twelve Apostles." And yet, they "did eventually succeed to these apostles in the exercise of pastoral care over the churches the apostles had founded." Therefore, he holds that the succession is more traceable to the work of the Spirit in the Church than to the historical Jesus. He concludes:

> The continuation of the functions of the Pauline apostle is the responsibility of the Church as a whole. A formal aspect of that responsibility has been entrusted to the bishop, but his succession to apostolic functions is qualified by the Church situation of our times. Only by drawing upon the larger resources of the Church can he make that succession realistic.[22]

In highlighting in this way the role of the whole community in apostolic succession, Brown is in accord with the insights of Protestant scholars. (Of course, that is not to say on them; rather, they are all dependent on the reading of Scripture with contemporary biblical and historical methods.) But, in stressing the "formal aspect of that responsibility," which is given to the bishop, he is affirming Catholic practice and understanding as well. Brown also realistically assesses the limits on the authority of the bishop, on the basis of both the testimony of the New Testament and the situation of the present-day Church.

MINISTRY TO WORD AND SACRAMENTS

While the authors considered thus far have generally focused on the earliest period of church history, Bernard Cooke's *Ministry to Word and Sacraments* is significant for the thoroughness of its historical treatment of ministry in six great periods of the Church. However, an analysis of that dimension of Cooke's work would go beyond the design for this study. Therefore, only key theological aspects will be highlighted.

Theologically, Cooke situates his perspectives on ministry within Christology. He states that the basic question for Christianity is "What did Christ do and what if anything, is he still doing?" Regarding ministry, he says: "All Christian ministry finds its origin in the salvific ministry of Jesus himself . . . (A)ll authentic Christian ministry involves a participation in Christ's own ministerial mission and power." As in Schweizer, the emphasis here is on both the historical Jesus and the Risen Lord. Therefore, Cooke can say that participation in the ministry of Christ "means an ongoing cooperation between Christ and the community in the work of establishing the Kingdom of God" because Jesus "remains actively present to and operative through the Christian community."[23]

Cooke's reflections on "What did Christ do and what . . . is he still doing?" give the organizational framework for his book. The basic category is that of community; a theology of ministry evolves within an ecclesiology. Jesus created a community in his life, death, and resurrection; his work is continued by this community. In the New Testament period, "the early Christians saw themselves as charged with the task of building up the community that Jesus had initiated." Today, because of their Baptism, the corporate ministry of the Church "pertains to all baptized Christians." For this reason, Cooke finds it preferable to speak in terms of ministries, recognizing that:

> (T)he Spirit has given throughout history and will give at the present moment a plurality of gifts which exist in autonomy and complementarity. What unifies and orders these charisms and passes upon their genuineness is the community as a whole and the one Spirit working in the community.

One corollary of this perspective is the realization that "new ministries will come into existence" and others "might cease to have a purpose and should disappear." Another corollary is that it is the community that is in the first instance "the heir to the 'apostolic succession' and the bearer of the 'apostolic tradition.'" Finally, these ministries may be classed into two broad groups: those "that exist to provide for the church's service to the world and the ministries that exist to nurture the church's own internal well-being."[24] These two categories, in turn, provide the framework for the remainder of Cooke's work.

In analyzing the ministry of Jesus and the ministry of the Twelve, Cooke sees their witness to the saving act of divine love as a basic dimension of their activity; "such witness involves a ministry of word."

(T)he understanding of the community as prophetic is deepened by the realization that the community is this as Christ's own Body. Thus we have a radical unification of word and sacrament: the church is sacrament precisely insofar as it is word.

Among the ministries of the Word, Cooke groups the witness, the prophet, the preacher, the apostle, the teacher, those who do theology, writers (and all communicators), the liturgical celebrant, and the episcopacy.[25]

Another aspect of ministry is service to the people of God. The underlying theological theme is similar to that shown above:

Since loving concern for all men and women is the most basic precept of the Christian ethic, the entire church is diakonal. Delegation of special service functions to some within the community, if such delegations seem an effective way of helping people, does not free any member of the church from the continuing obligation of caring for others.

However, because "Jesus as the Christ is redeemer of the entire world 'from within,'" such an incarnational understanding "denies Christianity any ministerial monopoly and points to some sharing of 'ministry to the world' by Christians and all others who work to better the human situation." The specialized ministries of service include stewardship of the community's possessions, the ministry of healing (from that of a doctor to that of a spiritual director), and the ministry of governing.[26]

Next, Cooke discusses "ministering to God's judgment." In this context, within the New Testament he considers judgment on truth (a function of the community, the teachers, and the prophets), judgment on behavior (a function of the Twelve, the other apostles, and presbyters of the early church, always informed by the prophetic charism), and judgment on sin (essentially, as forgiveness of sin). Applying this to the Church today, Cooke emphasizes the role of the discernment of the Spirit. Characteristically, he says:

Unquestionably, the entire community's faith experience must be consulted in the attempt to discover the Spirit's action. . . For this reason, the traditional faith and historical experience of Christianity must always be one of the sources of insight that shape the church's search for the presence of the Spirit in its life.[27]

A dimension of this discussion is a consideration of authority in the Church. In assessing the New Testament evidence for the exercise of authority, Cooke sees it in the context of witness to the truth, rooted in a service of others, and having the Eucharistic self-gift of Christ as the norm. In applying this to the Church today, he discusses differing bases for the authority to exercise judgment: knowledge (including witness), religious experience (especially when shared by many), theological competence, prophetic charism, and the authority of love.[28]

In his final section, Cooke analyzes "ministry to the Church's sacramentality." The New Testament record is acultic, Cooke states, and yet Jesus' priesthood and victimhood are implicit in his entire life. And so, too, "because he abides with his brethren whom he joins to himself in his Body. . . the entirety of Christian existence is caught up into a cultic context, the whole of Christian life is meant to be an act of worship." He states further: "Christians are a priestly people because they are the Body of him who is the one high priest." In the Church today, Cooke sees this radical sacramentality operative: "Christ as sacrament makes his Father present; the Church as sacrament makes Christ present, and it does so most formally in those symbolic activities that have traditionally been called the sacraments." Within this community of the Church, the role of the celebrant is "to help bring into being a deepened community of faith and worship in the very act of Eucharist so that the assembled community can more authentically and profoundly celebrate the Eucharistic mystery." The Eucharistic ministry symbolizes "the assembled community and the liturgical leadership collegium. . . and. . . acts as the sacrament of Christ."[29]

From this overview, it can be seen that Cooke develops more completely and in a more nuanced fashion some of the key theological concepts already encountered in this chapter. First, he stresses the role of the entire community. Küng did also, but in his work, the "priesthood of the faithful" was the starting point, and the language used was consistently clerical. Küng seemed to be extending the role of the priest to include the layperson. In Cooke, the starting place is the whole community, as community. His insights proceed from his Christological and ecclesiological starting points. The entire exposition of ministry is developed out of this understanding of its being the work of the entire community, vivified by the Risen Christ. Within the community, specialized ministries exist to assist with this task. Furthermore, because the cosmic Christ vivifies all of reality, people who actively serve the needs of the world, whether as part of the Christian community or not, are also involved in this ministry.

Second, his approach is at the same time both radically Word-oriented and radically sacramental. Even the power of office is interpreted in this context: "Because a man through his ordination possesses public recognition as a witness to the church's faith he is enabled to act as a 'word' of the church; but the effectiveness of his action comes from that action being the Church's *word* and not from some other power that is attached to the office which the man occupies.[30] The primacy of a ministry of the Word is clear. Individual ministries partake in both these dimensions of ministry: the witness testifies to the truth, yet in his life as disciple also sacramentalizes it; the liturgical celebrant both preaches the Word and serves as a multivalent symbol in the community. The centrality of a sacramental ministry is also clear. The entire community ministers "to Word and Sacraments," as the title of his volume so cogently states; specialized ministries exist within this context.

MINISTRY AND LEADERSHIP

In the volume *Ministry: Leadership in the Community of Jesus Christ*, Edward Schillebeeckx distills twenty-five years of his work on the topic of ministry. It is only possible to highlight a few aspects of his thought that have particular relevance when considering the new ministers.

Schillebeeckx's starting point is "the living life of the communities which take initiatives," because he thinks that the practice of the ministry is "formed from theological reflection on new human and cultural situations. . . .[A]uthoritative documents are always prepared for by new practices which arise from the grass-roots." He thinks we have entered a fourth phase in the history of ministry, the first three being the first millennium, the feudal period, and the Tridentine period.[31]

Schillebeeckx begins with "the story of New Testament communities." It is helpful to reflect on his conclusion. In considering the Pauline and "Matthean" communities, he notes the difference between a gradual institutionalization of ministry in the first and an emphasis on charismatic leadership in the second. He concludes:

> Ministry without charisma becomes starved and threatens to turn into a power institution; charisma without any institutionalization threatens to be volatilized into fanaticism and pure subjectivity . . . so the stress is placed by the post-apostolic churches of the New Testament on the apostolicity of the communities, which ask for ministers; that is an essentially Christian intuition.[32]

In assessing the Johannine community, Schillebeeckx notes that the presbyters did not seem to have the kind of authority which that office has in Paul and Matthew. However, he does see authority (in this case, that of Peter) as being an issue in chapter 21, a later addition to the Gospels. Therefore, he says:

> Thus in Johannine theology there is certainly a structure of ministry, but to begin with this was in no way a teaching authority. Only gradually does Johannine theology arrive at the experience that a mere reference to the anointing of each believer with the Spirit (1 John 2:27) is insufficient to keep the community true to the gospel. . . even the Johannnine church accepts the authority of ministers in teaching and discipline, but nevertheless makes these structures relative . . .[33]

Schillebeeckx draws conclusions about what ministry was in the New Testament period. First "the ministry did not develop from and around the eucharist or the liturgy, but from the apostolic building up of the community through preaching, admonition and leadership." Second, "ministry is a constituent part of the church . . . necessary for building up the church along apostolic lines. . . The ministry is a service to this apostolicity." Third, this apostolicity is vested in "the gospel of the community, which also has the right to ministers who make sure that it remains in line with this apostolic origin." Fourth, "the particular character of the ministry is set against the background of many different, non-ministerial services in the Church. In this sense the ministry is not a status but in fact a function."[34]

Schillebeeckx sees two aspects of the tradition as central for clarifying the Church's understanding of ministry in the first ten centuries: canon six of the Council of Chalcedon, declaring invalid "absolute consecration," and the *Apostolic Tradition* of Hippolytus. The first shows there was an essential link between the community and its leader. Ordination did not give the power to preside over the community and at the Eucharist. Rather, "the minister appointed by the community already received, by virtue of his appointment, all the powers which are necessary for the leadership of a Christian community." The second links appointment by the Church and the charisma of the Spirit. He concludes that "the recognition of someone as a minister by the church (people and leaders) is decisive."[35]

Schillebeeckx's central concern is leadership in the community, which he sees as linked with ordination. He does not see the varied services that exist in the Church as part of "the ministry." Therefore, he considers the situation of the new pastoral workers as an anomaly. "[T]heir actual pastoral situation has not been completely 'institutionalized' (often it is also without appropriate legal, let alone financial guarantees)." He holds that it is important "to recognize the ecclesial implications of their charisma (which is in fact that of a minister) accepted by the community: their *pneuma hegemonikon* or charisma of leadership."[36]

Schillebeeckx's starting point is the "new human and cultural situation," represented by both priestless communities and the new pastoral workers. His primary concern is focused on the right of communities to Eucharist and the need for official ecclesial recognition of pastoral workers. In *Ministry* he seems to favor ordination of pastoral workers as priests,[37] whereas in *Church with a Human Face* he posits that a fourth kind of ministry (in addition to episcopacy, presbyterate, and diaconate) may be emerging in our age.[38]

Schillebeeckx's viewpoint is primarily ecclesial: it is the community that is apostolic, a view already noted several times in this study, but here seen to have further implications. It is also pneumatological: the Spirit acts both in the giving of the charisma of leadership and in the community's recognition of that gift and consequent designation of the leader.

MINISTRY AS A THEOLOGY OF GRACE

The starting place for Thomas O'Meara is the "cultural phenomenology" of ministry today, and throughout history. His thesis is that a description of ministry is "a theology of grace which views God's presence in the world as the source, milieu and goal of ministry." He brings together many of the issues, questions, and tensions we have already considered, from the perspective of this "theology of grace." While cultural history is central to his exposition, this overview will comment primarily on the theological conclusions he draws.[39]

Characteristic of his theology of grace is his assessment of "the explosion of ministry" throughout the world: it "suggests that the Holy Spirit is intent upon a wider service, a more diverse ministry for a church life that will be broader in quantity and richer in quality." Characteristic of his cultural history perspective is his assessment of the need for this expansion in ministry, rooted in "a new church which is, for the first time in many centuries, worldwide." And, characteristic of his assessment of the world of laity and sisters involved in ministry throughout the world (the phenomenological data) is his statement: "The experience of the diversification of ministries appears like a life-plan sprung from the sub-conscious of the church. It is a collective charism intent upon realization."[40] His theology is a dialogue between spirit and world.

O'Meara defines tradition as "the history of Christian community manifest in cultural forms and articulated in theology, liturgy and prayer." Therefore, he draws on various "sources" to understand ministry in any age:

(1) the world of the thought-forms of the time expressed abstractly in philosophy; (2) the teaching of the church at this time (theology); (3) the services provided in ordinary church life; (4) the social context in which people live.[41]

O'Meara focuses on the centrality of the Kingdom of God in Jesus' preaching, concluding: "The Kingdom of God is the horizon of ministry. The Kingdom of God is the source, the milieu, the goal of ministry." Hence, "*pneuma, charisma,* and then *diakonia* are realizations of the wider, intimate horizon Scripture calls 'the Kingdom of God.'" Jesus invited others to share in his work. Therefore, the Church "is a community of ministers to the Kingdom, a limited but sacramental anticipation of God's presence." A theology of ministry is rooted in ecclesiology, but ministry does not simply point back to the Church. Rather, ministry is servant of the Kingdom, a universal servant (not just on behalf of church members, but of the Kingdom as present in various degrees through all people) and a sacramental servant (because the Church and ministry have "an incarnational nature" *and* manifest the power of the Spirit). Therefore, ministry is rooted in freedom to serve and not in self-serving (even of religion).[42]

O'Meara considers "the mode in which the risen Christ lives and works" since Pentecost as the Holy Spirit. He emphasizes the pneumatological: "ministry is grounded not so much in the imitation of the historical Jesus as in the personal response to the charismatic call of his Spirit." Because of the coming of the Spirit, the Christian lives in freedom, especially a "freedom for giving of self;" "the mode of this giving is service." Therefore, "ministry results from the Spirit and its freedom given in baptismal initiation."[43]

The "bridge between freedom and ministry" is charism, "the presence of the Spirit of Christ in an individual." Charismatic gifts are of many kinds, and are closely related to ministries. O'Meara links charism and official ministry (with its consequent authority), and argues against the division set up by, for example, Käsemann.

> Ministry is not an institutional product of the church but a realization of the pneumatic life of the community present in structure, diversity and unity. The church is the place, but not the solitary creator of ministry.

Charisms can range "from momentary inspirations to life-long decisions." "Not all charisms are diaconal, but at times in a Christian's life . . . invitations will be given to serve the Church." At the same time, "not all charisms are church ministry, but all church ministry is grounded in charism." Charisms are diverse, according to their immediate goal (e.g. healing, preaching), but have a common goal—building up the community. This analysis leads to a critical principle:

> The contemporary rediscovery of the word "ministry" with its sharp etymological challenge in service as well as its dynamics of

a diversified ministry looks towards a theological reappreciation of every church office as activity serving grace, and of the style of that activity as inescapably one of service—service of people, service of the Spirit in people.[44]

Treating the New Testament period, O'Meara's primary focus is the actual "actions and people" involved in ministry; these "functions and people appear in various forms." He finds ministry "is richer than the subsequent centuries of Christian reflection and practice." Following Lemaire, he cites three types of ministry: listed services in a community; Paul's co-workers and their goals; leadership in the community. And, he identifies four characteristics of ministry: it is not sacral office; it is action; it is service to the Kingdom of God; it is universal and diverse.[45]

O'Meara titles his historical overview, "The Metamorphoses of Ministry," emphasizing the changing performance and understanding of ministry. He examines "the services provided in ordinary church life;" some examples are helpful for giving a sense of the ebb and flow, expansion and diminishment of ministry and particular ministries. During the second century, new diaconal (readers, caretakers) and liturgical (singers, ascetics, assisting ministers, readers, and widows) ministers "swelled the ranks." In the sixth to eleventh centuries, he names "the monastery as minister" (not solely, of course, but significantly). However, parallel to such movements was the sacralization of the clergy and a frequent "diminishing" of ministry. By the twelfth century, the hierarchical vision began to dominate, with an emphasis on individual priesthood; the laity's role is increasingly passive. And yet, there were offices other than deacon, priest, and bishop: abbess, abbot, archbishop, archdeacon, pope, canon, friar, and provincial. "Ecclesial ministry was a public dignity and a state of life inserted into the wider social hierarchy." Within the Reformed traditions, the role of the pastor was emphasized; in the Catholic-Reformation period, the role of the spiritual director and the evangelist/missionary were given great prominence. This period also saw the rise of the modern congregations of vowed men and women. The early nineteenth century saw "a rediscovery of church charism and life," but in the latter part of the century these hopes faded. In the twentieth century, the American sister is "a paragon of ministry. The large and numerous achievements in institutions of education and health care, and the high level of office in education and in other areas of public life attained by these women indicate that something radically new appeared." O'Meara concludes:

> The lesson of the history of ministry is that one should not claim an eternal superiority. The life of the Spirit in the church never ceases; the corporate service of Jesus Christ in his Body continues.[46]

Having described ministry as rooted in the charisms of the Spirit, and having situated the reality of ministry historically, O'Meara formulates his definition of ministry:

> Christian ministry is the public activity of a baptized follower of Jesus Christ flowing from the Spirit's charism and an individual personality on behalf of a Christian community to witness to, serve and realize the Kingdom of God.

This definition collapses the traditional distinctions of lay and clerical or ordained and non-ordained ministry. It sees the possibility "that baptism will lead all Christians to some ministerial activity during their lives" and that some will "enter upon professional ministries." The latter category is important to his view of the future Church, with the emphasis on "a serious call and extensive preparation," full-time, perhaps lifetime commitment to service, which is for ministries that are central, important, foundational for the Church in its full life. These ministries will vary from church to church because:

> . . . Ministry begins with the community's consciousness of its needs; communal goals lead into an ecclesiology, i.e. into a plan of ministry . . . While ministries should not be too easily moved in and out of church order, the nature and number of the ministries expand and diminish as culture and church need them.[47]

O'Meara proposes a schema of concentric circles to picture the ministry of the Christian community. At the center he places the ministry of leadership, performed by the bishop, pastor, or vicar. In the next circle appear the ministries of peace and justice, health and aging, counseling, liturgy, education, evangelism, performed by full-time, professional ministers who have made a lengthy or lifetime commitment. Next, the same ministries as in the second circle are repeated in a third, these performed by part-time ministers, with varied intensity during stages of their lives, and brief but adequate preparation. Finally, the outer circle, beyond ministry, suggests the services offered to each other and the world by all Christians. These flow from their Baptism, and function as signs rather than ministries.[48] The typology of ministries developed here is different from those offered by authors previously treated. In keeping with his cultural history perspective, it flows from an assessment of current needs.

O'Meara argues that public and liturgical recognition, public commissionings for ministry are needed. While these could take various forms, he sees an appropriateness in an expansion of diaconal ordination, especially for full-time ministers. He defines ordination as "a communal liturgy of public commissioning to a specific ministry." Several forms of diaconate, for instance, deacon for education, deacon for peace and justice, would help specify the role to which an individual is called.[49]

O'Meara sees three sources of ministry: Jesus, "the summoner to and pattern of discipleship"; His Spirit, because: "By Baptism that Spirit is already present as source of all that is to come"; and God, through "the ontic and charismatic structure given to a personality by birth." The community and its leadership "point to the rightness and hope in a new minister." Individuals test the call, as does the process of training and evaluating the new ministers.

> All of these forces come together in placing a minister in the community . . . Canonical rubrics have long held the first place in constituting ministry. They are, however, only of tertiary interest. Ultimately, it is a theology of grace which can explore the sources of ministry.[50]

O'Meara's study strongly emphasizes ministry as service, a recurring theme in the literature today, here rooted in a theology of grace. He sees a diversity of ministries and ministers in our time and throughout history. These arise not only because of the needs of the community, but by the action of the Spirit. For this reason, ministries will be shaped locally by the needs and vision of particular churches. He collapses the kinds of tensions between charism and order and charism and authority set up in the 1960s, and transcends the issue of "priesthood" and "priesthood of all believers," seeing the need for various and complementary ministries, all part of the one ministry, in the community. He emphasizes the importance of the role of leaders of the local churches, bishops and priests, including their enabling of the ministries of others as central. And he recognizes that a liturgical installation or ordination of some new ministers is desirable.

NOTES

1. *Ministry to Word and Sacraments* (Philadelphia: Fortress Press, 1976), pp. 1, 5, and note 13.

2. Kenneth Kirk, ed., *The Apostolic Ministry* (London: Hodder and Stoughton, 1946), pp. v–vii, 7–14.

3. Gregory Dix, "The Ministry in the Early Church" in *The Apostolic Ministry*, pp. 237–240.

4. Ernest Käsemann, *Essays on New Testament Themes* (Philadelphia: Fortress Press, 1982. Originally published in 1964), pp. 64–65.

5. Ibid., pp. 71–76. For a critique from a Catholic of the way in which Käsemann relies on an analysis of the Church at Corinth, see Myles Bourke, "Reflections on Church Order in the New Testament," *Catholic Biblical Quarterly*, vol. 30, 1968, pp. 459–511. Peter Kearney's "New Testament Incentives for a Different Ecclesial Order" (in *Office and Ministry in the Church*, eds. Bas Van Iersel and Roland Murphy, New York: Herder and Herder, 1972, pp. 50–62) gives a Catholic view of these themes. He concludes: "the issue is not a dichotomy between spirit-filled authority and human structures" but an adaptation of the "new situation of the Church, which sought to secure stability in the face of waning eschatological expectation and of emerging theologies seen as dangerous to the tradition," p. 56. A scriptural study helpful on this theme is John H. Elliott, "Ministry and Church Order in the New Testament: A Traditio-Historical Analysis" (*The Catholic Biblical Quarterly*, vol. 33:3, July 1970, pp. 367–391), an analysis of 1 Peter 5:1–5.

6. Eduard Schweizer, *Church Order in the New Testament* (London: SCM Press Ltd., 1961), pp. 7, 13–14. For a similar overview from a Catholic perspective, see John McKenzie, "Ministerial Structures in the New Testament" in *The Plurality of Ministries*, Hans Küng and Walter Kasper, eds. (New York: Herder & Herder, 1972), pp. 13–22.

7. Ibid., pp. 20–50.

8. Ibid., pp. 51–60.

9. Ibid., pp. 63–75.

10. Ibid., pp. 78–88. For an exploration of the stewardship of tradition as both an adaptive and a preserving task, and one which sees this attended to throughout the New Testament, see Richard Dillon,

"Ministry as Stewardship of the Tradition in the New Testament," *Catholic Theological Society of America Proceedings*, vol. 24, 1969, pp. 10–62.

11. Ibid., pp. 106–116. A more recent Catholic study of the subapostolic era, Raymond Brown's *The Churches the Apostles Left Behind* (London: Geoffrey Chapman, 1984) sheds further light on the individuality of the various New Testament communities.

12. Ibid., pp. 164–169.

13. Bourke, p. 493.

14. Rudolf Schnackenburg, *The Church in the New Testament* (New York: Herder and Herder, 1965), pp. 22–26.

15. Ibid., pp. 34–36.

16. Ibid., p. 35.

17. Hans Küng, *The Church* (New York: Sheed & Ward, 1967), pp. 363, 370–387. For a helpful probing of the role of the whole community, see David Power, *The Christian Priest: Elder and Prophet* (London: Sheed & Ward, 1973). He begins with an assessment of the declining number of priests, the loss of status for the priesthood, and the confusion that exists about the functions to be expected of the ordained ministry. Reflecting on the last point, he says: "One of the reasons why the functions of the priest are questioned is that the laity have begun to take a much more active part in the life of the church. They are also more conscious of their own mission, coming from Christian initiation, and hence see their actions as belonging rightfully to them and not depending on a delegation from the hierarchy. . . Call to the ministry of the Word and pastoral care as well as a call to other diaconal ministries, is not necessarily linked with ordination. . . Moreover, all of this stems from the part in Christ's mission given to them at baptism and from the special gifts of the Spirit which forms the dynamic element of Christian life," pp. 1–5.

18. Ibid., pp. 388–394.

19. Ibid., pp. 395–405.

20. Ibid., pp. 441–442. Küng's reflections on the Petrine ministry (pp. 444, f.) go beyond the focus of our particular study.

21. Raymond Brown, *Priest and Bishop: Biblical Reflections* (New York: Paulist, 1970), p. 54.

22. Ibid., pp. 56–78. For another viewpoint on the role of the community in defining its ministries, see René Laurentin, "The New

Testament and the Present Crisis of the Ministry," pp. 7–18. *Office and Ministry in the Church.*

23. Cooke, pp. 23, 197. An historical overview which focuses on the role of laity in ministry throughout our history is given by Kenan B. Osborne in *Ministry: Lay Ministry in the Catholic Church: Its History and Theology* (New York: Paulist, 1993).

24. Ibid., pp. 37, 23, 38, 203, 204.

25. Ibid., pp. 219, 230, 330–337.

26. Ibid., pp. 390, 395, 397, 399–400. Richard McBrien, too, posits a ministry broader than that of the Christian community. *Ministry: A Theological, Pastoral Handbook* (San Francisco: Harper & Row, 1987), pp. 7–22.

27. Ibid., pp. 406–410, 511.

28. Ibid., pp. 411, 513–515.

29. Ibid., pp. 525–528, 530, 640, 646, 647.

30. Ibid., p. 199.

31. New York: Crossroad, 1981, pp. 2–3. In *The Church with a Human Face* (New York: Crossroad, 1985), he expands this initial book. The conclusions presented in *Ministry* are not substantially changed, but much of his argument is presented in both more nuanced and more developed fashion. The fact that his primary concern is priestly ministry also is clearer in the second book, although he does see the possibility of a fourth ordained ministry (see especially pp. 265–266).

32. Ibid., p. 24.

33. Ibid., pp. 28–29.

34. Ibid., pp. 29–31, 35.

35. Ibid., pp. 38–45.

36. Ibid., pp. 139–141.

37. Ibid., pp. 136–142.

38. Especially p. 262. The context for his assessment of something new emerging was set earlier in this volume: "Changes in the forms of ministry never seem to be deliberate in the first place, but only appear as a consequence of social changes in the church and the world: the rise of a new spirituality, different views of the church, society and the world," p. 2.

39. *Theology of Ministry* (New York: Paulist, 1983), p. 1. This is difficult because O'Meara's thought is so rooted in history. As he says, "The situation of the church is history. A *Theology of Ministry* is first and

foremost a study of history" p. 17. In 1999, Paulist published a "completely revised edition" of O'Meara's work. This insight, of a "theology of grace," is central in the new volume as well.

40. Ibid., pp. 5, 9, 11. In the revised edition, the description in chapter 1 of new developments is expanded, the conviction that these are positive even more clearly expressed. For example, "the expansion of ministry is not, then, a random or annoying occurrence but an aspect of a new church that is comprehending itself anew in its biblical sources and in its commission to be not just Italian or French but worldwide," (p. 18). William Rademacher also takes as his starting place the emergence of new ministers. *Lay Ministry: A Theological, Spiritual and Pastoral Handbook* (New York: Crossroad, 1991). "So there is no shortage of vocations. God may, however, be calling the baptized to many new ministries and the church may be failing miserably in recognizing, discerning and supporting these new vocations. It is possible that the 'shortage' of vocations is, at least partly a sign of the failure of the church's leaders, not the failure of the baptized," p. 30.

41. Ibid., p. 23–24.

42. Ibid., pp. 29–35, 44. Furthermore, this service is a task of many. "This diversification of the ministry inviting the theologically educated and the committed parishioner to full-time and part-time ministry is integral to healthy church life," p. 22, 1999 edition.

43. Ibid., pp. 48, 52. He says further, "The mission of the Spirit bears in it a drive toward activity, and this service—a being sent to serve—flows out of the freedom and community of the Christians. Nothing is more basic to a theology of ministry than to see how Christian service is grounded in the Spirit," p. 52. This theme, too, is expanded in the new edition. O'Meara also recognizes that we may fail in responding to these gifts. He says the Church could be held back by "a failure of nerve to follow the Council, the gift of the Spirit, into new ways and to retreat into small corners of the past," p. 25.

44. Ibid., p. 52, 60, 62–66, 67–70. Carolyn Osiek, in "Relation of Charism to Rights and Duties in the New Testament Church" (in *Official Ministry*), relates Paul's vision and that of the *Decree on the Apostolate of the Laity*. Like O'Meara, she links ministry and charism (p. 59) and the role of charisms in building up the Body. However, she also stresses that: "The rights and responsibilities inherent in

membership in the Body are the same ones inherent in the possession of charisms, for the charisms are simply the expression of the reality of the Body" (p. 58). For Osiek, it is precisely the rights and responsibilities of laity in the Church, not just in the world, that are insufficiently explored.

45. Ibid., pp. 71, 81–90, 93.

46. Ibid., pp. 95–128. O'Meara explains that "all of these forms of ministry have survived. They live on . . ." p. 128.

47. Ibid., pp. 142, 144–145, 148-150, 153.

48. For a study which views service to the world as a central form of lay ministry, see Robert Kinast's, *Caring For Society: A Theological Interpretation of Lay Ministry* (Chicago: The Thomas More Press, 1985).

49. Ibid., pp. 152–153, 198. In his revised edition, O'Meara slightly modifies this view. While still seeing diaconal ordination as an option, he also says: "Certain ministries, considered important by local or regional churches, may warrant recognition as professional types of ministry, that is, they begin after lengthy training. Their permanence and preparation might call forth a serious installation or ordination in the church," pp. 182–183. Rademacher, too, favors a new ordination, arguing from both the history of the tradition and sociological insights. However, the ordination he envisions would not be to a clerical state, and would include specification of a particular function, for example teaching or caring for the sick, pp. 96–102. See also Schillebeeckx, as described above, especially footnote 31.

50. Ibid., pp. 176–178.

CHAPTER NINE

THEOLOGICAL DIALOGUE

INTRODUCTION

As the work done by various groups has progressed, articulating our experience of the new ministers and reflecting on it, there has been significant intra-group dialogue. For example, this is clearly evident in the work of the canonists, through the permanent seminar, and the convening of ministry educators (including those working with deacon, priest, and lay formation) by AGPIM. In addition to such work, there have been two significant efforts to reflect theologically on the meaning of the new ministers by drawing together a group for in-depth reflection. The first was a theological colloquium, sponsored by the Subcommittee on Lay Ministry, held in Dayton in May 1997, the second a ministry seminary sponsored by St. John's School of Theology Seminary, Collegeville, in August 2001. Each fostered dialogue, and sought to identify points of consensus or convergence in the conversation. An overview of the process followed for each, the papers presented and the conclusions reached gives a picture of the unfolding of theological thought about the new ministers. The papers are outlined at some length in order to give an overview of the issues being addressed, the questions raised, and the areas needing further development, in the judgment of the theologians involved.

THEOLOGICAL COLLOQUIUM: THE PLANNING PROCESS

When the Subcommittee for Lay Ministry surveyed bishops about their questions regarding lay ministry, "the theology of lay ministry" was the highest ranked item. The highest ranked questions identified from the survey within that topic were: What is the theological basis for lay ministry?

What theological issues exist when a lay minister leads a parish without a resident pastor? How can the distinction between the vocation of the ordained and lay minister be further clarified? Many additional questions were submitted by respondents, including some related to baptism (how can we more clearly support the charisms that have their roots in baptism?), ecclesiology (what is the relationship (theologically) between ministry (service) and Eucharist?), vocation or call to ministry (how can the likeness of the vocation of ordained and lay be clarified?), and the emergence of lay ministry itself (investigate our own beginning assumptions— that is, do we see lay ministry as expedient due to shortage of priests or are we at least open to seeing lay ministry as valid in its own right?)[1] The subcommittee determined that a theological colloquium, with theologians and bishop-theologians, would provide a way to give a more adequate theological basis for ecclesial lay ministry in order to meet the stated needs of the bishops. The project was titled, "Toward a Theology of Ecclesial Lay Ministry," indicating the understanding that such an effort was, necessarily, one step in a longer process. To plan the colloquium, a steering committee of theologians and bishop-theologians was formed.

Several decisions taken by the steering committee are worth noting. They determined that the starting place for the investigation should be the new reality, the experience of the Church today, the new ministers. Therefore, the work of the colloquium would need to be inductive, not deductive, and a model of discernment, of mutual dialogue and reflection, was essential. These decisions were informed by the perspective that new developments in the life of the Church cannot be deduced from existing teaching, though relating them to the tradition, as a way of "testing what is good," is necessary. The committee concluded that papers on designated topics would be written and read beforehand (and not presented), and that the work of the colloquium would be conducted in small groups and the group as a whole. Two facilitators planned a process to assist this dialogue. The goals set for the event were the identification of theological issues raised by the experience of ecclesial lay ministry and of next steps for the subcommittee to take. A further goal was to model how bishops and theologians can work together in fostering the mission of Jesus Christ. Participation was by invitation, invitees identified by competence and particular interest, with the intention of having a group of varied positions in the Church (vowed religious, clergy, lay), theological viewpoints, and ethnic origins.

THEOLOGICAL COLLOQUIUM: THE PREPARATORY PAPERS

The first paper offered a description of who the new ministers are, drawing on various sociological studies. What positions they hold and functions they perform in ministry, demographic data, their paths to ministry, their education and formation, the support and supervision they receive, their collegial style of working and theological self-understanding were outlined.[2] A draft of the paper was critiqued by the steering committee, then by representatives of lay associations and organizations. The judgment was that the paper reflected the situation in the Church, and was a valid starting point for the work of the colloquium. It was then sent to the other writers, to serve as a point of reference as they developed their papers.

The purpose of the second preliminary paper was to outline a model for theological reflection, initially to share with the other writers, and then to inform the work of the symposium. Beginning with the present situation, James Heft indicated that a differentiation between ecclesial lay ministry and lay ministry broadly conceived is needed—but acknowledged that full agreement on what should be included in ecclesial lay ministry does not exist. Some key developments relative to both of these categories were sketched. Second, Heft outlined the sources to which we must turn in order to theologically interpret the new reality, including Scripture, church history, and tradition, and the teaching of the *magisterium*. Finally, he presented several steps for the theological reflection process. First, in order to adequately interpret our situation, the experience in the United States must be placed in the context of developments in the world Church. Second, the cultural context in the United States and its impact on the new development must be weighed ("reading the signs of the times"). Third and fourth, official church teaching, and lessons from history and tradition need consideration. Finally, from this process of reflection, the relevant insights for a theology of ecclesial lay ministry can be identified. In an appendix, Heft presented three specific issues that emerge from the research on ecclesial lay ministry, each of which has theological implications. These are the description of what ecclesial lay ministry is (he noted some of the varied descriptions, both theological and pastoral, which have been offered), the language chosen to name it (he indicated difficulties inherent in the designation "ecclesial lay ministry"), and the question of professionalization (he names some objections to this categorization, made by bishops).[3] These points still need further theological reflection.

Recognizing Baptism as central to the topic, the steering committee asked that a paper be developed addressing such issues as the leadership roles laity are fulfilling, how those are related to their baptismal call, and what processes of discernment, choice, and appointment are used. Zoila Diaz reflects first on the nature of the sacrament of baptism and then on the call to ministry. With both, the communal dimensions are stressed; the principle that "ministry has to be recognized by the Christian community" is developed. Many of the areas of ministry in which ecclesial lay ministers provide leadership are delineated, with an emphasis on their role in forming Christian community. The multicultural and multiethnic nature of the Church in the United States is outlined, and Diaz draws upon her own extensive experience of many years with the diverse communities of South Florida to illustrate. Of particular import is the divergence she sees between the professional lay ministers and "the poorly educated Hispanics who are the natural leaders of their communities and who are affirmed by them." Conclusions include: an affirmation of a more official lay ministry, distinct from the general lay ministry, as consonant with the teaching of Vatican II; the importance of discernment, and some tenets central to it; the desirability of a rite of commissioning or installation, because of "the need for some sort of validation or recognition by the community for a ministry to be legitimate." Diaz concludes with three issues needing further exploration. Should the category ecclesial lay ministry include volunteers who are graduates of lay ministry programs? (She questions whether *professionalism* could create a new clericalism.) What is the role of the Christian community in the process of discernment for the call to ministry? What does the data on the great majority of new ministers being white say about a multicultural Church?[4]

The steering committee wanted colloquium participants to be able to draw on our historical tradition, and so requested a paper that would identify historical precedents for lay ministry, including the theological understanding of ministry and vocation, in several periods of church history. Thomas O'Meara approached the task with the perspective that new forms and theologies in church life are "born of the intersections between faith and culture," and emerge in a saving history in which God acts, through revelation and grace. Therefore, history has a positive valuation.

"(T)he historical realizations of the Church in Edessa in the fifth century or in Naples in the sixteenth century are ways of continuing the Incarnation." The period since the council has been particularly rich in bringing forth new forms and ideas, only implicit in the documents, because the council invited a new look at ministerial needs and at the variety of ecclesiologies in biblical and patristic times. From these understandings, O'Meara developed five "trajectories of church and ministry." First, he described the Church of Paul, and his theology, emphasizing the centrality of charism, and Paul's welcome of "all ecclesial gifts, refusing to be embarrassed by or hostile to whatever was useful to the ministry of the Church." Second, he traces the emergence of the distinctions, clergy and lay, and the consequence: "While the clergy became an elevated, sacral state, the laity became a passive group." But today, large numbers of baptized Christians undertake various ministries. "One cannot make sense of today's parish in light of the clergy/laity distinction interpreted in a strict dualism." That there is a distinction of ministries, and that the pastor is central, are affirmed, as well as the grounding of all ministries upon a common faith and baptismal commissioning. Third, he traces a trajectory for the ministries of women, which "reaches from the New Testament to the present day, but it also passes through centuries of neglect and minimalization." O'Meara gives examples of the women of the twelfth century who came forth to imitate Jesus' life and preaching—"but the Church led the female counterparts to the friars back into cloistered life." He noted the seventeenth century development of communities with some active ministry, and the vast expansion of Catholic institutional ministries begun by congregations of active women religious in the United States in modern times. He concludes this mini-history by noting that starting in the early 1970s, "women not belonging to religious congregations are prominent in ministry." Fourth, O'Meara delineates the characteristics of the Baroque period, and its impact into the present time. "Ministry was done by parish priests limited largely to sacraments and by members of religious orders who conducted a number and variety of ministries... other baptized Christians might help in the physical support of running a hospital or preaching the Gospel in a foreign country, but they were kept at a distance from the real public ministry, just as they were kept from the sanctuary." Today, O'Meara envisions the emergence of "broader modes and kinds of ministry... a Church of ministers." Fifth, O'Meara notes the contemporary rapid changes in ministry, with great numbers studying theology, studying for the ministry, their involvement in "the essential ministries" of the Church, and the expansion of what is done. "The expansion of ministry did not come from the decline in the number of priests: the ministries of baptized men and women were often ministries that had not existed for some centuries." He concludes, "To reflect upon the expansion of ecclesial ministry in the past few decades is to conclude that the Spirit is determined to bestow on more people more ministries, and to disclose to the world Church how much there remains to be done."[5]

Scripture is for the Church a primary source for its life, and its theological reflection. Dianne Bergant was asked to develop a paper which would summarize notions and developments that would be important in understanding ecclesial lay ministry today. She began by noting the contemporary revitalization of biblical theology and the consequent desire "to discover the biblical foundation or justification of current pastoral practice." But, she cautions, "looking for precedents or biblical foundations is both enhancing and limiting . . . [because] the ongoing presence of the Spirit frequently brings forth realties that are new." She then explores a number of leadership roles found in the Old Testament, observing that all "grew out of the needs of the people and enjoyed certain religious legitimation, [but] some became part of the religio-political structure of Israel and others did not." Bergant focuses on those roles that are considered charismatic: the judge, the king, the prophet, and the priest. She noted that sometimes one is in tension with the other (prophet and king), that they acted in different ways (judges as military deliverers, kings as social and political administrators) and came to their roles differently (priests appointed or born into a priestly family, judges, early kings and prophets called by God). Within the Old Testament a central theme is that of the messianic age, when "the Spirit will no longer be given only to specific individuals, for a specific period of time, in order to perform some specific function. Rather, *all* flesh will receive the Spirit." In Jesus, the messianic age has dawned; he models what Christian ministry is: service. Reflecting on Paul, she notes the variety of gifts given and says, "All Christians must realize the social character of their God-given talents or gifts and must employ them without jealousy or envy." In today's Church, the Spirit has been conferred on all the baptized, "those who receive the Spirit are thus commissioned to act within the community in a charismatic manner." For this reason Bergant says that "one will have to look elsewhere [than the New Testament] for the specific roots of ecclesial lay ministry as defined for this colloquium."[6]

The steering committee asked John Beal to develop a paper drawing on canon law, addressing such concerns as governance and authority, and their relationship to baptism, office/delegation, and the mission of the Church. Beginning with Vatican II's insight of the sharing in Christ's priestly, prophetic, and royal office by all the faithful, he states that the Code incorporated this teaching and therefore "'opened wide the door for a wide variety of forms of participation by lay people in the Church's sanctifying and teaching missions." However, this is less true regarding governance, for a variety of historical and unresolved canonical reasons. Beal first examines opportunities named in the code for laypeople to play consultative roles in diocesan and parish governance, including roles at a diocesan synod and as part of a diocesan pastoral council or a parish finance council. He observes that various other consultative bodies and mechanisms have evolved. While the opportunities are for consultation, not decision making, Beal says, "they can and do have broad opportunities for sharing responsibility for ecclesial decision making with their bishops and pastors through their generation of alternative strategies, assembly of information, and implementation and evaluation of choices. Despite its reservation of most choice-making authority to bishops and pastors, the code evidences a strong preference for collaborative rather than unilateral decision making." This is a marked change in emphasis in canon law. Second, Beal presents the varied directive roles that laypeople may hold, including those of pastoral administrator (he notes that this experience has not yet been subjected to critical scrutiny), principals of parish schools and parish directors of religious education, some business managers. (He does not see pastoral ministers and youth ministers in the same way, judging them not to be ecclesiastical offices in the canonical sense.) At the diocesan level, most offices in the judicial section of the diocesan curia are open to laymen and women. Other offices such as diocesan chancellor and diocesan finance officer are permitted in the Code, and particular law and organizational documents have created a variety of offices to deal with the multitude of activities in the typical diocesan bureaucracy. Finally, Beal treats the complex question of laypeople and the power of governance, presenting the diverse opinions on this topic. His own analysis is that "lay people can cooperate in the exercise of the power of governance as delegates of their pastors and diocesan bishops." He goes on to say that while a diocesan bishop cannot delegate his legislative authority, there are few restrictions on his freedom to delegate his executive authority. "The critical criteria for such delegation are the competence of the proposed delegate for the task in question and the pastoral needs of the portion of the People of God entrusted to the bishop's care." He concludes that in light of the complexity of issues and challenges facing the Church, and the declining number of clergy, two things are needed: a coherent canonico-theological rationale that transcends the current doctrinal impasse about the participation of laypeople in the exercise of governance, and making consultative bodies and processes effective vehicles for building consensus and facilitating decision making in the local church.[7]

Francis Cardinal George was asked to develop a paper relating ecclesial lay ministry to recent magisterial teaching. His work opens with a reiteration of the Vatican II teaching, that there is an "intrinsic, sacramental relationship between the mystery of Christ and the Church." All of the documents assumed and built upon this dynamic of universal communion, which encompasses "the mysterious union of each human being with the blessed Trinity . . . Christ, the center of communion, joins the baptized together through the gift of the Spirit." Cardinal George roots ecclesial lay ministry in this context, and affirms that it "serves ecclesial communion through teaching, liturgical ministry, administration, pastoral care, and the outreach of charity and justice." This ministry arises out of personal charism and, more fundamentally, baptism and confirmation. However, "any ministry must be identified and delegated subsequently by the ordained pastors according to the nature of the ministry and an individual's state within the communion." He concludes this section stating, "if the relationships rooted in sacramental communion are respected, ministerial functions sort themselves out." Many of the documents reviewed by George are treated elsewhere in this volume: *Constitution on the Church, Decree on the Apostolate of the Laity*, the final report of the Synod of Bishops, *Christifideles Laici*, John Paul II's encyclical on missionary activity, a letter from the congregation for the Doctrine of the Faith on the Church as communion, and John Paul II's address on the participation of laity in the priestly ministry.[8]

Finally, two bishops were asked to reflect on ecclesial lay ministry as now experienced in United States dioceses. Their charge was: "As you listen to the data, as you live the experience in your diocese in this area of ecclesial lay ministry, what theological issues surface and how is the diocese currently addressing those theological issues? Are there theological insights that speak to this experience?"

Bishop James Hoffman, of Toledo began his paper with a description of one parish in 1960, and then in 1993. He noted the explosion of ministries, and their greater degree of specialization, attributing the changes to Vatican II's vision, a well-educated Catholic community, the emergence of women in new roles, and the aging of vowed religious and priests. Bishop Hoffman briefly described his ministry formation program, and told the stories of two participants, their discernment of their call, and subsequent journey in ministry. He also briefly outlined his fourteen years of experience with the role of parish life coordinator, placing it within the context of an ecclesiology of communion. He concludes with three questions: Has the conciliar teaching about the priesthood of the faithful been adequately emphasized? How do we understand the difference between the common priesthood of the faithful and the ordained priesthood? What are the implications of that difference for questions of governance?[9]

Bishop Howard Hubbard shared his experience: "In the Diocese of Albany, we have been seeking to promote the ministry that belongs to all the faithful by virtue of baptism, confirmation, and eucharist." In pastoral letters in 1978 and 1988 he presented a vision in which "collegiality, collaboration and shared responsibility have been the predominant themes." He has taught that all are called to be co-creators with God, and that every person's contribution is vitally needed, giving a vision of a universally ministering Church. For the vision to be realized, it must be prepared for carefully; people, especially in leadership, need the skills to function in such a model, so it must be "nurtured and implemented patiently and sensitively." Ordained ministers and other parish staff are key to its implementation. To foster this vision, two steps have been taken: the development of a broad continuum of educational and formational opportunities, and a diocesan policy that specifies which church entities finance these opportunities. The diocese and parishes bear the cost of the Formation for Ministry program; graduate study is financed equally by the diocese, parish, and participants, with scholarships available. A plethora of ministries have emerged as a result; "efforts to promote collaborative ministry only beget further ministry." Furthermore,

Hubbard sees them as responsive to the signs of the times. He notes that while the diocese is, indeed, dealing with the reality of ecclesial lay ministry, they have not focused on this group. Borrowing from O'Meara, Hubbard offers a possible definition: "Ecclesial lay ministry is the public activity of a baptized follower of Jesus Christ flowing from an inner awareness of one's baptismal call and of a responsiveness to the Spirit's charism and authorized or commissioned by the bishop or his delegate in direct service to the community of faith." He particularly emphasized the dimension of vocation (and not simply a response to a shortage of priests); authorization or deputation by the bishop or his delegate (for example, pastor, pastoral life director, or diocesan official) to assure assessment of competency, character, and good standing within the faith community; and that the activity to be exercised has been evaluated by some ecclesiastical authority as being an ecclesial lay ministry. This definition could apply to volunteers or professionals, if they have the requisite skills and personal characteristics required for the particular public task. Recognizing that "the development of lay ministry—mostly salaried and at the parish level—requires a more careful assessment of what is happening with regard to the activities being performed and the nomenclature being employed . . .", a task force of clergy, religious, and laity was established. They determined that those serving in ministry be classified in one of three categories: parish life coordinator, pastoral associate (a professional minister, usually full time, responsible for a specific area of pastoral life), and pastoral minister (a volunteer giving service in a specific area). Of these, the bishop appoints the first, and the pastor or pastoral life coordinator the other two. The task force also suggested that, in addition to the present academic model of formation and spiritual development, a second, with mentoring, service and learning (such as exists in many monastic communities) be used as well. In addition, they said that guidelines were needed for recruitment and interviewing, for job descriptions and ministerial agreements, wages, benefits, evaluation and grievance procedures, and help for pastors in using diocesan human resource resources and guidelines.

It would seem, as well, that this establishment of clear diocesan guidelines and nomenclature, ministerial criteria, hiring protocol, evaluation procedures, and grievance mechanisms would do much to preserve the necessary distinction between the ordained

and nonordained articulated in the Vatican Instruction . . . and
to guard against the development of a congregational mentality
or to combat the lack of relationships between ecclesial lay ministers and the diocese . . .

Bishop Hubbard observes that there are sometimes tensions that lay
ministers experience in their relationships with pastors and other church
authorities. However, he points out that this is true for others as well,
such as deacons and associate pastors. He attributes this in part to the
tension between two aspects of the reality of Church: the radical equality of all the members within a hierarchically structured Church. At all
levels of the diocesan church, this reality calls for interdependence, partnership, collaborative ministry. In conclusion, he names some concerns:
that we not exclude laity serving in extraparochial ministries from a consideration of who qualifies as an ecclesial lay minister; that we not foster
a new clericalism, viewing ecclesial ministers as better or more noble,
contributing to a passivity among other laity; that we not define ecclesial
lay ministry in a way that de-emphasizes or detracts from the role of laity
in the world; and that the definition of ecclesial lay ministry not be made
prematurely, for "while it is imperative that we study, reflect, clarify and
theologize about ecclesial lay ministry, at this point in history, we ought
not to attempt to finalize what is still a developing reality."[10]

THEOLOGICAL COLLOQUIUM: POINTS OF CONSENSUS

Before the colloquium, the papers were read by participants, who formulated questions for discussion at the gathering. The staff grouped the
questions into six categories. These were an appropriate and adequate definition of ecclesial lay ministry; relationship of the baptized and the
ordained in light of the needs and mission of the Church; theologizing
from the present experience, focusing on the signs of the times; appropriateness of forms of ecclesial sponsorship and recognition; evolution of
magisterial teaching on the laity in and since Vatican II; ecclesial lay ministry
within the context of the Church as communion, hierarchy, and Spirit-led.[11]
The questions do indicate what many of the unresolved issues are.

In small groups, participants developed consensus statements relevant to a theology of ecclesial lay ministry. These were presented to the

larger group for discussion, and then further refined in the small groups. Finally, all statements were posted on newsprint, and participants used a coding system to indicate their level of agreement with each.

The evaluations indicate that overall the total experience was overwhelmingly positive. Some comments about what was most helpful included: "The genuine spirit of collaboration, especially maintaining respect despite divergences of view;" "Good preparation. Good mix of people. Great willingness to work. This meeting sets a model of cooperation between bishops and theologians/theoretical thinkers and practical workers." However, the evaluations also point out some difficulties: "The scope was too broad. Abstract aims (define, etc.) were not sufficiently separated from concrete practical problems;" "Inability to offer reason for divergent positions in large group; no ordered debate on foundational issues." These evalations help to explain the results of the colloquium: although there were many points of consensus, no comprehensive statement of the work of the group was published. Certainly, the work informed the subcommittee, and helped to shape *State of the Questions*. Certainly, too, participants were influenced by the dialogue. But more theological reflection, and more development of consensus on specific questions and issues was needed. As one bishop observed on his evaluation form: "I was frustrated by the embryonic state of the theology and reflection on what is such a common pastoral reality."

What were the areas of agreement? First, a willingness to accept the concept of a group of laity within the larger body of laity who could be designated by the name "ecclesial lay ministers." Of course, this was the stated focus of the colloquium. However, there was debate about the category, and some ongoing discussion about language, but nonetheless there was essential agreement about this. Important, however, is that the larger theological context was in many ways primary in the discussions. That the Church is an organic communion, that because of baptism all are called into mission, and that this mission is the transformation of the world were foundational statements. Also central were statements more directly relevant to ecclesial lay ministry: that the ordained and laity, including ecclesial lay ministers, share in the mission; that the teaching and canon law of the Church authorizes official lay ministry; that some ministerial offices must be fulfilled by a bishop or a priest and others may be fulfilled by a layperson; that lay ministry is a call from God and flows from charism; and that, in addition to ministry, laity participate in synodal consultative structures of church governance. Some areas in which a clear consensus did not emerge included: the secular quality of the laity; and the application of that principle; particular understandings of the role of ordained ministers and ecclesial lay ministers; the relationship of charisms and ministry; the role of the community in the selection of ecclesial lay ministers; and what recognition of ecclesial lay ministers is appropriate.

MINISTRY SEMINAR: THE PROCESS

With the help of a grant from the Lilly Endowment, Inc., St. John's planned the summer research seminar entitled, "Envisioning a Theology of Ordained and Lay Ministry." Their starting point was that "we need an ecclesiology and theology of ministry that affirm the distinctive ministries of ordained and lay in the context of their shared baptism." A particular focus was promoting "a common understanding of the distinctive identities of ordained and lay ministers." In order to develop such a theology they invited ten theologians for an eight day seminar; each wrote a paper on an aspect of the topic entirely chosen by the individual. Papers were submitted and read beforehand; group dialogue and feedback about the papers and supplemental reading (*The State of the Questions; As I Have Done for You*; "Some Questions Regarding Collaboration of Nonordained Faithful in Priests' Sacred Ministry") preceded an effort to identify points of convergence. The work of the seminar will be shared at two national conferences in the summer of 2002, and will be published by The Liturgical Press (tentatively titled *Ordered Ministries*). The original papers were revised by the writers after the seminar.

MINISTRY SEMINAR: THE PREPARATORY PAPERS

Michael Downey begins by naming what he says some term a vocations crisis, but what he sees as a more participatory exercise of ministry. He noted that in the face of these changes, there is tension, and a felt need to strengthen identity, but that too often this is done by a contrastive method, or by a focus on skills, on doing. He offers some illustrations, and an alternative—an emphasis on the common foundations of ministry:

baptism, a sharing in mission and the call to holiness, a common ecclesiological spirituality. He is particularly concerned with "a recognition of the importance of ministry as a way of being, of knowing and loving and living within the tradition, and inviting others to live within it, so that they too might share in the mission of Word and Spirit." The path to such a way of being is an ecclesiological spirituality, which is marked by 1) being washed in the Word; 2) living what we say and do at liturgy; 3) understanding ourselves as first and finally members of God's Holy People. Downey offers a meditation on each of these. He concludes with a reflection on "ministerial iconicity," suggesting that lay ecclesial ministers are an "icon of the Church ad-vent-ing" and the priest the "icon of the community's pondering heart."[12]

Two seminar papers focused on the laity, and in particular the secular character of the laity. In the first, the underlying concern is the way in which the teaching about the secular character is interpreted so as to cause questioning of the validity of the emergence of lay ecclesial ministry. Therefore the paper traces the evolution of the concept from the early work of Yves Congar, through debates at the council, the relevant Vatican II documents, and the later work of Congar. The author places *Lay People in the Church* in the context of his time; his desire to more positively develop the role of the laity is shown. He emphasized that the laity are baptized Christians, and therefore exercise sacred activities; their participation in the priestly, kingly, and prophetic functions of Christ are performed particularly in the world. An examination of council speeches show that many bishops wanted to give a positive theology of the laity, though some had serious hesitations about concepts such as the laity's share in the mission of Christ, the priesthood of the faithful, and an articulation of more freedom for the laity. Some of this ambivalence remains in the council texts, although the role of the laity is certainly emphasized, including that of some laity "devoted to the service of the Church." Some documents issued since the council are also described; continued ambivalence can be seen. As a way of resolving the theological dilemma posed by church practice today, the later work of Congar is used. He begins with the concept of the church community, formed by Christ and His Spirit. In this community there are multiple ministries— "They do actually exist but up to now were not called by their true name . . . nor were their place and status in ecclesiology recognized." The development of lay ecclesial ministry is seen as congruent with the

Council's effort to move beyond a negative dichotomizing of sacred and secular, Church and world. "Symbolizing the shared call to mission, in their lives, as people who are married or single, living 'in the world,' not 'set apart' in monastery or rectory, yet ministering in the church, they are one embodiment of the church *in* the world, in a particular dialogue with the joys and hopes, sorrows and aspirations of the world."[13]

Noting the present situation in the Church in which the "reality generally referred to as 'lay ministry' has leapt ahead of theological reflection. . . ," Richard Gaillardetz articulates an ecclesiological foundation for a theology of church ministry. He draws three points from what he calls the council's emergent ecclesiology: the priority of the baptismal call; the Church's call to mission in the world; and the Church as an ordered communion. Each is developed, drawing on conciliar texts. His emphasis on all the baptized bound together in a common mission to the world avoids a dichotomizing separation between the Church *ad intra*, and *ad extra*. The emphasis on the Church as *koinonia*, united at Eucharist, *and* as a communion of Eucharistic communions, highlights the role of the parish community, and the local church in relationship to the universal Church. This communion is animated by the Holy Spirit; it is an "hierarchical communion." Gaillardetz sees this "ordering" of the Church as intrinsic to her life "as it receives its life from the God who, in Christian faith, is ordered in eternal self-giving as a triune communion of persons." "To be initiated into the Church is to take one's place, one's 'ordo,' within the community." This effects communion with God in Christ, with all believers and a movement outward toward the world. The second dimension of ordering refers to ministry. Ordered ministry includes the ordained and "any and all ministries that, once formally undertaken, draw one into a new ecclesial relationship...; one is ecclesially repositioned." This involves a call, ecclesial discernment and recognition of a genuine charism, and appropriate formation, authorization, and ritualization (as a prayer for assistance of the Spirit and a sending forth on behalf of the community). Drawing on the work of John Zizioulas, Gaillardetz outlines a "relational ontology of ministry," in which relationship with the community is central, and holy orders marks reconfiguration into a new ecclesial relation. By examining the evidence of other "orders" in the history of the Church (for example, readers, catechumens), he goes beyond Zizioulas and concludes: "From parish catechists to diocesan directors of Christian formation, from parishioners who bring communion to the sick on behalf of their community to full-time campus ministers and hospital chaplains, we are witnessing today a diverse ordering of ministries. . . " He suggests the categories of ordained, installed, and commissioned ministries, moving away from the designation "lay" or "lay ecclesial ministry." Installation of those now being called "lay ecclesial ministers" would restore the liturgical dimension to their ecclesial repositioning. "Installed ministries demand significant ministerial formation and a high degree of stability. Commissioned ministries also indicate a repositioning, and imply a new degree of accountability, a specialized formation and a demand for some formal authorization." He summarizes his paper by noting that "the specific ordering of ministries has changed dramatically in the past and will doubtless change further in the future." What is consistent is "the fundamental orientation of the whole Church to the fulfillment of the mission of Christ and the ordering of ministries in service of this mission."[14]

The second paper on the secular character of the laity was developed by Aurelie Hagstrom. She asks whether the call for laity to transform the secular order negates intra-ecclesial lay ministry? Or might it enhance and enrich it? She says that there are three common interpretations of the notion of secular character in recent magisterial documents; two can be supported by Vatican II documents, one by Pope John Paul II's *Christifideles Laici*. The first interpretation is typological or phenomenological, referring to the life situation of the laity. The second is theological or ontological, seeing their secularity as stemming from their vocation in Christ; laity's participation in the mission of Christ is characterized by their secularity, which is rooted in the Incarnation and the nature of the Church. The third sees secularity as both a sociological fact and a theological condition. However, the secular character of the laity is within the wider secular dimension of the whole Church. Various documents are surveyed to trace the development of the theme of secular character: *Lumen Gentium, Apostolicam Actuositatem, Gaudium et Spes,* the 1983 Code of Canon Law, *Christifideles Laici* and the 1997 Instruction on Ministry. In her analysis Hagstrom notes that *Lumen Gentium's* theological interpretation of the secular character is given in light of the laity's baptismal vocation in Christ, and that the laity are not secular people, but members of the Church in the temporal order; "they are the Church in the world." Therefore, "This secular character must be an essential part of any theology of the laity since it gives the specific element in any description of the laity's identity and function." *Apostolicam Actuositatem* adds the idea that "the life of the laity should be considered in itself as an instrument of the apostolate." The everyday activities of the laity can have a redemptive value. *Gaudium et Spes* emphasizes the secular mission of the entire Church. Reviewing the documents she concludes: "the secular character is not just a form of the apostolate, but it is something which qualifies the whole life of the laity, in the Church and in the world." Therefore, in intra-ecclesial functions, the secular character is a gift laity (including ecclesial lay ministers) bring to the Church. The *Code of Canon Law* "reflects the theological or ontological approach of the conciliar documents." *Christifideles Laici* expands these themes, placing them in the context of Creation and Redemption: God "handed the world over to men and women so that they might participate in the work of creation. The task of the laity is to free creation from the influence of sin..." Secularity, then, is a theological mission, for the laity. The 1997 *Instruction* "apparently goes back to the pre-conciliar understanding of 'two realms'—sacred and secular . . . the temporal sphere belongs to the laity and the sacred to the clergy." This contrasts with *Christifideles*. Hagstrom sees the vision of *Christifideles* as most helpful, and views it as compatible with ecclesial lay ministry.[15]

Kenan Osborne's essay probes the historical origins of the ambiguity in recent church documents and pastoral relationships regarding the interrelationship of "lay/cleric ministers." First he gives an overview of major theological events of the twentieth century that have challenged traditional forms of differentiation between clergy and laity. These are historical research on the sacraments ("the differentiation of cleric and lay has never been uniform in the history of the church"); Jesus as the primordial sacrament and the Church as the foundational sacrament; the liturgical renewal (this "refocused both the sacramental and non-sacramental ministries of clerics and lay men and women"); *la nouvella théologic* (leading to a questioning of the origins of ministry); existential, phenomenological, and postmodern philosophies ("Temporality, historicity, linguistic relativity, and a form of subjectivity have had a serious impact on the theology of ministry"); the documents of Vatican II; liberation theology (issues are raised by its kingdom-centered theology, highlighting the lack of priestly ministry for the majority of Catholics and the influence of inter-religious dialogue); feminist theology (raising the issue of "the role of women in all ministries in the church"); the renewal of the permanent diaconate (surfacing issues such as celibacy, gender, and collaborative forms of ministry); the *Catechism of the Catholic Church* (a problem is the great emphasis on Thomistic and Neo-Thomistic theologies, to the exclusion of other theological traditions); a multicultural Church (inviting a radical reformulation of theology drawing upon the thought patterns and experiences of varied cultural groups); and the hermeneutics of biblical studies (opening the way to new interpretations of traditional formulations). Second, he examines causes for the clashes between clerical and lay ministers. Some are practical (such as personality conflicts or gender differences), some theological. Of the latter, the first is insufficient understanding of the common ministry rooted in baptism; presenting this Osborne outlines key teachings from Vatican II, especially emphasizing the rooting of all ministry in Jesus, the servant, and the high priest. Jesus as priest is related to both the priesthood of all believers and the ministerial priesthood. "The current theological inadequacy of these relationships is one of the primary systemic reasons why there are symptomatic clashes between ordained and non-ordained ministries." The second theological issue explored is the disjuncture between contemporary historical research on ordained ministries and sacraments on the one hand, and magisterial documents on the other, leading to "contemporary clashes between ordained and lay ministers" regarding sacramental issues and ecclesiastical authority. He argues that, "A clear boundary between what only a bishop or priest does in sacramental life and what a lay person might do is not that clear," illustrating this with some historical notes of the evaluation of the roles of bishop and priest in five historical periods. In conclusion, he says that the Church needs to take more seriously a number of issues: the history of the sacraments; the understanding of the Church as sacrament (and its relationship to an understanding of ministry); Jesus as sacrament (and the rooting of all ministry in Jesus the minister); a renewal of liturgy in keeping with a multicultural Church; the concreteness of space, time, individuals, and communities as central to liturgical celebrations; the integration of multicultural diversity and integrity into the life of the Church; justice issues raised from the standpoint of liberation theology; opening the permanent diaconate to women; and the "porosity and immutability of all ministry."[16]

In his essay, David Power examines concepts of priesthood in the Scriptures, the patristic era, the medieval Latin West, the sixteenth century, and the period before Vatican II in Catholic theology. His intention is to show how present usage of priestly terms has emerged over time, and to retrieve some understandings that could assist us today toward "an inclusive sense of mission that respects diversities within oneness." He begins by sketching the perspective of Vatican Council documents, then stating that "prevailing assumptions about the priesthood of Christ and its distinction from the offices of King and Prophet, and about the priesthood of the Church's members, do not accord well with pre-medieval tradition, east and west." The scriptural texts Power focuses on are the letter to the Hebrews and 1 Peter. In Hebrews "the exercise of [Christ's] priesthood. . . first is the death through obedience and the shedding of his blood, the piercing of the veil of the flesh into the heavenly sanctuary . . . second is what results from this, the eternal priestly intercession which Christ makes for his own at the right hand of the Father." Furthermore, attentive to the sufferings of the faithful to whom he writes, the author makes this priesthood and its sacrifice the foundation of their spiritual life. Through suffering they can gain their salvation; "they must however risk . . . infamy, in communion with him. . . " 1 Peter also strives to encourage the followers of Christ in their suffering, especially as aliens and the disregarded, reminding them that they are a chosen people (evoking the Exodus experience) and therefore a royal priesthood, who can engage in true worship, a people "that has spiritual dominance and which can announce the good news of salvation . . . a people in which each and all are kings and priests. . . The terms apply to their whole lives." The texts are not applied to community leaders, but are about Christ and his mediation, and about the dignity and salvation and hope given to God's people. He concludes: "It is also clear that the language of kingship and priesthood has nothing to do with distinctions within the body of Christ, either of kind or of degree." In the fathers, understandings of Christ as priest and king are within the context of his work of mediation and role of mediator. Priest and king are symbolic terms used to bring out the meaning and power of Christ's mediation. The teaching of the royal priesthood of the Church is rooted in the Church's sacramental communion with Christ as his Body. "From this sacramental communion there follows the spiritual communion, whereby the Church and all its members offer the sacrifice of a life lived according to the Gospel, the service which they render to the poor and their songs of praise and thanksgiving." It is within this context of the Church as royal priesthood and living sacrifice that the title of priest is assigned to bishops; the title must be seen in relation to all of his ministry, including the suffering that he endures through its exercise. In the thought of Pseudo-Dionysius, who speaks of the bishop as hierarch, Power discerns an emphasis on the idea that, "what renders a person capable of leading others to Christ is his own closeness to him." In the medieval Latin West, "thinking about priesthood took a new turn . . . with the accentuation of the priesthood of bishop and presbyter and then the limitation of this language to eucharistic and sacramental actions." Gradually, "priesthood was defined in terms of the power to consecrate and the power to offer sacrifice," and "the exercise of the Church community's royal priesthood was diminished." The role of the diverse laity in the Church was kept through the notion of order within the Body—and there were many and varied examples. However, gradually "priesthood and order became more and more elements in a strictly clerical vocabulary." In the sixteenth century the Reformers strove to overcome the distinction between the baptized and ordained ministers; Luther and Calvin each "retrieved elements of an earlier patristic tradition." But, "Trent seemed unable to incorporate these into its own perspectives on order and ministry, given its desire to keep the distinction between laity and ordained firmly intact." In the early twentieth century, shifts in understanding began to account for an active part of all the baptized in the life, liturgy, and mission of the Church, but even in Vatican II "writers seemed, as it were, stuck with the application of priestly terminology to liturgy, extended beyond this at best to include spiritual sacrifices." Power concludes that this history shows what was lost: "the association of Christ's priesthood and kingship, taken together, with suffering and combat with sin and death, in the service of humankind's deification, and of what it means for his followers to be one with him in this *kenosis*." An emphasis on cultic aspects of priesthood contributes to this, and does not focus on the Church's mission in the world. Power suggests that new language may be needed "to express the communion of the Church in the service of a way of being whereby life, love and reconciliation, even through suffering, prevail over hatred, divisions and death." He advocates "the notion of order and ordering within the one body and communion, in pursuit of the one mission" as helpful. This also avoids the sacred/secular dichotomy. "The body as such is in the world, and for the world, and is internally ordered into groups. . . " Power explores the ways in which new orders, designated and not, are emerging in our own time, such as the order of catechumens and "order" of baptized persons sent on mission to countries in need of aid and human development. He concludes, "A preferable use of language may be to distinguish the complementarity of orders and ministries in mission and service. It would be more respectful of the first, fundamental and most original language of priesthood."[17]

Noting various understandings of ministry in contemporary theology, Thomas Rausch observes that "part of the difficulty stems from the fact that the New Testament is open to different interpretations." Therefore he begins his exploration with an examination of Scripture. First he traces the origin of the word *ministry*, which originally meant service, and then referred to "those whose particular form of service places them in leadership roles in the community." He notes that the example of Jesus, who saw his own life and death as a service on behalf of others, was the ultimate inspiration for the adaptation of the word. Second, he examines the diversity of ministries evident in this early period and a certain fluidity of terminology. However, "there was leadership from the beginning, even a certain order in the ministries." While it is difficult to speak of a ministerial office in the earliest New Testament letters "there were structuring principles." All ministry is grounded in some charism, so "institutionalized" and "charismatic" ministries should not be opposed to each other. In the later books of the New Testament, "one can discern a pastoral office in the process of emerging," and a certain concern about a type of "nascent clericalism" (see, for example, Matt. 23:5–10 and Mark 10:35–40). Rausch cites Brown and says that in the churches associated with Paul, James, and Peter, presbyters were known and established in the last third of the century; the threefold ministry of a bishop "was in place throughout the church by the end of the second century." In this development, there was some loss: of the Pauline concept of the multiplicity of charisms, and the openness to women in ministerial roles. And, there was gradual sacralization or sacerdotalization. "As the church became more aware of the sacrificial dimension of its Eucharist, it began using sacerdotal language for its eucharistic presiders." In the contemporary Church, the impact of the council's development of a theology of the laity and attention to the vocation of the layperson is unfolding. All are part of the People of God, all are called to holiness, there are spiritual gifts "both hierarchical and charismatic," both ordained ministers and all the faithful share in the priesthood of Christ, though in different ways.

"In the years after the Council the rediscovery of the laity's participation in the mission of the church focused primarily on the question of ministry." Rausch sees three positions relative to this issue. One "seeks to expand the concept of ministry beyond its restriction to the ordained," and is found in both Protestant and Catholic theology, including *Ministeria Quaedam*. While Paul VI envisioned an expansion focused on particular roles, there had been a ministry explosion in the 1980s, and a theological emphasis on baptism as the grounding for ministry. A second current, developed by some feminist scholars, seeks "to deconstruct what was perceived as being at the foundation of the church's hierarchical structure and ordained ministry, the apostolic office." These scholars emphasize egalitarian aspects of the earliest church communities. Other scholars have sought to reinterpret the eucharistic role of ordained ministers, in various ways. A third approach, "evident in more recent post conciliar documents issuing from Rome, seeks to limit the terms 'minister' and 'ministry' to the ordained." The Roman Instruction views the laity as participating in the ministry of priests, which is sacred; the laity's mission is secular. Laity assist or collaborate in the sacred ministry. Similarly, the 1999 letter from the Congregation of the Clergy "fails to show how the ordained priesthood is to serve the priesthood of all the faithful." Rausch seeks to foster an understanding of ministry that would move us beyond the "traditional dichotomies—clerical and lay, religious and secular, institution and charism, ordained and nonordained" because they reinforce the false church/world dichotomy. He states that a "solid argument can be made that the Second Vatican Council was moving towards a more inclusive understanding of ministry," rooted in baptism. He notes a growing theological consensus on this point, and says that Pope John Paul II gives "a carefully qualified acknowledgement of lay ministry in two of his writings," rooted in baptism and the baptismal priesthood. Rausch also wishes "to safeguard the unique meaning of ordination." The sacrament of orders incorporates men into the Church's apostolic ministry or office, enabling them to act in the name of the Church and thus in the person of Christ, its head. Ordained ministry is not merely a function; "it is rooted in a received identity." Rausch concludes that both baptized and ordained ministers share in the one priesthood of Christ, though in different ways; Vatican II was moving towards a more inclusive concept of ministry; some laypeople are called to a specific lay ministry, distinct from the vocation of all the baptized; ordination gives a special role, not a higher status; the ordained priesthood serves the common priesthood, especially at Eucharist; and the priest symbolizes and maintains the communion between the local congregation and the local church, with the worldwide communion of the Church.[18]

As a canon lawyer, Elissa Rinere chose to focus on "the care of souls (*cura animarum*)," tracing differences between the Codes of 1917 and 1983 and documents from Vatican II relative to the involvement of laity in ministerial activities. In light of the fact that "lay ministry is flourishing and in some ways running far ahead of any theological or canonical foundation," she explored this area of ministry. Traditionally associated exclusively with ordained ministry, today care of souls is being exercised by laity. Although the care of souls is not defined in the 1917 Code, it is referred to as the pastoral activity, "in all its complexity" of pastors (bishops or priests); it was exercised "only through ecclesiastical office and ecclesiastical offices were entrusted only to clergy." The role of pastor of a parish included a wide range of activities (for example, celebrating the sacraments, catechetical instruction, and leading public processions); there was a "territoriality" involved, each officeholder tending to his own people. A change occurred at Vatican II: "although not completely consistent in its statements, [it] set out with deliberation to include laity in the pastoral activity of the Church." *Christus Dominus* explicates the role of the bishop, his office of governing, teaching, and sanctifying; clergy and laity alike cooperate with him in his work. It also focuses on the parish as a particular locus for care of souls, and of the multiple roles of pastors, including, for example, "Knowing the people of the parish personally . . . and encouraging the works of the apostolate." However, "a missionary spirit" should also characterize parish life, and priests and laypeople should both strive to make contact with groups of people, exercising the cooperation of clergy and laity in the care of souls. *Ad Gentes*, too, mentions laypeople as lay missionaries—"an extraordinary development . . . [since] traditionally, only priests were considered to be missionaries"—and refers to the care of souls they give. *Apostolicam actuositatem* "establishes the parish as the primary site for lay activity . . . and also links . . . the priesthood of the baptized with the priesthood of the ordained by pointing out the necessity of collaboration between the two for the sake of the care of souls." It also expands the range of possibilities for lay involvement, and includes "individual laity in the pastoral work of the hierarchy based, not on need, but on the giftedness of the individual lay person for the work in question." The Code of 1983 treats care of souls in ten canons and, unlike the earlier code, these are not all in sections dealing only with clergy. This code redefines ecclesiastical office, implicitly making it possible for laity to hold office and to participate in some aspects of the care of souls (though not "the full care of souls"). Rinere concludes this overview: "Based on the richness of the documents of Vatican II, the law, although adequate, is somewhat disappointing." However, she says that the broader area of pastoral care must also be considered, and here notes especially Canon 517.2, which permits what is sometimes referred to as a pastoral administrator of a parish. Rinere evaluates this, saying, "The canon, while on the one hand providing so many opportunities for lay participation in the pastoral office, allows this only if needed to supply for a lack of priests." On the other hand, she notes that in the documents of Vatican II explored in the paper "none of the texts cited, especially those which allow for individual invitation or authorization from the hierarchy, makes any mention of laity undertaking these sundry functions because of a shortage of clergy "but is rooted in their baptismal call to take an active role in the Church's life and work." Her judgment is that while in many ways the 1983 Code reflects the conciliar understanding of care of souls, its focus on clergy, including laity only as exceptions to ordinary practice, "obscures the clear intent in the conciliar documents to give laity a proper inclusion" in the care of souls. There is a tension, therefore, between what is unfolding in the life of the Church, out of the Council's understanding of pastoral care, and canon law. She sees the 1997 Roman Instruction as a response to the tension, a tension understood as necessary in a vital society, the Church. "Only time and attention to mission will bring us to clarity about how the priesthood of the ordained and the priesthood of the baptized must work together for the sake of *cura animarum*."[19]

Kevin Seasoltz explored the meaning of institutes of consecrated life in the contemporary Church. He notes that since the Council "the magisterium has tried to deepen and enrich the renewed vision of religious community," with an emphasis on "the spiritual dimension and the bonds of community which must unite all the members in charity." Community life includes both the spiritual communion of the members, and a life in common "through fidelity to the same norms, taking part in common acts and collaboration in common services." Basic to religious institutes are a public profession of the evangelical counsels and three characteristics: a commitment to prayer, to community life, and to ministry. He is concerned, however, that many members are living lives more consonant with the norms of a secular institute, and that there is confusion concerning "their commitments, their identity and their ministry." To bring clarity, he outlines the general history of religious life. He explores the shamans and prophets of the Old Testament, and notes that in the New Testament the emphasis is less on individuals and more on community witness. This "has bearing on the appropriate life style of contemporary members of institutes of consecrated life." Seasoltz's view is in contrast to those who see the origins of religious life primarily in the eremitical life understood as an individualistic experience of God. (Seasoltz underlines their rootedness in community.) "The early Christian men and women responded above all to a call to discipleship, not to a call to *diakonia*." At the margins of Church and society, they "became centers radiating counter-cultural values." However, the prophetic role of communities was lost when their dominant frame of reference became the Church as an institution, rather than the reign of God. To regain their prophetic role, they must once more become marginal communities, "but they must also retrieve their own proper institutional or communal identity and witness." Other historical influences are outlined. The contribution of Pachomius (who influenced the development of an ordered community, with obedience as an essential component), the impact of Augustine (who organized the life of his clergy around himself with a common life), and the development of Benedictine monasticism are three; the evolution from monasticism as more a lay movement to its clericalization is also noted. Seasoltz also traces the stories of developments relative to women and religious life, both positive (the founding of many early monasteries) and negative (the emphasis on the monastery as a place of enclosure which "became refuges for widows, undowried and consequently unmarriageable daughters, wives of priests and bishops, captives who had been abused by conquering soldiers, and women seeking sanctuary after refusing to marry, and even children"). Other notable developments in monasticism include the strong commitment to the liturgy that grew at Cluny (still an influence in Benedictine monasticism), new communities with an emphasis on the eremitical life (with a strict separation from the wider world) and an outgrowth of monasticism, and clerical religious (with a priestly ministry and life in community according to prescribed vows). In the thirteenth century the mendicant orders

(Dominicans, Franciscans) adopted a rule of community poverty, "a radical departure from the monastic tradition." They also "abandoned the seclusion and withdrawal of the cloister in order to engage whole-heartedly in pastoral ministry." They preached that salvation "could be found by faithfully fulfilling one's normal obligations in the secular world." Seasoltz looks in particular at the Dominicans, their ministry of preaching and the particularity of their bondedness, located not in a place (for example, a monastery) but in a union of persons (as a community). He also chronicles their work with women, and the founding of an order for women as well as a third for persons "living in the secular world." The founding of the Franciscans, and later the Jesuits (their precisely non-monastic characteristics are noted, as well as their strongly hierarchical organization, and, "in essence a vow of mobility. . . to travel anywhere in the world 'to save souls'") is sketched. Various women strove to develop new forms of religious life; St. Angela Merici's sisters would be returned to strict enclosure by Trent and Mary Ward could receive no ecclesiastical approval. St. Louise de Marillac, under the direction of St. Vincent de Paul, formed a community with common life under a superior, but committed to social and charitable ministries outside the convent. In succeeding centuries, many communities of various kinds were formed. Eventually the 1917 Code of Canon Law defined the nature of and laws for religious life. But evolution continued—secular institutes arose. Seasoltz says, "they are distinguished from traditional religious institutes by their general abandonment of common life and their work in secular professions. In general they manifest little or no institutional witness." In the United States, religious institutes began many educational, healthcare, and social service institutions; as the Catholic population grew, so did these institutions. The size, number, and professional standing of these institutions represented a concrete response to the pastoral and social needs of people, have embodied standards of excellence (a reality tied to a sense of mission), are not separatist but an inculturation of Catholic faith in a pluralistic culture (they have been a tool of the Church's strong influence on society), and today have largely passed into the hands of laymen and women. In conclusion, Seasoltz quotes a Vatican document on community life that raised points of concern such as emphasizing mission over community and taking on too much work, "thus leaving less time for common life." He reiterates Gottemoeller's concerns: about those clear boundaries which promote organizational health, creativity, and prophetic witness; and the emphasis on parish life leading to both men and women religious focusing their energies there with "less and less time and energy in their own religious institutes." He regrets the loss of "what might be described as a common work consonant with the charism of the institute." A primary need is "the task of beginning once again to rebuild community life in common," even though the task may appear daunting.[20]

Because so much of priestly identity is focused on the celebration of the Eucharist, Susan Wood decided to approach the question from another perspective. Drawing on an insight from the Lutheran-Catholic dialogue, regarding communion, she focused on the parish as a baptismal community. She notes that presbyteral identity is usually addressed as a question of priestly identity, to the neglect of the roles of pastoral leadership or prophetic function. Wood chose to develop the pastoral role, which "implies a flock, a community, and a church with which the ordained is in relationship." She states that this approach allows a focus on the contextualized character of the presbyterate in its historical, particular, pluralistic, and contingent particularity. The presbyter stands in relation to his bishop, and his pastoral charge. His relation to the bishop is a dimension of the communion of the Church, which is served at various levels with various ordained ministries. "Presbyters serve the internal communion of parishes and their communion with the particular church." (However, this conceptualization does not address the identity of all priests, for example, members of religious communities.) Wood observes that while Vatican II documents develop a theology of the particular Church (diocese), most Catholics experience Church in the parish. She sees a need for the development of a theology of parish, a lack which she illustrates with texts from the Council. Vatican II also developed the teaching about bishops, seen as having "the fullness of the priesthood." A consequence of this is that "now the priest [is] perceived as something less than a bishop," which may contribute to the search for priestly identity today. In this search for identity, a distinguishing characteristic of the presbyter is his presiding over a grouping of the faithful (the parish). Toward a theology of the parish, Wood draws on Rahner. For example: "The parish is not a division of a larger segment of the church, 'but the concentration of the Church into its own event-fullness.'" Vatican II affirmed that Christ is present in local congregations, as has Pope John Paul II. While Rahner develops his idea of parish around the celebration of Eucharist, an event common to other groups as well, Wood observes that a more differentiating dimension can be drawn from baptismal theology. Other groups "do not generally evangelize, prepare catechumens, baptize them, and then continue to nurture them in the context of a stable faith community." Wood indicates that historically, baptismal churches were distinguished from other kinds of congregations. As a baptismal community, the parish "is a formation community in Christian living." And the parish is apostolic, sent in mission. The duty of missionaries described in the *Decree on the Church's Missionary Activity* "is the responsibility of a presbyter charged with the pastoral leadership of a parish." The presbyter ministers in the parish along with various others, but he has been ordained to represent the community and its ministers in "communions corresponding to the threefold office." Therefore a presbyter's identity is defined representationally, rather than functionally. An aspect of this work is "ministry to the apostolicity and communion of the church," through his relationship with his bishop. Another aspect is pastoral care of his church. "As the parish has an ecclesial identity, so the presbyter finds his identity in relationship to this segment of the church." Here he presides at Eucharist, discerns and oversees other ministries, which are exercised collegially, and exercises his prophetic function by preaching the gospel and witnessing to the apostolicity of the text and the community hearing it. "A baptismal community lives in the power of the Spirit," within the concrete, historical, particular circumstances of the parish, along with its presbyter.

MINISTRY SEMINAR: POINTS OF CONVERGENCE

Unlike the theological colloquium, the seminar did not have a structured process designed to identify points of convergence. Rather, after discussing each of the papers once, and the supplemental documents, then revisiting each of the papers, participants were invited to name what they saw as an emerging consensus. Statements were listed on newsprint, discussed, refined, discussed again. The final list was to be further refined for the publication. The summary given here is personal, based on notes, and the typed summary of the full discussion and summarized "Points of Convergence."

The first topic in the *discussion* was baptism, but in the *points of convergence* the group decided that a conversation about ministry today must begin with an experiential description of ministry as it is now exercised in the Church. The discussion about baptism was far reaching, with easily a dozen aspects identified. Gradually the focus became that baptism is an initiation into the life of Christ and the way of discipleship in the Church by which all participate in the mission of the Church; it is the ground for all discussion and exercise of ministry. The discussion about ministry was also wide-ranging and multifaceted, raising many of the questions and points from earlier work in the group, including the Church's relationship to the world and the variety of ministries in the Church. The final statement: Ministry, grounded in baptism, is the building up of the body of Christ for the mission of the Church. Ministry not only serves the internal needs of the Church but enables the Church to pursue its mission for the transformation of the world. Concurrent with the discussions about baptism and ministry was that about mission, the relationship of mission to Christ (or Jesus, following Francis of Assisi), and the Trinity. Two points emerged from this conversation: 1) Mission is grounded in the divine missions of Word and Spirit for the transformation of the world and the service of the reign of God; 2) which flow from God's love for the world. When considering the concrete manifestations of ministry in the community, one aspect of the discussion focused on the traditional forms of ministry (bishop, priest, deacon) and another on emergent ministries such as that of religious education, social justice, and the environment. The group kept returning to the fact that the Church has always ordered its ministries, and that the present situation needs a new ordering. The points developed from this were: 1) Within the diversity of the Spirit's gifts the life, communion, and mission of the Church has been served by ordered ministries. 2) What is constant historically is the principle of sacramental order. What changes is how ministries evolve and are ordered. This dynamic of change is the eventing of the Church as the risen body of Christ. 3) These principles call us to an ongoing ecclesial discernment and a fresh articulation of an ordering of ministries (for example, installation, commissioning) in the Church in order to recognize emerging ministries and changes in actual practice. Further reflection on the idea of an ordered ministry noted its helpfulness in preserving the unity of community, in moving away from the language "lay ecclesial ministry," and in taking us beyond a lay/ordained dichotomy.

Finally, the group said: Among the ordered ministries there is a particular need for an apostolic episcope; ordered ministries constitute a repositioning within the Church, the components of which include personal call, ecclesial discernment, formation, and authorization.

CONCLUSION

This chapter records the work of two groups of theologians. It is clear that in each group, and in both groups together, there is considerable agreement about ministry, lay ministry, new ministries in today's Church, and theological principles to shape understanding of these realities and to facilitate an adequate and appropriate response by the official Church and the community as a whole. In both groups, conveners sought to represent different disciplines, theological viewpoints, and states in life. In both groups, there were questions left unanswered. What the work represents is a corporate effort to respond to the new ministers, and a corporate challenge to others to address the questions and continue the dialogue.

NOTES

1. *Lay Ministry Survey Report*, NCCB Lay Ministry Subcommittee, a document of the subcommittee, April 16, 1996, p. 4.

2. Zeni Fox, "Ecclesial Lay Ministers: An Overview." The paper summarized chapters 1 to 4 of the original edition of this book. All papers from the colloquium were published in *Together in God's Service: Toward a Theology of Ecclesial Lay Ministry* (Washington, D.C.: United States Catholic Conference, 1998); this paper, pp. 3–22.

3. James Heft, "Toward a Theology of Ecclesial Lay Ministry," *Together in God's Service*, pp. 23–50.

4. Zoila Diaz, "Baptism and the Baptized in Church Leadership," *Together in God's Service*, pp. 51–69.

5. Thomas O'Meara, "Ministry in the Catholic Church Today: The Gift of Some Historical Trajectories," *Together in God's Service*, pp. 70–86.

6. Dianne Bergant, "Biblical Foundations for Christian Ministry," *Together in God's Service*, pp. 87–102.

7. John Beal, "Lay People and Church Governance: Oxymoron or Opportunity," *Together in God's Service*, pp. 103–129. A statistical survey of women who exercise governance (their roles, their responsibilities) and the questions raised by this is offered in *Women and Jurisdiction: An Unfolding Reality: The LCWR Study of Selected Church Leadership Roles*, Anne Munley, Rosemary Smith, Helen Maher Garvey, Lois McGillivray, Mary Milligan (Silver Spring, MD: Leadership Conference of Women Religious, 2001).

8. Francis Cardinal George, "Magisterial Teaching," *Together in God's Service*, pp. 130–157.

9. James T. Hoffman, "Ecclesial Lay Ministry in a Local Church," *Together in God's Service*, pp. 158–167.

10. Howard T. Hubbard, "Reflections on the Experience of Ecclesial Lay Ministry," *Together in God's Service*, pp. 168–183.

11. A listing of all the questions submitted is given in *State of the Questions*, pp. 184–195.

12. Michael Downey, "Ministerial Identity: A Question of Common Foundations," unpublished paper.

13. Zeni Fox, "Laity, Ministry and Secular Character, unpublished paper."

14. Richard R. Gaillardetz, "The Ecclesiological Foundations of Ministry within an Ordered Communion," unpublished paper.

15. Aurelie A. Hagstrom,"The Secular Character of the Vocation and Mission of the Laity: Towards a Theology of Ecclesial Lay Ministry," unpublished paper.

16. Kenan B. Osborne, "Lay-Ordained Ministry: Current Issues of Ambiguity," unpublished paper.

17. David Power, "Priesthood Revisited: Mission and Ministries in the Royal Priesthood," unpublished paper.

18. Thomas P. Rausch, "Ministry and Ministries," unpublished paper.

19. Elissa Rinere, "The Exercise of *cura animarum* through the 20th Century and Beyond," unpublished paper.

20. R. Kevin Seasoltz, "Institutes of Consecrated Life: Identity, Integrity and Ministry," unpublished paper.

✥

PART TWO

PERSPECTIVES
FROM THE TRADITION

✥

Section One

Scripture

INTRODUCTION

As the Church engages in theological reflection, probing the meaning of the emergence of the new ministers, the New Testament is an important source for us. We do not turn to the experience of the early church in order to copy what existed then, even if such a response were possible. Rather we study the life and thought of the first Christians both because the words of Scripture are inspired, and because those who were closest in time to Jesus of Nazareth have a privileged place in Christian tradition. We look to their experience, their words, for inspiration in our life today, for clarification about what is faithful in our following and what needs conversion, for models that might be newly appropriated, for wisdom in our discernment process.

In these opening years of the twenty-first century, we stand in a new relationship to the Bible. The work of modern scripture scholarship began at the end of the nineteenth century. Since the encouragement given to Catholic scholarship by Pius XII's *Divino Afflante Spiritu* in 1943, prodigious work has been done, exploring the original meanings of the texts. In addition, extensive historical research has enabled us to understand more fully the life of the early church communities. Systematic theologians today draw on these resources from other theological disciplines. It is not possible here to even briefly review the many aspects of this scholarship that bear on the topic of this study. Rather, some general descriptions which have particular bearing on the topic of the new ministers will be presented in schematic fashion. The intention is to provide a scriptural context for the assessment of this new reality.

CHAPTER TEN

MANY MINISTERS

Although the New Testament is quite small, in terms of numbers of pages, nonetheless we meet many ministers, presented by function, role, and even personal name. A few examples will illustrate this richness.

PROPHETS

Some scholars have chosen to emphasize the prophetic spirit of the entire Christian community,[1] but most authors view the prophet as a distinct minister within the early church.[2] Evidence of prophets and their activity in the community is traced back to very old sources, with references presumed to have been present in the "Q" tradition.[3] Prophets are mentioned in Matthew, Luke, and Paul, but not in John. The writer of the Book of Revelation calls himself a prophet attesting to a late reference to prophets,[4] but it was especially in the very early life of the Church that the prophets played an important role. Both men and women were prophets.

The prophets were enthusiasts, or charismatics,[5] but they spoke in a language that all could understand.[6] Their service was a dimension of the ministry of the Word.[7] The prophet proclaimed God's Word in the liturgical assembly, and it was heard as "a word of actuality coming from God."[8] The special role of the prophet in proclaiming the Word was the task of making revelation relevant to any given situation.[9] The prophet spoke out on contemporary issues, proclaiming what God intends to do and what God would have the people do.[10] There is, therefore, an element of disclosure and prediction in the prophets' words,[11] at times predicting things to come, especially in the proximate future. Their proclamation was based on a special "inspired insight" which they possessed.[12]

A perspective on the inspired, intuitive nature of their ministry is offered by Dillon. He traces their contribution to the tradition of Jesus'

191

sayings. He notes that "even within this most ancient layer of the Synoptics . . . there are the clearest traces of change and adaptation by the post-Easter congregations." Dillon asks, who would have the daring to take such initiatives with the Lord's own sayings, and concludes, it was the prophets.[13]

The purpose of the work of the prophets is the building up, the encouragement, and the consolation of others in the community.[14] With the apostles, they had a founding function in the missionary congregations.[15] Part of their work was the movement of the Church from Judaism to universality. Perhaps prophets presided over the Eucharist at times; this may have been linked to their presiding over the community.[16] Therefore, it is possible that the prophets, who were involved in a ministry of the Word, were also involved in sacramental ministry and a ministry of oversight. There is evidence of prophets who were itinerants, and others who were leading figures in their own local communities.[17]

What authority did the prophets have for their ministry? It would seem clear that they were authoritative figures. Dillon characterizes them by saying:

> The eschatological necessity of responding to both the founding prophet and his followers has—as is characteristic of the enthusiastic era—no historical or rigorously reasoned basis . . . The compelling power of the prophetic call is just *there*, in the event of the Spirit working though him.[18]

But, did they have authority over the community? Since the community was called upon to test the authenticity of the prophet's words, even as the prophet spoke with a sense of God-given authority, this is a difficult question. Küng's perspective is helpful: the prophet "has authority in the community, as a member of the community in communion with the other prophets who have the same authority."[19]

Did the prophets disappear early in the life of the Church? Dillon states, "A new generation, concerned with stability and legitimacy of beliefs, would not long endure the techniques of pneumatic prophetism; hence the prophets as such have no significant role in the churches of the later New Testament literature."[20] As the Church became more institutionalized, the functions of the prophets and teachers gradually were taken up by presbyters.[21] Nonetheless, in his "The Succession of Prophets in the

Church," Dulles points out that throughout church history great prophets like Bernard of Clairvaux, Francis of Assisi, and Catherine of Siena have arisen in our midst.[22]

The historical changes in ministry that occurred in New Testament times are clear in the example of the role of the prophet. Originally an enthusiast, a charismatic function of prophecy was gradually assumed into a more institutionalized role. One could see this as a change from an eschatological period in which the Spirit operated more directly in the Church, or a change in the perceptions of the Church, with an emphasis less on an imminent parousia and more on a Church for future ages. In our own day, when the "already" dimension of the reign of God has been reaffirmed, perhaps there will be a new valuing of the role of the prophet. But even if there is not such an explicit valuing, the voices of the Bernards, Francises, and Catherines of our time will surely not be stilled, even if persecution and martyrdom eventually silence them.

TEACHERS

Statistically the description of Jesus as a prophet is not very common in the New Testament. Usually, when he is so designated, it is the people who call him a prophet.[23] On the other hand, the most used title for Jesus is that of teacher.[24] In John, Jesus refers to himself as Teacher. The function of teaching and the role of teachers is broadly attested to in the New Testament. However, the ministry of the teacher is "attested in a fragmentary way" and "thinly studied."[25] The result is that there are many questions that remain unresolved about their ministry.

Although some writers emphasize the function of teaching, and assign that to the apostles,[26] it is generally thought that the teachers were a distinct group.[27] As with the prophets, their role is presumed to have been mentioned in the "Q" tradition,[28] and is found also in later New Testament works such as Matthew and Hebrews. Their's was a ministry of the Word,[29] probably addressed to believers only.[30] They were probably not pneumatics, because in 1 Corinthians 14:29, ff. they seem to be named as interpreters of ecstatics, and so were not of that group.[31] In fact, Dillon holds that they were anti-enthusiast.[32]

A diversity exists around the issue of what they taught, the content of their teaching. On the one hand, their work is seen as "catechetical instruction and development,[33] while, on the other hand, it is paralleled with the theologians of later church periods.[34] Bourke concludes that their teaching was not simply "catechetical repetition of the gospel, devoid of intellectual depth."[35]

The teacher's task was to transmit the didache "in a sequential form to those desirous of a deeper knowledge," probably modeled on the Jewish way of teaching of the period.[36] The teaching had a moral dimension, the moral implications of the Christian faith[37] or instruction in the new law. Some would see an emphasis on "the exegesis of the Old Testament as understood by the young church."[38] Most would emphasize a doctrinal orientation in the teaching.[39] In addition to their teaching role, some would say that the teachers may also have celebrated the Eucharist.[40]

The Christian teacher is sometimes compared to the Jewish rabbi.[41] If the parallel correctly describes the reality in the early church, it would mean that the teachers had a certain identity as a group and that they were trained for their role.[42] However, this may only apply to a later development of the role, especially as described in Matthew.[43] Another important aspect of the Hebrew tradition is that the teacher was conceived of as a revealer. Acceptance of the teaching is acceptance of the revealing of Yahweh's very self.[44] "Perhaps [the teachers] drew occasionally on their own revelation, charismatically received, and transmitted new insights into the truth."[45]

The qualities required by the teacher included knowledge and, especially in Hebrews, an inward growth that is inspired by the Spirit.[46] The role presupposes a life lived in accordance with what is taught, as is stated by James. The Jewish teacher was normally accorded many honors,[47] but the Christian teacher exists in a community where "the only hierarchy is the paradoxical one that the highest is the one who renders most service. . . and that the 'little ones' are the most important members of the Church."[48] Therefore, most would say that they did not hold an office in the Church.[49] The Jewish rabbi was not an officer of the congregation. Although he was ordained by the laying on of hands of his rabbinical teacher, the meaning of the rite was the conveying of "a private and personal qualification which lent weight to his words, but no public function or authority in the Jewish church."[50]

Like the ministry of the prophet, that of the teacher changed in the different periods of the New Testament. Schillebeeckx deftly outlines this development, highlighting their role as local leaders in the earliest days of the Church, their role in building on the foundation of the apostles and prophets in the early post-apostolic period, and the gradual assumption of their function by the presbyters at the end of the New Testament period.[51] Despite the fact that official teaching became a function of the clergy, the tradition of the teacher as it continues through the life of the Church embraces many laity, from theologians to catechists, and also parents. In our own day, the formal teaching ministry is continued by various individuals through different structures, including religious education directors in parishes and teachers in Catholic schools.

PAUL'S CHURCHES

In considering the "many ministers" of the New Testament period, it is helpful to look at Paul's churches. Clearly, there were varied ministries and many ministers—and Paul seems to have delighted in thinking of them, for he lists them often, in various ways. 1 Corinthians gives a central tenet of Paul's thinking:

> There is a variety of gifts but always the same spirit; there are all sorts of service to be done, but always to the same life; working in all sorts of different ways in different people, it is the same God who is working in all of them. The particular way in which the Spirit is given to each person is for a good purpose (12:4–7).

Paul continues with an enumeration of many gifts such as preaching with wisdom and healing, and concludes, "All these are the work of one and the same Spirit, who distributes different gifts to different people just as he chooses" (12:11). He ends this reflection with the analogy of the human body, in which each separate part is needed by the whole, and the parts are to work together for the good of all. It is not clear how the ministries he names differ one from another, and his list here is not exhaustive, even of his own naming of ministries.[52] However, Paul's sense of a diversity of ministries all serving the common good, each requiring positive regard by all, every one a gift of the Spirit, is abundantly clear.

An overview of Paul's work yields a picture in harmony with the goal he presented in 1 Corinthians. Many are associated with him in his ministry. E. Earle Ellis notes that the names of one hundred individuals are linked with the Apostle; they are designated by various titles.[53] The most used descriptions are fellow-worker, brother/sister, servant, and apostle.[54] These titles capture a sense of working together collegially; they connote a valuing of the contributions of each person. The group includes men and women. Some, like Mark, travel with Paul; some, such as Phoebe, are workers in local congregations.[55] Paul recognizes that at least some of these ministers should be supported by the congregation, and that they are distinguishable from the congregation. Ellis thinks that these men and women were a "professional 'class' . . . with a recognizable form, however varied or imprecise the vocabulary by which they were identified."[56]

One group of ministers mentioned uniquely by Paul are the house church leaders, apparently married couples. Prisca and Aquila are named in Romans and 1 Corinthians, Apphia and Archippus in Philomon. Paul does not give them a title, but he does describe functions they performed. Prisca and Aquila instructed Apollos, apparently exercising a ministry of the Word. Paul clearly values their ministry.[57] Audet observes that because traditionally we have focused so much of our attention on the hierarchy, the "micromorphology" of pastoral service in the early church has not received sufficient consideration. Therefore we miss much of what helped to make up the effectiveness and continuity of pastoral service in the early period. It was in the homes of couples like Prisca and Aquila that the Christian assembly was received, once the support of the synagogue had failed.

> The domestic framework assured, both to the ekklesia and to the itinerant service of the word, not only stability and security, but also the flexibility and mobility which made it possible for the gospel to continue its advance . . . Home and marriage were, both, and in a single sweep, profoundly integrated into the life of the apostolic church.[58]

The house church leaders may be seen as models for the leaders of base communities today,[59] or for the couples who minister together in various roles in their communities.

As Paul's churches evolved after his death, the need to more fully develop the institutional dimensions, the structural dimensions, gave rise to different emphases in ministry. The dispersal of ministries among many members was seen as problematic, and the type of charismatic leadership that characterized Paul and his co-workers is frowned upon in the Pastorals. Rather, in the epistles to Timothy and Titus we find that the appointment of a prudent, sober, balanced presbyter-bishop for every town is required in order to provide authoritative leadership for all the communities.[60] Changing circumstances led to changes in ministry. The needs of the communities helped to shape ministry, even in the earliest times.

CONCLUSION

While many other ministers could be considered, this brief introduction to the prophets, teachers, and house church leaders illustrates some of the diversity found in the early church. It is from Paul that we have the clearest picture of the many ministers who served the communities. One characteristic that can be noted is the way in which different functions are performed by different ministers. The teachers taught; the house church leaders convened a community. The roles involved called for different gifts; different persons took on the roles. A second characteristic is that it seems the functions were performed because of the gifts, the charisms, that were given by the Spirit. This is clearest with the prophets, but Paul emphasizes that all of the services flow from the gifts with which the Spirit endows some, for the good of all.

NOTES

1. So, for example, Gerhard Friedrich, "Prophets and Prophecies, in the New Testament," *Theological Dictionary of the New Testament*, vol. 6 (Grand Rapids: Wm. B. Eerdmans Publishing Co., 1968), p. 849.

2. For example, Avery Dulles, "The Succession of Prophets in the Church" in *Apostolic Succession*, ed. Hans Küng (New York: Paulist Press, 1968).

3. Krodel, Gerhard, "Forms and Functions of Ministries in the New Testament," *Dialog* 8 (Winter 1969), p. 197.

4. Edward Schillebeeckx, *Ministry: Leadership in the Community of Jesus Christ* (New York: Crossroad, 1981), n. 9, p. 145.

5. Richard J. Dillon "Ministry as Stewardship of the Tradition in the New Testament," *Catholic Theological Society Proceedings* 24 (1969), p. 18.

6. Dulles, p. 54.

7. David Power, *The Christian Priest: Elder and Prophet* (London: Sheed and Ward, 1973), p. 27.

8. André Lemaire, "The Ministries in the New Testament: Recent Research," *Theology Bulletin* 3 (June 1973), p. 144.

9. Power, *Christian Priest*, p. 27.

10. Friedrich, p. 848.

11. Myles Bourke, "Reflections on Church Order in the New Testament," *Catholic Biblical Quarterly* 30 (1968), p. 500.

12. Dulles, "Prophets," p. 54.

13. Dillon, p. 27.

14. Bourke, pp. 499–500.

15. Dillon, p. 18.

16. Hervé-Marie Legrand, "The Presidency of the Eucharist According to the Ancient Tradition," *Worship* 53 (September 1979), p. 416.

17. Dulles, p. 53.

18. Dillon p. 29.

19. Hans Küng, *The Church* (New York: Sheed & Ward, 1967), p. 396.

20. Dillon, p. 38.

21. Schillebeeckx, pp. 15–16.

22. Dulles, "Prophets," p. 56.

23. Friedrich, p. 841.

24. *Dictionary of the Bible*, 1965, s.v. "Teach, Teaching," John L. McKenzie, p. 870.

25. Lemaire, "Ministries," p. 143.

26. Rudolf Schnackenburg, *The Church in the New Testament* (New York: Herder and Herder, 1965), p. 38.

27. Bourke, p. 500.

28. Krodel, p. 197.

29. Küng, *Church*, p. 397.

30. John McKenzie, "Ministerial Structures," in *The Plurality of Ministries,* Hans Küng and Walter Kasper, eds. (New York: Herder and Herder, 1982), p. 21.

31. Karl Rengstorf, *Theological Dictionary of the New Testament*, vol. 6 (Grand Rapids: Wm. B. Eerdmans Publishing Co., 1968), p. 158.

32. Dillon, p. 44.

33. Power, *Christian Priest*, p. 27. Echoing this is Krodel, p. 198, who says that teachers transmitted moral catechisms, tables of duties, kerygmatic traditions, and Jesus traditions.

34. Küng, *Church*, p. 434.

35. Bourke, p. 501.

36. Lemaire, "Ministries," p. 144.

37. Bourke, p. 500.

38. Hans von Campenhausen, *Ecclesiastical Authority and Spiritual Power in the Church of the First Three Centuries* (London: Adam and Charles Black, 1969), p. 61.

39. For example, Dulles, who says teachers were concerned with "general points of doctrine"—unlike prophets, who spoke "on the basis of an inspired insight" ("Succession of Prophets," p. 54).

40. Bourke, p. 507; with certainty, Legrand, "Presidency of the Eucharist," pp. 415–416.

41. Anton Houtepen, "Gospel, Church, Ministry" in *Minister? Pastor? Prophet?*, Lucas Grollenberg, et al. (New York: Crossroad, 1981), p. 35.

42. Campenhausen, p. 61.

43. Schweizer, p. 198.

44. McKenzie, "Teach, Teaching," p. 870.

45. Arnold van Ruler, "Is There a 'Succession of Teachers'?" in *Apostolic Succession: Rethinking a Barrier to Unity*, ed. Hans Küng (New York: Paulist, Concilium vol. 34, 1968), p. 64.

46. Schweizer, p. 114. See also James D. G. Dunn, *Unity and Diversity in the New Testament* (Philadelphia: Westminster Press, 1977), p. 119, who emphasizes "spiritual maturity."

47. Rengstorf, p. 154. He cites examples that echo the treatment of Jesus by His disciples.

48. Schweizer, p. 60.

49. McKenzie, "Ministerial Structures," p. 18; Schweizer, p. 60.

50. Gregory Dix, ed., *The Treatise on the Apostolic Tradition of St. Hippolytus of Rome* (London: SPCK Press, 1968), p. 236.

51. Schillebeeckx, *Ministry*, pp. 10–16.

52. Jerome Murphy-O'Connor, "The First Letter to the Corinthians," *The Jerome Biblical Commentary*, Raymond Brown, Joseph Fitzmyer, Roland Murphy, eds. (Englewood Cliffs: Prentice Hall, 1990), p. 810.

53. "Paul and His Co-Workers," *New Testament Studies*, vol. 17, 1971, pp. 437–438.

54. Ibid., p. 440.

55. Ibid., p. 442.

56. Ibid., pp. 443–444. (The noun translated in Ellis as "brothers" can also be translated as siblings. It is common gender, and includes sisters.)

57. Jean Paul Audet, *Structures of Christian Priesthood* (Macmillan: New York, 1968), p. 35.

58. Ibid., pp. 49–50, 57.

59. Ibid., p. 104.

60. Brown, *The Churches the Apostles Left Behind*, pp. 31–37.

CHAPTER ELEVEN

MANY MINISTRIES

THE TWELVE

Most Scripture scholars today would agree that the designation "The Twelve" belongs to the language of the most ancient sources, probably dating to the Galilean ministry of Jesus. However, the designation "The Twelve Apostles," found in Luke, probably dates to the postapostolic period.[1] Because they had known Jesus during his historical ministry, and because they were also witnesses to his Resurrection, the Twelve held a special position in the early church. The significance of their being precisely twelve suggests the eschatological function they fulfilled, symbolizing at once the twelve tribes of ancient Israel and the convening of a new Israel. It was around the Twelve, perhaps convened by them, that the new community formed. And it was they who were to play a definitive role in the final eschatological time, sitting on twelve thrones and judging the nations.[2]

What additional functions they held is difficult to determine. There is no evidence that most of them ever left the Jerusalem area, so they were not missionaries. Apparently, they also were not bishops, not even in the early sense of overseer of a community. ". . . (W)hile the Twelve themselves may have baptized, presided at the Eucharist and forgiven sins, the Church may also have recognized the sacramental authority of others who were not ordained by the Twelve."[3]

Although Scripture records the replacement of Judas by the casting of lots, so that the Twelve continued with their original significance as twelve, there is no record of further replacements of the original members of the group. In fact, recollection of them appears to have been dim, even at the time of the writing of the Gospels. There are variant lists of their names, but most have no clearly defined personality.[4] As an institution, a particular form of ministry, the Twelve as such dies out.

This may be because "their role was thought of more in relation to the Resurrection and return of the Christ, and was less suited to the continuing community of the interval."[5] Whatever the reason, that this earliest form of ministry disappears shows the fluidity of ministerial forms which characterizes the New Testament period.

APOSTLES

Both the title and the functions associated with "apostle" are the cause of much debate. Schillebeeckx states the issue succinctly: "While the concept of 'apostleship' has a clearly defined nucleus, it is more fluid at the periphery."[6] Part of the reason for this is the varying usages of the word by different New Testament authors. In Luke, *the* apostles were eyewitnesses of the historical Jesus; the Twelve are the apostles. In Paul, his own apostleship is constituted by his mission from the Risen Jesus. In Mark and Matthew, each using the word only once, it denotes a function, not a title. In Revelation, the Twelve are the Apostles; in the Pastorals, Paul is the Apostle. For Luke, the idea of the Twelve Apostles is important for his theology; he uses this compilation of the Twelve and apostle to underline the historical nature of the Church, and her authoritative voice.[7]

In Paul's letters, references are made to "apostles" in such a way as to allow varying interpretations of who should be included in this circle. Certainly, Paul presents himself as an apostle, frequently using the title. Andronicus and Junia are named as apostles, as are Peter, Barnabas, and possibly Silvanus. In 1 Corinthians 15:5–8a, Paul says that Jesus appeared first to Cephas, secondly to the Twelve, then to various other groups and individuals, "then to all the apostles" and last of all to himself. Clearly, there were apostles other than the Twelve, and at least one, Junia, was a woman.[8]

The functions of the apostles are also described differently in the varying strata of New Testament evidence. The primitive sources emphasize the role of the apostle as a missionary, a delegate. The apostle was sent by his or her church to proclaim the good news to other communities.[9] In the Pauline perspective, the mandate given the apostles in their encounter with the risen Christ makes them instruments of revelation of God's present and future saving act towards humanity. Therefore, they did not simply use traditional formulae, repeating in rabbinic style, but adopted the message to the circumstances and needs of the churches. Apostleship is an intensely present credential. It is in Luke, written in post-apostolic times, that the emphasis is placed on the apostle's role as reporting on a past experience of the historical Jesus, rather than on the present revelation.[10]

With a power of word and action, the apostles were founders of communities.[11] Paul's letters show us the relationship which he maintained with his communities. We see him teaching and exercising guidance in the communities, even from afar.[12] Although there were other ministries exercised in the communities, to some extent, "he himself remained the father and leader of the church."[13]

An aspect of the experience of the apostle is that of suffering and persecution.[14] Paul rejoices in this dimension, seeing it as a sharing in the suffering of Christ. Clearly, his stance is not one of glorying in his status as an apostle, but rather of sharing in the suffering of the Lord.

A debated aspect of the role of the apostles is the extent to which they exercised authority. It is helpful to examine this question in two ways, first, their speaking with authority or speaking authoritatively, second, their exercising authority over the early Christian communities. Viewing authority in the first sense, it could be said to flow directly from their experience of the risen Lord, and to be manifested in the power in word and action with which they communicated the *kerygma*. Many writers speak of the apostles' authority from this perspective, either explicitly or implicitly.[15]

The debate more properly concerns the exercise of authority in the second sense. For example, Dix, while viewing the apostles as having great prestige and influence, describes their role as advising, as arguing, but not as being part of the local government of the Church.[16] On the other hand, Schnackenburg sees in the fact that the Church at Corinth submitted questions to Paul for his decision an indication that he exercised authority over that congregation.[17] Other writers strive to de-emphasize the "exercising of authority." This viewpoint is found in Dillon, who states that "itinerant enthusiasts like Paul drew converts by ecstatic words and deeds, then left churches to develop according to their own cultural situation."[18] In a similar view, Käsemann argues that an authoritarian relationship "has no place in the ordering of the Church and . . . indeed is the precise target of the polemic found in such passages as Matthew 20:25, f; 23:11; 1 Corinthians 3:5, and 1 Peter 5:3 against claims to domination and to positions of power."[19]

Campenhausen provides an essential link between the two views of authority that have been outlined here. He says:

> . . . Paul, who both as one called to be an apostle of Christ and as a teacher of his churches is a man of the very highest authority, nevertheless does not develop this authority of his in the obvious and straightforward way by building up a sacral relationship of spiritual control and subordination . . . Rather, he stresses the freedom in the Spirit of his congregations, both against the old, Jewish law and also any new personal authorities that arise within the congregation itself and seek to domineer over men's faith . . . This means that the power of command which he exercises is from the outset fundamentally limited . . . the congregation of those who possess the Spirit must follow him in freedom . . .[20]

The issue of who were the apostles and what were their functions has considerable importance for understanding the question of ministry today. Apostolic succession, authority in the Church, and the meaning of tradition are some of the theological issues associated with these questions. For this study, however, those questions cannot be dealt with as such. The main point here is that "The decisive thing about the apostles is their personal meeting with the Lord, whom they all, in one form or another, knew as someone who had been dead and was alive again."[21] Theirs was an experience, and a commission, which was part of the eschatological moment that embraced the earthly ministry and post-Easter manifestation of the Lord Jesus. Their words and deeds of power had a uniqueness; they shared in the saving act of the Christ in an unrepeatable way. Therefore, they are the foundation stones, the founders, the fathers, even the nursemaids, as Paul says, of the Church. Their ministry was once-and-for all.

Of significance when reflecting on the new ministries is the fact that some apostles were missionaries, but not the only missionaries; ministers of the Word, among others, such as prophets and teachers; leaders of their communities, as were elders and bishops; disciples of the Lord, just as all of the early followers of The Way were called. The picture that emerges from the New Testament of the ministry of the apostles is that it was one of great importance, yet still one that is a ministry among other ministries.

THE SEVEN

In Acts 6:1–6, we read of a ministry established in the earliest days of the life of the Christian community, perhaps the second ministry of the Church.[22] Most commentators concur that this account is not about the deacons whom we will meet later in the history of the Church.[23] Furthermore, the passage records both an event in the life of the primitive community in Jerusalem and an interpretation of that event by Luke at a later period in the Church's history.

The exegetical study of this passage by Lienhard proposes that verses 5 and 6 are traditional, based on an historical event.[24] Difficulties had arisen in the Jerusalem community between the Aramaic-speaking Christians (the Hebrews) and the Greek-speaking Christians (the Hellenists). Ostensibly, the quarrel was about the material help provided to the Greek-speaking Jewish-Christian members of the community.[25] The Hellenists probably represented a theological position, rooted both in Jewish sectarianism and in the diaspora. They were opposed to the domination of Judaism by Jerusalem, and brought this perspective with them to Christianity. To them Christianity was a sign of divine rejection of the Jerusalem Temple. Therefore, the resolution of the conflict by the appointment of Hellenist leaders for the Hellenist community marked an effort by the early church to allow pluralism on the question of the relations of the community to the Temple.[26]

Relying again on Lienhard's exegesis, it would appear that the naming of the Seven early in the history of the Christian community marked their authoritative appointment.[27] It is reasonable to expect that they had already demonstrated their leadership in the community before that. Dunn maintains that before the appointment theirs was a charismatic authority.[28] In their role, they supervised, preached, and taught,[29] and, therefore, shared in the ministry of the Word.[30] They baptized as well and, of course, cared for the poor.[31]

Subsequently, Hellenists were persecuted by the Jewish Sanhedrin (the Hebrews were not) causing them to flee to Samaria and Syria. Throughout the Jewish diaspora, along the Mediterranean coast, they founded Christian communities.[32] "Thus, the Hellenists became the earliest missionaries."[33]

An interesting aspect of the role of the Seven is the relationship between their administrative responsibilities in the Hellenist community and the developments in other communities of the New Testament period. Although Scripture gives us their names, it does not indicate whether they had a title. We also don't know whether the Hebrew community also received administrators. However, the fact that later elders are mentioned in relation to those communities (Acts 11:30) makes it seem likely that they did.[34] It is possible to identify the Seven with the later presbyters or elders found in the New Testament churches.[35]

When Luke narrated the story of the Seven, he added to the traditional elements. Some say, he used an "Antioch source" for the "Stephen cycle," including this section; others hold that he wrote an independent narrative that he joined to the episode of the institution of the Seven. Luke's redaction added its own emphasis: "the community chooses the candidates and 'the Twelve'—the authoritative body in the community—commissions them in office."[36] This accords with a central theological concern of Luke, that of the legitimate tradition. He wants to show how the ministry of the word was passed on to the post-apostolic Church and so uses this opportunity, among others, to show the Twelve's role in commissioning others to service.[37] Another concern that may be evidenced in Luke's account is the description of the Christian contribution to social and material development, embodied in the task of caring for the widows.[38]

A striking note about the ministry of the Seven is that the official designation was made as an effort to resolve a conflict in the Church. To meet the needs of theological diversity, cultural enclaves, and material need, out of the fire of conflict, a new official ministry was forged. Those chosen for this new role were already active leaders in the community. And their authorization was for service, not in a carefully delimited way, separating this role from that of the apostle, but in a way that called for sensitivity to the movement of the Spirit. So we read that Stephen "was filled with grace and power" (Acts 6:8) and that "the angel of the Lord spoke to Philip" (Acts 8:26). The early church, led by the Spirit, created ministries, and designated ministers. The ministers, led by the Spirit, exercised their service to the Church.

CONCLUSION

Even such a brief overview as this indicates the vibrancy of service in the early church, manifested in a multiplicity of ministries. Although the differentiating norms are not altogether clear to us today, the ministries of "The Twelve" and "The Seven" were recognized as different. We can also note that the norms for different ministries varied somewhat from one local community to another, as the varying understandings of "apostle" show us. While there are indications that as in all human relationships there were tensions at times (for example, why else did Paul feel such a need to defend himself precisely as an apostle?), it is also clear that the varying ministries worked together for the building up of the Church.

NOTES

1. Lemaire, "Ministries," p. 141.
2. Brown, *Priest and Bishop*, pp. 49, 55.
3. Ibid., pp. 49, 52–54.
4. Walter Schmithals, *The Office of Apostle in the Early Church* (New York: Abingdon, 1969), p. 70.
5. Dunn, p. 108.
6. Schillebeeckx, *Ministry*, p. 6.
7. Schweizer, pp. 194–195; 63–70.
8. Campenhausen, p. 22.
9. Lemaire, "Ministries," p. 143.
10. Dillon, pp. 19–21.
11. Campenhausen, p. 23; also Dillon, p. 18.
12. Brown, *Priest and Bishop*, p. 35.
13. Schnackenburg, pp. 29–30.
14. Raymond Brown, "Episkopé and Episkopos: The New Testament Evidence," *Theological Studies* 41 (June 1980), p. 328.
15. For example, Dillon explicitly speaks of the apostles' "peculiar mandate and authority. . . conferred in a single initial encounter with the risen Christ" (p. 19). Schmithals says that the authority of the apostle rested not in his person but in his message (p. 40), and Campenhausen that the apostles proclaim the word with confidence and reinforce it with miraculous signs, so sharing the authority of Jesus (p. 24).
16. Dix, pp. 243–244.
17. Schnackenburg, p. 29. He argues further that Paul's appointment of elders as recorded in Acts 14:23 is a sign of such exercise of authority (p. 30).
18. Dillon, pp. 16–17.
19. Käsemann, *New Testament Themes*, p. 63. And yet, Käsemann sees Paul acting to regulate the communities and charisma, concluding, "Thus [Paul] does not hesitate to set limits to the Pneuma which indwells the community and its worship and to do it in the declaratory style characteristic of juridical pronouncements." The norm he used was not his personal authority but rather the concrete act of ministry as it occurs (pp. 82–83).

20. Campenhausen, pp. 46–47.

21. Küng, p. 354.

22. Lemaire, "Ministries" p. 36.

23. Lemaire states that "the majority of the experts think that the seven should not be considered as prototypes of the deacons" ("Ministries," p. 147).

24. Joseph T. Lienhard, "Acts 6:1–6: A Redactional View," *Catholic Biblical Quarterly*, 1975, p. 236.

25. Schillebeeckx, *Ministry*, pp. 6–7. Also Brown, *Priest and Bishop*, p. 56.

26. Brown, *Priest and Bishop*, p. 56. For a different view of their ministry see John N. Collins, *Are All Christians Ministers?* (Collegeville: The Liturgical Press, 1992), especially pp. 36–40.

27. Lienhard, p. 236.

28. Dunn, p. 107.

29. Brown, "Episkopé and Episkopos," p. 326.

30. McKenzie, "Ministerial Structures," p. 20.

31. Küng, *Church*, p. 401.

32. Schillebeeckx, *Ministry*, p. 7 and note 5.

33. Brown, *Priest and Bishop*, p. 57.

34. Brown, "Episkopé and Episkopos," p. 326.

35. Küng, *Church*, p. 401.

36. Lienhard, pp. 228–231.

37. Dillon, pp. 48–51. The same point is made by Schmithals, who comments on Luke's intention saying, "The laying on of hands . . . has to do simply with an ordination which underscores the self-evident fact that all power lies in the hands of the Twelve" (p. 249).

38. Power, *Elder and Prophet*, p. 32.

Chapter Twelve

Central Characteristics: Diakonia and Collegiality

Ministry: The Choice of Language

As can be determined from the analysis in previous chapters, what developed in church order in the first century can be traced to various structures and functions in the worlds of Judaism and Hellenism of the time. This fact, of course, does not deny the role of the Spirit, God's grace guiding this development. What is unique is the word that describes the whole enterprise, *diakonia*–translated as ministry or service.[1] And this choice, too, is guided by the Spirit!

Diakonia: Origin and Evolution

Various other words utilized in the Septuagint, in secular Greek, even in other parts of the New Testament, could have been chosen. Hans Küng suggests that several were not used because they express a relationship of rulers and ruled. Even *leitourgia*, which originally meant service to the community, and had gradually assumed a specialized sense of religious service (of service to the gods), was not used to describe those with a special role in the community. Rather, an unbiblical word, not used in this way in either Jewish or Hellenistic circles, was bent to a new use by the New Testament community.[2]

In its original usage, *diakonia* meant serving at table. In the eyes of the Greeks, this serving was not dignified; ruling was proper to man. Slaves, and women, served. Judaism did not have this same disdain of serving, especially if one served a great master.[3] Of course, in the Christian context, the word means the service of *all*, especially the poor and needy. "It is essentially being at the disposal of those who are at table and fulfilling their need."[4]

This is the starting point for the evolution of the term in the New Testament. Gradually, its meaning embraces any discharge of service in genuine love, a service of brother or sister and also of Christ. Finally, it referred to the discharge of certain obligations in the community: apostolic office, the office of the evangelist, the activity of Mark who combined personal service and assistance with missionary work.[5] Therefore, "the term *diakonia* can also be used for the service of leaders in the community . . . and also for the office of apostle."[6] It is for this reason that Ellis says that the appointment to ecclesial office "was, in the most literal sense, to be a worker and a servant.[7]

DIAKONIA: BIBLICAL AND THEOLOGICAL ASSOCIATIONS

This theme of service interconnects with and is informed by many other theological themes of the New Testament. Lemaire says, "This distinctive vocabulary carries a deep meaning and orientates the whole evangelical conception of the functions in the church."[8] Houtepen roots the language of service in the Christian fact of "a new relationship with God which is born out of sharing in the fate and destiny of Jesus." He shows that the New Testament names used for ministry "correspond with titles which were given to Jesus himself and thus have a Christological basis."[9]

Many of these themes are highlighted in a helpful historical–critical study of 1 Peter 5:1–5 by Elliott. Elliott sees the text as an exhortation to leaders in the community or "a primitive Christian instruction for office."[10] The key notes sounded are the need to "avoid exploitation of the power of office," and the "need for humility." The text reflects a still flexible church order tradition. He states, "As the Sitz-im-leben of this ministry and order tradition I would propose the baptismal catechesis of the early Church." He concludes, "The tradition indicates a concern to correlate Christological with ecclesiological motifs: Jesus as servant correlates to church leaders as servants or Jesus as Chief-Shepherd parallels to leaders as shepherds."[11]

Other authors develop the understanding of ministry by examining the scriptural use of *diakonia* in various contexts.[12] Schnackenburg's study is particularly helpful. He explores Luke's account of the Last Supper, in which the evangelist uses the language of serving, as he does again in Acts 6:2. Schnackenburg concludes that Luke was writing with his contemporary Church in mind.

> He is aiming at the overseers who had to attend to the serving of tables and look after the poor. He is concerned with "the task of those who have position and responsibility in the community" . . . Luke demands from them, in accordance with Jesus' words, readiness to serve and fidelity in small things . . ."[13]

Schnackenburg also examines the gospel of Matthew, especially chapter 18:1–20, the "so-called 'community rule.'" He sees the parable of the lost sheep as referring to the role of church leaders in caring for "those little ones," and the exhortation to "humble oneself" in v. 4 as perhaps the basis of all order in the Church. He concludes,

> The paradoxical requirement of service holds good throughout for all who "desire to be great" in the Church. At all events, Matthew knows and acknowledges presiding functions and offices in the Church but also subjects them all to the law of service and responsibility before the Lord.[14]

One result of this emphasis on ministry as radically oriented toward service is that authority is viewed in a different way. Therefore, in drawing seven conclusions from his overview of research on ministries in the New Testament, Lemaire states that "ecclesial authority is essentially a service."[15] Similarly, Ellis concludes that as long as the idea of being a worker and servant continued, "structure and authority in an official worldly sense remained subordinate and contingent."[16] Finally, when considering "ecclesiastical office as ministry" Küng says that

> . . . the only valid model is that of the man who serves at table, . . . a total existence in a life and death of service for others, as prefigured by the service of Jesus himself (Mk. 10:45; Mt. 20:28) and as demanded by Jesus himself of those who would serve him. "He who loves his life loses it, and he who hates his life in this world will keep it for eternal life. If anyone serves me, he

must follow me; and where I am, there shall my servant be also; if anyone serves me, the Father will honor him" (Jn. 12:35, ff.).[17]

CONCLUSION

An analysis of the origin of the word *diakonia* highlights the radical Christological orientation at the heart of the concept of ministry. Jesus Christ is the disciple of his Father, the Suffering Servant who gives himself for the sake of others. The Church, the Body of Christ, and the People of God, continues this mission of service. (In this sense, the Church is prior to and more important than its ministries.) Therefore, those with a special role in building up the community, its ministers, are called upon to imitate his humble, self-effacing, other-directed service to all. Even the exercise of authority is to be modeled on the one who girded himself and washed the feet of his disciples at the Last Supper.

COLLEGIALITY IN MINISTRY

It is interesting to realize that in McKenzie's 1965 *Dictionary of the Bible* there is no listing for "collegiality."[18] Of course, it is not a biblical word; nonetheless, in the years since Vatican II, the word has taken on increasing significance in the life of the Church. Various authors have reflected on this key characteristic of ministry in the New Testament period. Some focus on the collegiality of the Twelve and reflect on implications for the episcopacy; others study collegiality as a characteristic of the New Testament church in general. While the latter perspective is of greater significance for this study, the former is important enough to be examined briefly.

COLLEGIALITY OF THE TWELVE

In light of the Vatican Council's affirmative vote on collegiality in the Church, David Stanley wrote an important article exploring the New Testament basis for the concept. The focus of the article is on the Twelve; the argument is on behalf of episcopal collegiality. His most important point is that there is an emphasis on "twelveness" rather than on the individual role of each apostle. In support of this, he points out that the Synoptics record both the call of certain of the disciples as individual followers and the selection of the Twelve, "an action of Jesus [for] the *institution of a group*." He also sees the way the names are listed, suggesting a mnemonic and always including Judas, as a further sign of an emphasis on the group rather than the individuals.[19] He concludes that episcopal collegiality is founded on the tradition begun by Jesus, and continued in the New Testament church.[20] Brown also considers the central role of the Twelve, and concludes that they were counciliar (for our purposes, collegial).[21] In analyzing Acts 6 and Acts 15, he discerns a similar pattern:

> . . . the multitude had to join the Twelve in giving approval to the position defended by Peter and Paul. In Luke's description, then, the Twelve emerge as a type of council, presiding over the multitude when meetings are called affecting the destiny of Christianity.

Brown cites a similar form of government in the Qumran community. There, the "Session of the Many" was called together to exercise judicial and executive authority, and a permanent community council consisting of twelve men and three priests served as a higher authoritative body.[22]

COLLEGIALITY OF THE NEW TESTAMENT CHURCH

Many authors assert that collegiality was one of the principal characteristics of the New Testament church. Schillebeeckx states categorically: "For all its pluriformity the ministry in the Church is essentially collegiality, i.e., solidarity of Christians equipped with different charismata of ministry."[23] In his study emphasizing the presidency of the community, Power states that originally "the presidency was collegial," a body of elders, all of equal authority. And even when the bishop emerged, there was still a "presbyteral college."[24] In concluding his primarily New Testament study of ministry, Houtepen notes the "essentially collegial and brotherly structure of ministerial service."[25] Küng, considering both the relationship of local pastors and their chief pastor, and that of local pastors and their communities, says they must share a "brotherly fellowship (collegiality)."[26] Schillebeeckx's conclusion flows from a consideration of the charisms given the community, Houtepen's from a study of several ministries of the New Testament period, and Küng's from his emphasis on the radically diaconal, service-oriented dimension of ministry. Different starting points, but the same conclusion.

Other authors use less specific language in this regard. Lemaire says, "the ecclesial authority must serve the authority of Christ and has to be exercised, within the Christian community, in a fraternal relationship."[27] Some helpful theological perspectives are presented to show the reason for this collegial, fraternal relationship. Lynch emphasizes the role of the *koinonia*:

> The kingly function of the people of God necessarily involved participation in the government of the Church . . . the dignity and responsibility of the laity were recognized, their advice sought, their enthusiasm welcomed, yet the decisive authority of the bishop was not threatened.[28]

Arguing that all members of the Church are part of the People of God, and no one belongs to a ruling group who are not People, Werdt says,

> Ministry is such only when it is related to the whole. If it turns into the opposite and becomes a claim to power, making the whole subordinate to itself, it no longer serves the whole and is no longer an ecclesial ministry. No ministry is exclusive in such a way as to render the others superfluous.[29]

COLLEGIALITY IN PAUL AND JOHN

To further elucidate this New Testament theme, it is helpful to examine some perspectives on Paul and John. In considering the Pauline church, during Paul's lifetime, Schillebeeckx states that they were "communities which understood themselves as brotherhoods, without rank or status . . ."[30] In a quite different vein, in his study on collegiality, Stanley concludes; "Paul in his turn attests the collegial character of the original apostles' role in the church . . . (he) constantly acknowledges his indebtedness to the apostolic traditions 'handed on' to him by the apostolic college . . ."[31]

A helpful study in this regard is the exegetical analysis of Paul's co-workers by Ellis. For the 100 persons named as associated with the Apostle, Ellis identifies nine designations given these colleagues: brother (sister), apostle, servant, slave, companion, worker, soldier, fellow-prisoner, and fellow-worker. None are named prophet, teacher, pastor, elder, or bishop. Ellis concludes:

> Probably in response to their Lord's command, they eschew titles of eminence. With reference to their task they are the workers, the servants, the special messengers; with reference to one another, they are the brothers [and sisters].[32]

Each of these authors helps focus the collegial nature of the Church Paul knew.

In a similar vein, Brown in particular helps us glimpse the collegial nature of the late first century Johannine church. Groups of presbyters were responsible for the administration and pastoral care of a church. The emphasis in the epistles is always on the presbyter as "part of a collective we who bear witness." Sometimes this collective means all of the brothers (the whole community) and sometimes a distinct group which represents the tradition bearers and interpreters.[33] Again, as Küng stressed, there is a collegiality between the leaders and the community, and among the leaders themselves.

Delimiting Collegiality

It is helpful to explore the limits on the meaning of collegiality. As Houtepen stresses,

> The one paramount factor is a conviction of the need to be faithful to the one paradosis, which must be safeguarded by the whole community, but which is the special concern of those who are chosen from the community to work within that community and to interact with it. Here they are more than democratic representatives; they are servants of Christ, themselves sent by Christ, stewards of the mysteries of God, grasped and seized by the Spirit.[34]

Collegiality is not democracy; leaders are not merely representatives of the community. Their role is to bear a special responsibility in the safeguarding of the tradition.

This perspective is borne out further in the New Testament history of the concern for "apostolic succession" as described by Schillebeeckx. He points out that:

> The sending of Timothy (Phil. 2:19–24) is one which goes above the local leaders and shows all the marks of being a "succession" to the apostle Paul. However, the basis of this succession is the "community of faith" between Paul and Timothy. Only the Pastorals Epistles will reflect on this further.[35]

CONCLUSION

Collegiality appears in the New Testament first as a spirit, evidenced in the choice of language: fellow-workers, brothers/sisters. It is a parallel development to that of the language of ministry: service. It is also manifest in the first ministerial group, the Twelve. Gradually, as structures emerge, it is enfleshed in them: councils of elders, and later councils of the Church, provincial, regional, universal. Both the spirit and the structures are important legacies of the New Testament church.

NOTES

1. For an extensive argument against this way of translating diakonia, see John N. Collins, *Diakonia: Re-interpreting the Ancient Sources* (New York: Oxford, 1990).

2. Küng, *Church*, pp. 388–389. Houtepen underlines this perspective, saying, "[The New Testament] ethic is characterized by the key words brotherliness and service; *diakonia* is the most general term for the service of the ministry in the New Testament" (p. 31). Lemaire also points out that sacerdotal language was not chosen, rather *doulos* (slave) and *diakonos* (servant) ("Ministries," pp. 134–135). Audet (p. 78) makes the same point. Schweizer stresses that the word chosen is unbiblical, non-religious and "never includes association with a particular dignity or position" (p. 174).

3. Beyer, p. 81. For a cogent argument against Beyer (and some of the understanding of *diakonia* presented in this chapter), see Collins, especially pp. 6–8, 26–41, and 253–263.

4. Houtepen, p. 33.

5. Beyer, p. 87–88. The use of the word in the New Testament is even more complex than indicated here, embracing many such actions of love such as the collection of monies for the community at Jerusalem (cf. Küng, *Church*, p. 393) but because of the focus of this study, this brief statement of the evolution of the term serves the purpose.

6. Houtepen, p. 33. He stresses the fact that for every Christian "being available" is based on sharing fully in Jesus' own service; all are called to serve. See also Schweizer, "on principle, everyone is engaged in service, and there is no point in distinguishing between ordinary believers and those called to service" (p. 32).

7. Ellis, p. 452.

8. Lemaire, "Ministries," p. 135.

9. Houtepen, p. 32. He gives as examples: servant, apostle, evangelist, prophet, teacher, shepherd, and priest.

10. Elliott, "Ministry and Church Order," pp. 369, 372.

11. Ibid., pp. 374–390.

12. See, for example, Schillebeeckx, especially *Ministry*, p. 21; Küng, Church, pp. 390–393.

13. Schnackenburg, p. 69. He also refers to other passages in the gospel which he thinks refer to the later pastors of the Church: Lk. 6:39 ff.; 12:39 ff.; 42 to 46, 47f.

14. Ibid., pp. 75–76.

15. Lemaire, "Ministries," p. 166. He says of his conclusion, "Detailed studies of some New Testament writings have confirmed these various conclusions. Consequently, these can be considered as sufficiently founded exegetically to be used as a starting point for a biblical theology of the ministries, yet to be undertaken or developed."

16. Ellis, p. 452.

17. Küng, *Church*, p. 392.

18. McKenzie, *Dictionary of the Bible*.

19. David M. Stanley, "The New Testament Basis for the Concept of Collegiality," *Theological Studies* 25 (1964), pp. 199–201.

20. Stanley, p. 202.

21. Brown seems to accord the Twelve more importance than many other authors, especially in *Priest and Bishop*. Of course, this may be due to the nature of his investigation in that volume.

22. Brown, *Priest and Bishop*, pp. 57–58.

23. Schillebeeckx, "Ministry in the Future," p. 65. See also, *Ministry*, p. 13.

24. Power, *Elder and Prophet*, p. 31.

25. Houtepen, p. 38.

26. Küng, *Church*, pp. 430 and 436.

27. Lemaire, "Ministries," p. 139.

28. John E. Lynch, "Co-Responsibility in the First Five Centuries: Presbyteral Colleges and the Election of Bishops," in *Who Decides for the Church: Studies in Co-Responsibility*, James A. Coriden, ed. (Hartford, CT: The Canon Law Society of America, 1971), p. 17. Although his article examines the history of the first five centuries, and this quotation is from the conclusion, it is faithful to his analysis of the period of the Pastorals, where he emphasized both the role of the college of presbyters and that of others in the community.

29. Joseph Duss-von Werdt, "What Can the Layman Do without the Priest," in *Apostolic Succession*, p. 111.

30. Schillebeeckx, *Ministry*, p. 9.

31. Stanley, p. 212.

32. Ellis, pp. 437–440. (See chapter 10, footnote 56, re: common gender.) Audet also emphasizes the roles of the many collaborators of Paul, including "those less well-known workers" (p. 36).
33. Brown, *Beloved Disciple*, pp. 99–102.
34. Houtepen, pp. 29–30.
35. Schillebeeckx, *Ministry*, p. 11.

CHAPTER THIRTEEN

CHARISM AND ORDER

At one point in recent history, there was extensive debate over these two aspects of New Testament ministry, as we saw in chapter 8. For example, Protestant theologians, such as Harnack, opposed two groups: the institutionals, especially the Jewish-Christian communities of the Pastoral letters and the charismatics, especially the Gentiles of the Pauline churches. Most writers today do not see these two factors as being in opposition.[1] However, both represent important aspects of ministry, and each at times receives a greater emphasis. Furthermore, individually and together, they contribute much to a basic understanding of ministry.

THE TERMINOLOGY

Until recently, the term *charism* did not have wide secular usage; in fact, it was not found in secular dictionaries in English, German, Italian, and French. However, in religious circles, it has a long history. It was probably coined by St. Paul, linking the verb *charizomai* (meaning to please) with *charis* (meaning grace). The word is used seventeen times in the New Testament, primarily in Pauline texts, occasionally in deutero-Pauline sources. It is used in a general way to designate gifts bestowed by God gratuitously, and more often in a more specific sense for gifts used for the building up of the Christian community.[2]

In the New Testament, eight lists are given of these gifts intended for a function to be fulfilled in the community. Therefore, charisms may be defined as "free gifts of the Spirit intended for the building up of the Church, the Body of Christ."[3]

In this sense the charisms are slanted towards roles, function-sand ministries. At a deeper level they are Agape operating in one Spirit.

There is a great variety of charisms, from the inspiration of biblical authors to the apostolate of the Twelve, to the gifts of interpretation. What is important is that they are valued "by the charity which is their measure and their strength."[4]

It is more difficult to quickly delineate the meaning of order. The New Testament does not treat ideas of order or office.[5] Furthermore, theologians have basic differences of perspective on the concept, as we saw in chapter 8. The difference is easily seen by comparing Schweizer's and Schnackenburg's views. The former minimalizes the sense of "official ministry" in his consideration of order; he chooses to emphasize the role of each member of the community. He concludes that while the Church has the need to regulate individual ministries, a ministry that it does not regulate may be just as great and important.[6] On the other hand, Schnackenburg emphasizes the hierarchical structure of the Church, the role of special ministers in the Church, an order given by God. And yet he clearly states that this order is due to the guidance of the Spirit and the "absolute authority of Christ."[7] As shown above each author traces the history of order in the New Testament using his particular way of defining the question.

However, from either perspective the sense of the community *and* its official ministers, in relationship or order, and the sense of a regulation of ministries, or ordering of them, can be discerned. Therefore, in the idea of "order" we have a concept that of necessity stands in tension with the concept of "charism." Some theologians place greater emphasis on one concept, some on the other.

THEOLOGICAL PERSPECTIVES

It is not surprising that Ernst Käsemann, a theologian who sees "*libertas Christiana* as being the decisive mark of the disciples of Jesus,"[8] should see charism as a central defining element of ministry. He notes that office is not mentioned in the New Testament because it would have "implied the presupposition and recognition of an authoritative relationship which has no place in the ordering of the Church." Rather, he says, Paul chose a new word in order to present his theological perspective: "the emergence of a critical posture over against other early Christian views about the relation between the ministerial office and the community."

The dominant image for describing the charismata is that of the Body of Christ.

> Insofar as the Church understands itself as the dynamic unity of charismata and of those endowed with them, she cannot find her order in uniformity and rationalization. Neither must she give so much prominence to individuals among her members that others are overshadowed and condemned to passivity; otherwise she would be transgressing against her God-given order . . .

This perspective is a radically christological one. Furthermore, each person's task in the community is defined by the gift that person has been given. Order flows from this; ". . . as gift and task, grace and ministry coincide, so do freedom and order."[9]

Dillon places Käsemann's conclusions in a more sharply focused historical perspective:

> The Church's enthusiastic response to Easter, coupled with her expectation of a proximate end of the ages in Jesus' return explains the absence of structured offices and transmitted authority from the earliest testimonies.

The experience of the power of the Spirit was such that it couldn't be charted or controlled. Moreover, "geographical factors likewise encouraged an open and unstructured church order" as itinerant enthusiasts, like Paul, drew converts by ecstatic words and deeds, then left churches to develop according to their own cultural situation. In considering the period of the apostles and prophets, Dillon concludes:

> Church order and ministries of the earliest communities were not custodial and defensive but charismatic and creative . . . Such "order" as there was, as 1 Cor. 14:26 ff. makes clear, was an obedience *afterwards* to the *de facto* action of the Spirit in her minister, rather than an appointed mediation beforehand of the divine initiatives.[10]

Myles Bourke speaks specifically to some of the issues raised by Käsemann, and helps to focus the emphasis on church order in the New

Testament. One problem he identifies is the high-valuation placed on the Church at Corinth by Käsemann,[11] an enthusiasm Bourke does not share. Bourke clearly presents the diversity of order in the New Testament, noting a movement from less structure in the early the-Parousia-is-imminent period, to more structure when the hope for an imminent Parousia had faded. When faced with the problem of how to maintain the purity of the apostolic faith,

> . . . the solution given by the Pastorals is that the work of the apostles will be carried on by others chosen for that task . . . There is surprising continuity between the duties of these men and those which belong to the apostle himself in the Pauline epistles . . . preaching . . . safeguarding the gospel.

In analyzing this development and in opposition to Käsemann, Bourke states that it is not an office set up over against the community, anymore than the apostle himself was over against the community. Like the apostle, they are to teach and to govern. He concludes,

> . . . what the Pastorals do present us with is an apostolic succession in which the preservation of the apostolic preaching, the teaching, and the leadership of the churches, which the apostles enjoyed in an eminent degree, are passed on by the laying-on of hands to those whom he has designated for that work.[12]

In a similar view, Brown also contends that "the strongly charismatic community at Corinth was not a viably structured church." He, too, places emphasis on order, stating,

> Recognition by the church is what is essential for sacred ministry; ordination by the laying on of a bishop's hands is simply the standard way of conferring recognition in episcopally structured churches . . .[13]

Most theologians today emphasize both charism and order.[14] For example, Daniélou states clearly: "It is not a case of charisma on one side and institution on the other, but rather that prophets and presbyters, *didascaloi* and *episcopi*, are all both ministers and charismata."[15]

Furthermore, while both teachers and prophets, and bishops and presbyters were active, it was not a "charismatic hierarchy" distinct from an "institutional hierarchy," but different ministerial patterns that developed in different geographic and ethnic settings.[16] In disagreeing with Harnack's position, Schweizer states,

> As far as we can see, it can only be said that even the primitive Church ordered certain ministries by means of appointment, while others were carried out more spontaneously. But this separation . . . is not that between "natural" and "charismatic" ministries . . .[17]

Because of the way theologians like Käsemann have stated the argument, stressing the free action of God, it is helpful to review how the charism-order tension is focused in regard to that point. Schillebeeckx states:

> The call by the community is the specific ecclesial form of the call by Christ. Ministry from below is ministry "from above" . . . the laying on of hands . . . is a liturgical and sacramental expression of the sense of the community that what happens in the *ecclesia* is a gift of God's Spirit and not an expression of the autonomy of the Church.[18]

In similar fashion, Kearney maintains that to say authority in the Church can only be legitimated by charismatic signs

> . . . is in effect to deny to the Church the authority to structure itself anew in human fashion to meet new human situations. Catholic tradition of the union of human and divine in the Incarnation would favor understanding the bestowal of charismatic gift and development of office as a fruitful interaction.[19]

Finally, Laurentin offers this perspective:

> The trinitarian presentation of 1 Cor. 12:4 suggests that the *forces* (energemata) which originate from the Father emerge in the form of *charisms* (charismata) of the Spirit, and take the form of ministries, referred to Christ, and they include the apostolic ministry.

He offers a final reflection on this trinitarian origin of charism and order, suggesting that theoretically there should be no conflict between charisms and legitimate authority. But, he concludes, because of human weakness, there often is conflict.[20]

New Testament Patterns

One reason for the theological debate on this topic is that varying New Testament communities developed in different ways. Contemporary scripture scholarship makes these patterns more clearly discernible than they had been in the past, contributing to the consensus on this issue noted above. Hence, we see the pattern in the Pauline communities, during his lifetime, of an emphasis on the more charismatic roles of prophets and teachers, and the local community leaders who appear to have arisen spontaneously when the apostle moved on to evangelize others.[21]

On the other hand, in the later New Testament period, as can be seen with special clarity in the Pastorals, "there was a church order according to which a group of 'presbyters' was responsible for the leadership and pastoral care of the local communities."[22] However, various scholars would argue that one need not look only to this late period for evidence of order. In a helpful study of Acts 6:1–6, Lienhard traces the redactional and traditional elements of the passage. He maintains that Luke joined an independent narrative about the institution of the Seven to the Stephen episode. Lienhard sees the speech of the Twelve as a redactional composition, but verses 5 and 6 as traditional. He says that the kernel of historical tradition is that there was a dispute between the Hellenists and Hebrews, and it was resolved by appointing seven men, whose names are preserved, to an office within the community. However, he thinks that it cannot be affirmed with certitude that the Twelve mediated. So he concludes that it is firmly established that

> . . . early in the history of the primitive community in Jerusalem, certain members of that community were authoritatively appointed to an office. [The redactor adds his own emphasis.] . . . the community chooses the candidates and the "Twelve"—the authoritative body in the community—commissions them in office. The pericope does not describe the institution of the

order of deacon. But it is a strong witness to the existence of office at an early date in the short-lived but influential Jerusalem community.[23]

Schweizer identifies some key ecclesiological concepts that implicitly shape the charism-order tension of the New Testament. On the one hand, the Church proclaims a message that is not yet fully realized and is rooted in the historical Jesus. On the other hand, the Church has already met the Risen Lord, and experiences His ongoing presence. So, there are two points of emphasis: first, historicity, tradition, and the link with Israel, which Luke and the Pastoral letters present; second, newness and the role of the Spirit, which John evidences. What was stressed was shaped by the historical situation of the time, specifically, the danger the Church faced in the particular time and place.[24]

In examining the New Testament evidence, Schnackenburg assesses the development at the time of the Pastorals and concludes,

> . . . as regards the conception of office, it is in fact possible to say that the institutional and charismatic components have fused into an organic unity in the pastoral epistles in as much as in them the "imposition of hands" confers the Spirit.[25]

BEYOND CHARISM AND ORDER

While the understanding of ministry can be sharpened by an analysis of the charism-order tension, it can be helpful to place the issue in a broader framework. One way of doing so is to focus on the Church as such, so that charism, order, office, authority are all aspects of the one life of the Church. Krodel offers this perspective:

> Does the proclamation of the Christ-event as salvation event determine the ministerial office, the ecclesiastical rules and institutions, or do these determine what constitutes legitimate or illegitimate proclamation? In the latter case, the Church as such is the institution of salvation which through its gifts, sacraments, etc., guarantees salvation. In the former case, the eschatological

nature of the Church is recognized. Being "in" the world demands institutions, being not "of" the world prohibits the divinization of institutions.[26]

Another approach is to use the Incarnation as the starting point for an understanding of charism and order. Doing so leads Kearney to conclude that, because Catholic tradition affirms the union of humanity and divinity in the Incarnation, both charismatic gift and the development of office are aspects of that tradition.[27] In a similar way, Schnackenburg bases some of his conclusions about the essential features of the Church on Christology. He says,

> Every exercise of office or service in the Church only takes place in virtue of the power . . . given to those he sent . . . Christ "gives" his Church the various men who are entrusted with services, who work together in building up "his body" . . . all qualification comes from God . . . In the early Church this qualification is often actually produced by the Holy Spirit (extraordinary charismata) and sometimes made known by prophecy . . . but even with the imposition of hands . . . it is always conferred by the Holy Spirit (charismatic grace of office).[28]

A final way to reflect on this is to place the charism-order tension at the service of the apostolic tradition. This is particularly clear when analyzing the Pastorals. Schillebeeckx sees the pseudonymity of these letters as a theological device chosen to underline the fact that ministers not only "work in the name of Christ and are in his service" (as the apostles were) but also "are under obligation to the apostolic heritage" and "responsible for the apostolicity of the community."[29] In similar fashion, Krodel says,

> Hence the essence of the office of the ministry is the function of being the guardian and transmitter of "sound" apostolic doctrine. And the ministry is subordinated to the Word. The offices of the ministry and the structures within the Church remain regulative offices and structures. What is constitutive in the Church of the Pastorals is the "sound" apostolic doctrine.[30]

CONCLUSION

The Church of the New Testament was characterized by both charism and order. Historical and exegetical studies make it possible to state that firmly. But theology also could bring us to this conclusion, as we reflect on the meaning of the Incarnation, or the Church, or the apostolic tradition of the Church. A community founded by the historical Jesus continues in an ordered fashion, referring back to his words and deeds. A community which lives as the Body of the Risen Lord continues to receive the gifts of his Spirit, the charisms for the building up of the community. Because this community is human and divine, tension, at times conflict, will exist between these two aspects of its life. A community faithful to the one Christ, historical and risen, will strive to value each of these aspects. But perhaps, as in the New Testament communities, particular churches will emphasize one or the other aspect at particular times in their history, because of local custom and circumstance.

NOTES

1. Lemaire, "Ministries," pp. 138 and 156.
2. René Laurentin, "Charisms, Terminological Precision" in *Charisms in the Church*, C. Duquoc and C. Floristan, eds. (New York: Seabury, 1978), pp. 3–5.
3. Ibid., p. 8.
4. Ibid., pp. 9, 10.
5. Käsemann, *New Testament Themes*, p. 63.
6. Schweizer, pp. 8 and 229. Küng emphasizes similar points; for example, *Church*, pp. 363–364.
7. Schnackenburg, pp. 125–127 and 26. Brown's position is similar, for example, *Priest and Bishop*, p. 85.
8. Käsemann, *New Testament Themes*, p. 7.
9. Ibid., pp. 63–64, 70, 74, 76–77.
10. Dillon, pp. 15–18.
11. Bourke, p. 493.
12. Ibid., pp. 503–504, 505–506.
13. Brown, *Priest and Bishop*, pp. 84–85. However, Brown is open to the possibility of an alternative form of recognition being introduced, if church union occurs.
14. Lemaire, "Ministries," p. 165. When stating that this is one of the consensus points in most studies of ministry today, he says that the (official) ministries are gifts, charisms bestowed on the Church.
15. Jean Daniélou, *The Theory of Jewish Christianity* (Chicago: The Henry Regnery Company, 1964), note on p. 350.
16. Daniélou, "The Priestly Ministry in the Greek Fathers," in *The Sacrament of Holy Orders* (Collegeville: The Liturgical Press, 1962), p. 121.
17. Schweizer, p. 184.
18. Schillebeeckx, "Ministry in the Future," pp. 73–74.
19. Kearney, p. 57.
20. Laurentin, "Charisms," p. 6.
21. Schillebeeckx, *Ministry*, pp. 9–10. Küng also emphasizes the Pauline developments, arguing from them to what he sees as a key characteristic of the Church, its charismatic structure.
22. Ibid., p. 15.

23. Lienhard, pp. 230–236. See also the discussion of this study in chapter 11, above.

24. Schweizer, pp. 164–68.

25. Schnackenburg, p. 102.

26. Krodel, p. 191.

27. Kearney, p. 57.

28. Schnackenburg, pp. 126–127.

29. Schillebeeckx, *Ministry*, pp. 12–13.

30. Krodel, pp. 200–201. The argument given by Dillon is very similar. He sees the Pastorals as offering "the prototype of a conservative stewardship of the tradition. . . Whereas in the original Pauline churches, order and ministry followed upon the Spirit's action, now it precedes and mediates that action; hence, charism and empirical ordination are inseparable, and the latter is prior. . . [Therefore]: it was always perceived, in other words, that tradition is not correctly stewarded when either meaningful adaptation or faithful preservation of the *tradita* is ignored" (pp. 54–62). So also Ellis, "But did unstructured function always precede the structured, i.e., appointed role? The above considerations have led me, rather reluctantly at times, to conclude that it did not. From the beginning charism and appointment sometimes went together. But the appointment was, in the most literal sense, to be a worker and a servant. As long as this conception continued, structure and authority in an official, worldly sense remained subordinate and contingent" (pp. 451–452).

✣

Section Two

Recent Church Teaching

INTRODUCTION

In the process of theological reflection, Scripture is important, and so, too, is the ongoing tradition of the Church. As a living people, a community, the Church is embodied in each age, and rooted in a vast variety of particular places. The Church is an organic body. Christ is its head, and it is enlivened by His Spirit. Therefore the Church is in a continual process of change, growth, renewal. At the same time, it is continually united to its apostolic tradition. The teaching office of the Church safeguards the authenticity of the developments in the life of this community.

In our continued reflection on the new ministers in the Church, in this section we turn to the Church's official teaching. First we will examine some relevant documents from Vatican Council II, and then some documents promulgated by Popes Paul VI and John Paul II, as well as the revised Code of Canon Law. In order to discern the way the Church strives to understand and interpret new developments, some of the work of the Synod on the Laity will be sketched.

Finally, because our focus is the church in the United States, the work of the United States bishops relative to the new ministers will be presented. Their work has particular import because our bishops are responding to the developments in their dioceses, the currents of change in the Church. They are striving to read the signs of the times, in light of the tradition which they are charged to safeguard. As these chapters will show, this is a work in progress.

CHAPTER FOURTEEN

VATICAN COUNCIL II

INTRODUCTION

The Second Vatican Council is recognized as the great seedbed for many developments in the Church today. The theological self-understanding of the new ministers and the response to these ministers by the larger Church, discussed above, are rooted in perspectives and ideals proclaimed by the council. A brief overview of key conciliar formulations will highlight the relationship between the vision of Vatican II and the emergence of the new ministers, and will contextualize the response of church groups and organizations. The purpose is not a full examination of the influence of the Council on contemporary developments, but a thematic exploration of some of the most significant aspects of the conciliar documents.

CONSTITUTION ON THE SACRED LITURGY

As the first of the documents formally approved by the council (December 4, 1963), the *Constitution on the Sacred Liturgy* presents perspectives which are both influential on and deepened in later documents. The opening paragraphs of the *Constitution* describe the liturgy as the work of all the faithful (not only of the clergy), a way of thinking about the Church as the total people, which will become a theme of the total conciliar corpus. It states that the purpose of the liturgy is building up those who are in the Church, "making of them a holy temple of the Lord, a dwelling-place for God in the Spirit," and increasing "their power to preach Christ." *All* of the faithful make up the temple of the Lord, *all* are empowered to preach,[1] with their very lives.

In article 14 this theme receives its full expression and theological grounding:

> Mother Church earnestly desires that all the faithful should be led to that full, conscious, and active participation in liturgical celebrations which is demanded by the very nature of the liturgy, and to which the Christian people, "a chosen race, a royal priesthood, a holy nation, a redeemed people" (1 Peter 2:9, 4-5) have a right and obligation by reason of their baptism.[2]

Jungmann called this "summons to active participation" the refrain of the *Constitution*; it is repeated at fifteen other places in this rather brief document.[3] In retrospect, it is clear that this vision awakened the Church, clergy and laity alike, to the right and duty of all the baptized to be active participants in the worship, the mission, the entire life of the Church.

A second important development is the way in which the *Constitution* differentiates between the general participation of the people, and those who have particular roles to play:

> In liturgical celebrations, each person, minister, or layman who has an office to perform, should carry out all and only those parts which pertain to his (sic) office by the nature of the rite and the norms of the liturgy.

> Servers, readers, commentators, and members of the choir also exercise a genuine liturgical function. They ought, therefore, to discharge their offices with the sincere piety and decorum demanded by so exalted a ministry and rightly expected of them by God's people.[4]

In light of the emergence of ecclesial ministers, this recognition of a variety of functions performed by particular members of the faithful is instructive. The choice of language is also significant: ". . . an office to perform . . . their offices . . . so exalted a ministry." The 1917 Code of Canon Law had limited office holders to the clergy alone; this, therefore, marks a breakthrough in church teaching about possible roles for laity. It also reintroduces the term ministry in Catholic circles, for at this time the word was not commonly used.

A final aspect of the *Constitution on the Sacred Liturgy* that has relevance for the new ministers is the granting of new powers to bishops' conferences, for their own areas.[5] The meaning of the local church is given enhanced significance, and there is an understanding that the local churches will respond to particular needs in individual ways. (Because of this, some areas of the world have catechists who are installed as official ministers. This, of course, has implications for our situation in the United States today.) As Jungmann states, the strict centralization enforced since the Council of Trent "was thus greatly relaxed after 400 years."[6]

CONSTITUTION ON THE CHURCH

"Among all the documents of Vatican II, probably none underwent more drastic revision between the first schema and the finally approved text." A tremendous development in the Church's self-understanding resulted from the dialogue in the council. "With something like unanimity it has been hailed as the most momentous achievement of the council . . ."[7] When approved in November 1964, this church document articulated a renewed understanding of itself as the People of God, the Body of Christ.

Bernard Cooke states that some of the most advanced thinking of the Council on ministry is found in this document, although in fragmentary fashion. (He adds that the decrees on the episcopal office and that on the ministry of ordained priests do not present the more fully developed thinking.)

> With its stress on the basic unity of all Christians as the people of God, its clear statements on the equality and responsibility of the laity within the community, and its teaching on the collegiality of the pastoral office, this decree provides the principles for a basic reconsideration of ministerial priesthood. If lay people in the Church are really to exercise the share in Christ's priesthood about which this decree speaks, it is clear that they will become involved in many forms of activities that were previously thought to be proper to the clergy.[8]

For the purposes of this study, the image of the Church as the people of God and the understanding of the equality and responsibility of the laity within the Church are of great significance. An interesting historical perspective on these developments is provided in a commentary on the document:

> The extension of "Church-mindedness" to the whole of the people of God had been prepared in recent years primarily by the successful launching of Catholic Action and then in the various forms of the apostolic activity of the laity—factors which have helped a growing number of Catholics to a greater sense of personal commitment to Christianity.[9]

It was the very life of the Church, including the involvement of laity in its mission, which contributed to this development in the Church's enriched self-understanding of its nature as a people, a body, a communion, in which all members share responsibility.

The unfolding of this vision in the entire document will only be presented briefly here. This understanding of the Church as the people of God has greatly influenced clergy and laity alike in recent decades. At the heart of the document is the description of the action of Christ and the Spirit described in article 7. Christ has redeemed us, formed us into a new creation. Christ mystically constitutes us as his body by communicating the Spirit. All members are united to Christ and each other. First, then, the unity of all in the Church is affirmed; only then are the differences explored. In the building up of Christ's body "there is engaged a diversity of members and functions." The spirit gives different gifts for the welfare of the Church, according to the needs of the ministries and the Spirit's own richness. Christ continually provides the Church "gifts of ministries through which, by his power, we serve each other unto salvation . . ." These gifts include the grace of the apostles and charisms given to others.[10] This Christocentric and Trinitarian understanding of the life of the Church emphasizes the free gifting of the Church by God with a rich diversity of gifts, and of ministries, all ordered so that we "may increase and attain to all the fullness of God." The council teaches that these gifts and ministries are given not only to the apostles and their successors, but to others as well, "who are endowed with charisms."

Articles 10 through 12 give further specification to the themes of article 7. The members of the People of God all share in the one priesthood of Christ; the common priesthood of the faithful and the ministerial or hierarchical priesthood are ordered to one another. Baptism incorporates individuals into the Church, and all the sacraments, including both orders and matrimony, contribute to developing "the priestly community." Second, all members of the Church also share in Christ's prophetic ministry. It is the "whole body of the faithful who have an anointing that comes from the holy one and cannot err in matters of belief." The *sensus fidei* is ascribed to the whole people, "from the bishops to the last of the faithful." Finally, all have a part in the Church's task of sanctification. The council indicates that it is not only the sacraments and church ministries which sanctify the people:

> Allotting his gifts according as he wills (cf. Cor. 12:11), he also distributes special graces among the faithful of every rank. By these gifts he makes them fit and ready to undertake various tasks and offices for the renewal and building up of the Church, as it is written, "the manifestation of the Spirit is given to everyone for profit" (1 Cor. 12:7). Whether these charisms be very remarkable or more simple and widely diffused, they are to be received with thanksgiving and consolation since they are fitting and useful for the needs of the Church.

Furthermore, those in authority "should judge the genuineness and proper use of these gifts . . . not indeed to extinguish the Spirit but to test all things and hold fast to what is good."[11] The Church, therefore, is called to accountability for testing and celebrating God's charisms.

This vision of the Church as the People of God is having an effect on the way in which both clerics and laity conceive and live their mission today. It is the Church as God's people that receives and bears Christ's mission and is his sacrament.

> The primary mission is not given to the hierarchy, nor can we distinguish between the mission of the apostles and the mission of the Spirit. Christ's mission and Spirit are given to the body of the Church, so that laity and clergy share in their respective ways

in the one mission of God's people, and in the triple office of Jesus Christ as Priest, Prophet and King.[12]

Chapter 3 sheds further light on the meaning of ministry. The topic is the episcopate, the emphasis is on service. "For those ministers who are endowed with sacred power are servants of their brethren . . ."[13] The language and spirit here move away from understanding ministry as dominion; this has had an impact pastorally. Kerhofs observes, "For many reasons, the most important of which is perhaps the shift of emphasis brought about by Vatican II, the ministries are now more generally seen as ways of *serving the Christian Community* rather than as exercises in a hierarchically structured power system."[14] Similarly, the emphasis on the collegial nature of the episcopate marks an important change, from viewing the bishops as isolated monarchs to emphasizing their collective responsibility. This shift in understanding ultimately affects other relationships in the Church as well. Häring states:

> In the sense of "a current pastoral authority" collegiality embraces only the College of Bishops with the Pope at its head. But as a structural eucharistic and sacerdotal principle, collegiality truly and absolutely includes the entire priesthood.[15]

This principle of collegiality emphasizes acting together, a norm in the discussion and practice of collaboration in the Church today.

The reinstitution of the permanent diaconate concludes this chapter. Some commentators stress the deacon's role as that of providing assistance to the priest in his ministry,[16] whereas others see this development as a broadening of the concept of ministry. O'Meara wonders, in the light of such a development, "Could there be other assistants in the ministry? Other ministers and other ordinations?"[17] Crucial questions in considering the new ministers.

Chapter 4 is devoted to the laity. Their role in the mission of the Church is affirmed. Pastors are instructed "that it is their noble duty so to shepherd the faithful and recognize their services and charismatic gifts that all according to their proper roles may cooperate in this common undertaking with one heart."[18] And now a new note is sounded. Laity share "in their own way" in the mission: "Their secular character is proper and peculiar to the laity . . . it belongs to the laity to seek the kingdom of God by engaging in temporal affairs and directing them according to God's will." Social and family life, every work and business, present their particular duties; by fulfilling these, "they may contribute to the sanctification of the world, as from within like leaven." The laity are "so to illuminate and order all temporal things with which they are so closely associated that these may be effected and grow according to Christ . . ." Those in Holy Orders, on the other hand, are "expressly ordained to the sacred ministry."[19]

As noted earlier, in the *Constitution on the Sacred Liturgy* the laity's role in the Eucharistic action was affirmed; those laity performing certain functions were said to be ministers. But here, the emphasis is on the laity's role in the temporal order. In this document, ministry, prefixed by "sacred," is the provence of the ordained. Article 32 affirms that through baptism and confirmation, the laity are appointed to the apostolate by the Lord himself. Yet, article 33 states:

> . . . the laity can be called in different ways to more immediate cooperation in the apostolate of the hierarchy, like those men and women who helped the apostle Paul in the Gospel, laboring much in the Lord (cf. Phil. 4:3; Rom. 16:3 ff). They have, moreover, the capacity of being appointed by the hierarchy to some ecclesiastical offices with a view to a spiritual end.[20]

In chapter 2, the mission of the whole people to the world was affirmed; in chapter 4 it seems as though only laypeople are sent into the world. Their work within the Church is envisioned as necessary only under certain conditions:

> . . . when there are no sacred ministers or when they are impeded under persecution, some lay people supply sacred functions to the best of their ability . . . , indeed, many of them expend all their energies in apostolic work . . .[21]

As has often been noted, the documents of the council were the work of many writers, influenced by the positions of varied theologians and bishops. Different points of emphasis are found in different places, as is evident in *The Constitution on the Church*, with implications, of course, for the life of the Church today.

Chapter 5, "The Call to Holiness," adds another interesting note to reflection on lay ministry. First, the council reminds bishops that by carrying out their ministry with holiness, eagerness, humility, and courage—imitating Christ—"they will thereby make this ministry the principal means of their own sanctification." It affirms that priests, deacons, and other clerics, too, are called to faithful service. And then a new category is considered:

> Close to them [clerics] are those lay men chosen by God, who are called by the bishop to give themselves fully [in Abbott: exclusively] to apostolic works, and carry out a very fruitful activity in the Lord's field.

Subsequently, married couples, Christian parents, laborers, and those who are oppressed are treated.[22] Reflecting on this section, Häring says that laity in apostolic service "occupy in the Church a position similar to those of clerics and therefore have a spirituality which is similar to theirs. Their path to holiness consists above all in this service, in this ecclesial diaconate, exercised in a spirit of humility and dedication."[23] Rahner is even stronger, saying that such a layman must be considered a cleric.[24] Clearly, the tension here is with the understanding of the laity's secular role. If the laity's particular task is in the world, how do we explain those working in the Church? This led one commentator at the time to say, "The vocation of the laity . . . can be understood only in terms of Christian involvement in temporal and secular affairs."[25] Certainly today far more laymen and women "give themselves fully to apostolic works" but our theology is caught in the tension noted here.

A final aspect of this chapter has indirect bearing on our topic: the emphasis throughout on the fact that Christian sanctification "is a thing achieved in and through one's state of life with its daily tasks, in and through the concrete circumstances and events of one's existence." This shift from an ascetical approach to spirituality, to one focused on the grace-given, charismatic nature of Christian life as itself a path to perfection has had far-reaching effects on the life of the Church today.[26] This also has many implications for the spirituality of lay ministers.

DECREE ON THE APOSTOLATE OF THE LAITY

This decree had an interesting history at the council. It went through several major revisions, during which time everything from its title to its length was challenged. The preparatory commission had wanted to involve laity as consultants, but were not able to. During the Council, permission to do this was granted, but not until two years after work began. In addition, permission was given to seek the assistance of laypersons in the re-editing of the text. And, in the debates on the text, a layman addressed the Council—for the first time. Gradually, a theology of the laity was evolving, embodied in the actions and the texts of the Council. When the final text was approved, in November of 1965, it had the fewest dissenting votes in the whole of the council.[27] In word and deed, the council proclaimed a new understanding of the role of the laity as active participants in the life of the Church. The vision first articulated almost two full years earlier, in the decree on the liturgy, is here brought to a certain fulfillment.

Despite the extensive debate on the document, its essential teachings were already implicit in *Church*. The emphasis in both documents is on the laity's "proper and indispensable role in the mission of the Church" flowing from the Christian vocation. However, new clarity emerges in this document: For example, article 2 states: "[The laity] exercise a genuine apostolate by their activity on behalf of bringing the gospel and holiness to men, and on behalf of penetrating and perfecting the temporal sphere of things through the spirit of the gospel."[28] Klostermann notes that in arriving at that formulation, the commission was "again and again in danger of being forced into extreme positions which were diametrically opposed to each other." On the one hand, there was a desire to limit the apostolate of the laity to the temporal order, and on the other, to limit it to that apostolate under the direction and authority of the hierarchy. He stresses that if the tasks of evangelization and sanctification are seen as belonging only to the hierarchy, while the orientation of all aspects of the world towards Christ belong only to the laity, we arrive at two types of Christians, the ecclesiastical and the worldly, the spiritual and the fleshly, the perfect and the imperfect. The final formulation avoids the sharp delineation of these tasks.[29] Furthermore, in article 3, the laity are reminded of their right and duty to use their charisms "in the Church and in the world."[30] What was implicit in *Church* here is made explicit; the perspective of *Sacred Liturgy* is more fully articulated. Developments in lay ministry since the council are rooted in this vision.

In article 3, the work of the Spirit is described in two ways: operating through "the ministry and the sacraments" (implicitly, the realm of the clergy) and also through the "special gifts," later called charisms, given to the faithful, the laity. The role of the laity in "the ministry and the sacraments" described, however briefly, in the *Constitution on the Sacred Liturgy*, is not found explicitly here. During the council, some even complained of the unsuitability of speaking of the charisms of the laity[31] The evolution of a theology of lay ministry is clearly not complete.

Several other themes of the document have an indirect bearing on questions we are considering. The tension between charism and order is implicit in the call to the laity to exercise their charisms "in the freedom of the Holy Spirit who 'breathes where he wills' (Jn 3:8), and at the same time in communion with his brothers in Christ, and with his pastors especially." Pastors are "to pass judgment on the authenticity and good use of these gifts, not certainly with a view to quenching the Spirit but to testing everything and keeping what is good." As one commentator says, pastors are "admonished not to use their supervisory functions as a fire-extinguisher, thus quenching the flames of the Spirit, which seems to be regarded as a danger."[32] The treatment of spirituality once again emphasizes that a path to sanctity is the performance of work according to God's will. Much of the focus is on the penetration and perfection of the temporal order.[33]

Chapters 3 and 4 present various fields and forms or methods of the apostolate. In light of the myriad ways laity are involved in ministry today, these seem a vague blueprint for what has emerged. The debate of interest for this study was about Catholic Action, and its relationship to the hierarchy. Some thought that Catholic Action should be carried out through associations founded and directed by the hierarchy; the Council presents that view in article 20. It emphasizes the "collaboration of the laity in the hierarchical apostolate," with the laity acting "under the superior direction of the hierarchy, which can authorize this cooperation, besides, with an explicit mandate."[34] In article 19, however, more authority is granted to the laity: "While preserving intact the necessary link with ecclesiastical authority, the laity have the right to establish and direct associations, and to join existing ones."[35]

Throughout this document, the role of the laity in the secular sphere has been stressed. However, in article 22 we once again meet a group of laypeople who do not fit the categories thus far developed. They "put their person and their professional competence at the service of institutions and their activities. . . " Since pastors are counselled to see that they have the "resources necessary for the maintenance of themselves and their families" they clearly are employed by the Church in professional roles. This group is an anomaly, in light of the definition of laity by the lay/secular themes in the document. Commenting on this article, Klostermann offers an interesting insight:

> A completely new "state" of Christians in the Church is developing, in which they can offer their own special type of service to the Church. We have already remarked that, strictly speaking, we are no longer concerned here with Christians in the world, but with a new category of Christians.[36]

The council treats of other forms of lay ministry as well. Chapter 5, article 34, when considering the relations with the hierarchy of various forms of the apostolate states:

> . . . the hierarchy entrusts the laity with certain charges more closely connected with the duties of pastors: in the teaching of Christian doctrine, for example, in certain liturgical actions, in the care of souls. In virtue of this mission the laity are fully subject to superior ecclesiastical control in regard to the exercise of these charges.

Klostermann says that the history of this text makes it clear that not only an official conferral of tasks is involved, but rather that of an office as such. Offices are mainly held by the hierarchy, but they may be conferred on a layperson without ecclesiastical ordination or divine commission. Klostermann says that this would not change the person's lay status. Examples which he cites include catechetical instruction, managerial positions in associations, and in church administration and pastoral tasks.[37]

In conclusion, we can say that the *Decree on the Laity*, as that on the Church, clearly affirms that the laity shares in the mission of the Church. However, an ongoing tension in the preparation of the document, in the conciliar debates, and in the text itself has to do with the exercise of their apostolate. To what extent does it include ministries within the Church? To what extent is their apostolate dependent on the hierarchy, and to what extent does it flow from their baptism, and charisms that they have received? To what extent is it a sharing in the one mission of the Church, and to what extent is it a sharing in a separate apostolate of the hierarchy? These issues are not resolved in this decree.

OTHER DOCUMENTS OF VATICAN II

Various other documents also affirm diverse roles and functions which laypeople may fill in the Church. The *Decree on the Church's Missionary Activity* declares that the vocation to missionary work includes priests, religious, and laypeople; when sent by legitimate authority, they go forth "as ministers of the Gospel, set aside for the work to which they have been called."[38] The *Decree on the Pastoral Office of Bishops in the Church* states, "Priests and laymen who are attached to the diocesan curia should be mindful that they are collaborating in the pastoral work of the bishop."[39] The term *ministry* is used to refer to teachers of doctrine, or even any teacher in a Catholic school (*Declaration on Christian Education*) and laypersons are presented as "ministers of the Word" (*Dogmatic Constitution on Divine Revelation*). In addition to these ministries within the Church, the ministry of the Christian in the world is stressed, especially in the *Decree on the Apostolate of Lay People* and the *Pastoral Constitution on the Church in the Modern World.*[40]

The *Decree on the Ministry and Life of Priests* also contributes to an understanding of ministry. The document has a pastoral rather than a theological focus. Cooke states that it is not a pioneering document, being more a summation of common opinions of the period.[41] However, it is worth noting that the ministry of the priest is understood primarily as a continuation of the mission of Jesus; it is broader than a cultic priesthood, and includes various functions. That the ministry be carried out in a spirit of service and brotherhood is stressed.

The *Pastoral Constitution on the Church in the Modern World* is a unique document, not only among the decrees of *this* Council, but all the councils of the Church. In it, the Church turns from a consideration of her own life, outward to her relationship with the world. Of particular interest for our study is the fact that for the first time, in the preparatory work and during the actual debate on the document, laity were involved in the dialogue.

One aspect of the teaching of the *Pastoral Constitution* that has influenced contemporary developments in lay ministry is a vision of the Church as both evangelical and diaconal. "The most distinctive note sounded in the text . . . is that of the Church putting itself consciously at the service of the family of man."[42] Congar believes that the image of the Church as the People of God radically affected the understanding of the Church's mission given here. When the dominant image was the Church as institution and hierarchy, the Church was seen as something other than the world, confronting it, over it. But as People of God, the Church is in the world and participates in its movement. "[The] faithful are not so much sent to it as find themselves in it and form part of it. They are simply asked to be Christians in all that they are."[43] A second important theme derives from the anthropology of the document, which understands the human person first as created by God, created as the image of God. Therefore, "Human reality is the substance in which God expresses the revelation of His grace . . . [Therefore] the social, cultural and human separation that has grown up between Church and world will have to be overcome."[44] In words that summarize this perspective, and pose a challenge to today's ministry questions, Power comments:

> In the terms of this Constitution, there is no dualism between the secular and the sacred, between sacred ministry and service of the world. The church . . . is here presented as the instrument of God's presence in the world for the sake of building up the kingdom of God. The Church as a people bears responsibility for this mission . . . Within this perspective, it might be possible to speak of the reciprocal responsibility of presbyter and lay person in the service of the one mission, rather than to pursue the implications of a distinction between presence in the ecclesial community and presence in the secular realm.[45]

CONCLUSION

Most laypeople involved in ministry today would not name particular articles or documents from Vatican II as having motivated them to the service they do, nor as helping to sustain the attitudes and thinking that inform their work. Nor would clergy do so, to support the actions they have taken encouraging people toward and inviting laypeople into ministry. And yet, key themes from the council have had this effect. Central among these is the conviction that all baptized Christians have a share in the mission of the Church. Also important is the understanding that God calls individuals to particular work in the Church, and grants the charisms needed to perform these ministries. The lived experience of the new ministers attests to this, and their acceptance by their pastors and the communities in which they work witnesses to this reality. Out of the vision of the council, the new ministries have emerged and flourished.

However, the nature of the relationship between these new ministers and their bishops, a pattern for ordering these new ministries, and a theological framework for understanding their place in the broad ministry of the Church, are issues that are not clearly treated in Vatican II. In fact, somewhat different ways of understanding each of these issues can be derived from various parts of the documents; the viewpoints of various commentators indicate that these divergences were already implicit in the conciliar debates. The task of the Church today, therefore, is to meditate on the texts of the council, but also to strive to discern what is God's action in the life of the Church in our time.

Notes
___

1. *Constitution on the Sacred Liturgy*, 1, 2. Vatican Council II: *The Conciliar and Post-Conciliar Documents*, Austin Flannery, ed. (Northport, NY: Costello Publishing Company, 1984), pp. 1–2. All quotations from Vatican II documents will be from Flannery, unless otherwise noted.

2. *Sacred Liturgy*, 14, pp. 7–8.

3. Josef Andreas Jungmann, "Constitution on the Sacred Liturgy" in *Commentary on the Documents of Vatican II*, Vol. I, Herbert Vorgrimler, ed. (New York: Herder and Herder, 1967), p. 8.

4. *Sacred Liturgy*, 28–30, p. 11.

5. *Sacred Liturgy*, 22, p. 9; also, 36 (p. 13) and 40 (p. 14).

6. Jungmann, p. 19. *The Constitution on the Church*, 13 and 26, develops this important idea more fully.

7. Avery Dulles in *The Documents of Vatican II*, Walter M. Abbott, ed. (New York: The America Press, 1966), pp. 10–11.

8. Bernard Cooke, *Ministry to Word and Sacraments* (Philadelphia: Fortress Press, 1976), p. 6.

9. Gerard Philips in *Commentary on the Documents of Vatican II*, Vol. I, p. 105.

10. *Dogmatic Constitution on the Church*, 7, *Vatican Council II*, pp. 355–356.

11. Ibid., 10–12, pp. 360–364. The linking of charisms and ministries made here, and the understanding that clergy and laity receive gifts is not pursued in chapter 3, which treats the episcopate. There, the "variety of ministries" refers to ordained ministry.

12. Power, *Gifts*, p. 44.

13. *Constitution on the Church*, 18, Abbott (ed.), p. 37

14. Jan Kerhofs in *New Ministries in the Church: An International Survey*, Ted Gresh, ed. (PCPM, Sp. No. 669, February 1977), p. 3.

15. Bernard Häring, *Road to Renewal* (Montreal: Palm Publishers, 1966), p. 180. Häring means here the ordained priesthood.

16. Vorgrimler, p. 229.

17. Thomas O'Meara, *Theology of Ministry* (New York: Paulist Press, 1983), p. 8.

18. *Church*, 30, Abbott (ed), p. 57.

19. *Church*, 31, pp. 388–389.

20. Ibid., 33, pp. 390–391. Commenting on this section, and others which envision a specific role of laity within the Church, Osiek observes: "But generally the assumption is operative that the spiritual gifts or charisms given to the People of God do not include that of ministry, which belongs only to those in sacred orders." Her paper posits that the New Testament evidence cannot support such a distinction between ministry and charisms. Carolyn Osiek, "Relation of Charism to Rights and Duties in the New Testament Church" in *Official Ministry in a New Age*, James H. Provost, ed. (Washington, D.C.: Canon Law Society of America, 1981), p. 42. Cf. chapter 5 of this work, which treats her thought further.

21. Ibid., 35, p. 392.

22. Ibid., 41, pp. 398–400.

23. Häring, p. 74.

24. Cited by Friedrich Wulf, in *Commentary on the Documents of Vatican II*, Vol. I, p. 269.

25. Patrick Masterson, p. 110.

26. Wulf, 268, 272.

27. Martin Work, in *The Documents of Vatican II*, Vol. I, pp. 481–487; Ferdinand Klostermannn, *Commentary on the Documents of Vatican II*, Vol. III, pp. 273–322.

28. *Decree on the Apostolate of Lay People, Vatican Council II*, 1, 2 pp. 766, 768.

29. Klostermann, pp. 308–309. See also Philips, pp. 120–121, for the discussions on this topic during consideration of the draft of *Church*.

30. *Laity*, 3, p. 769.

31. Klostermann, p. 318.

32. *Laity*, 4-8, pp. 769–776.

33. *Laity*, 20, p. 787.

34. For a discussion of these tensions, see both Work, p. 511, and Klostermann, especially p. 353. The latter indicates that part of the struggle was a conception of the laity primarily as "an extended arm of the hierarchy" instead of being seen within its own proper functions and responsibility in the Church (p. 355).

35. *Laity*, 19, p. 786.

36. Klostermann, 367.

37. Ibid., p. 382. A thorough exploration of "care of souls" and laity is offered by Elissa Rinere, "The Exercise of 'Cura Animarum' Through the 20th Century and Beyond." See chapter 9 of this volume.

38. Article 23, p. 841.

39. Article 27, p. 579.

40. James H. Provost, "Ministry: Reflection on Some Canonical Issues," *The Heythrop Journal,* XXIX (1988), p. 292.

41. Cooke, p. 7.

42. Donald R. Campion in *The Documents of Vatican II*, p. 185.

43. "Session VI: The Laity" in *Vatican II: An Interfaith Appraisal,* John H. Miller, ed. (Notre Dame: University of Notre Dame Press, 1966), p. 246.

44. Edward Schillebeeckx, "Christian Faith and the Future of the World" in *The Church Today: Commentaries on the Pastoral Constitution on the Church in the Modern World*, Group 2000, eds. (New York: Newman Press, 1968), pp. 81–83.

45. Power, *Gifts*, p. 181.

CHAPTER FIFTEEN

SINCE THE COUNCIL

MINISTERIA QUAEDAM

The *Constitution on the Sacred Liturgy* also opened the door to many other changes relevant to ecclesial ministry. The decree states that the liturgical books are to be revised as soon as possible, that experts should be employed for this task, and bishops throughout the world consulted. After the council, in the course of considering revision of the rites, the issue of the meaning of minor orders was studied. The commission recommended suppression of the orders not exercised by their recipients (exorcist and porter), and also that when seminarians were ordained as lectors and acolytes, they were to exercise these offices in pastoral work.[1] However, Pope Paul VI chose to suppress all use of the word order, and designated lector and acolyte as ministries. Furthermore, quoting article 14 of the *Constitution on the Sacred Liturgy*, he linked these ministries to baptism, and provided for laypeople to officially hold these roles. Conferral of these ministries would be by installation, not ordination, and would be limited to men. A description of the roles of lectors and acolytes indicates that they transcend their functions at the liturgical assembly. For example, lectors are "to instruct the faithful in the worthy reception of the sacraments" and acolytes may expose the Blessed Sacrament for veneration.[2]

Paul VI's action designating these as specifically lay offices and ministries is significant. These are the "only two liturgical offices outside the sacrament of order which have a canonical status and a rite of installation common to all parts of the Latin Church." Furthermore, the pope indicates that episcopal conferences may request the establishment of other offices from the Holy See.[3] These established lay ministries are a watershed in the Church's ordering of her life. They recall the image of the Church as Wisdom, taking forth from her treasury things old and new. Pope Paul VI's action demonstrates the Church's freedom in the ordering of her ministries.

EVANGELII NUNTIANDI

Pope Paul VI continued his reflection on lay ministry in the document he published in 1975, *On Evangelization in the Modern World*. His thoughts must be viewed in the context of the entire exhortation. For this pope, evangelization is not only the preaching of the Gospel to ever greater numbers of people, in ever wider geographic areas, but more fully than that, bringing the Good News into all the strata of humanity. Paul VI holds as the goal that the Gospel transform culture and cultures, everything that defines the life of the human community. In order to do this, both the witness given by a Christian life lived fully and explicit proclamation of the Good News to others are needed.[4]

Paul VI views the work of evangelization as belonging to the whole Church, as a duty of the People of God. Nonetheless, within the one body there are different evangelizing tasks to accomplish. The pope, bishops, priests, religious, and laity have a diversity of services in the unity of the one mission. Because laypeople are "in the midst of the world and in charge of the most varied temporal tasks" their field of activity is all the aspects of human life, such as the worlds of politics and the mass media and realities such as human lives and professional work. In stressing these temporal tasks, the pope specifically says of the laity: "Their primary and immediate task is not to establish and develop the ecclesial community—this is the specific role of the pastors."[5]

And yet Paul VI goes on to discuss diversified ministries. While stressing the importance of the laity's involvement in temporal affairs, he says we should not neglect or forget the other dimension:

> . . . the laity can also feel themselves called, or be called, to work with their pastors in the service of the ecclesial community, for its growth and life, by exercising a great variety of ministries according to the grace and charisms which the Lord is pleased to give them.

Paul VI says that while ordained ministers consecrate themselves in a special way to the service of the community, the Church also recognizes "the place of non-ordained ministries which are able to offer a particular service to the Church."[6]

The pope goes on to present a methodology for theological reflection on new ministries. He invites us to look to the origins of the Church, for "an early experience in the matter of ministries" as well as to the present needs of humanity and the Church. Such a reflection makes possible an adaptation to the demands and needs of today, a way of discovering "the ministries which the Church needs and which many of her members will gladly embrace for the sake of ensuring greater vitality in the ecclesial community." These ministries should be established with "absolute respect for unity and adhering to the directives of the pastors, who are the ones who are responsible for the Church's unity and the builders thereof."

> These ministries, apparently new but closely tied up with the Church's living experience down the centuries—such as catechists, directors of prayer and chant, Christians devoted to the service of God's Word or to assisting their brethren in need, the heads of small communities, or other persons charged with the responsibility of apostolic movements—these ministries are valuable for the establishment, life, and growth of the Church, and for her capacity to influence her surroundings and to reach those who are remote from her. We owe also our special esteem to all the lay people who accept to consecrate a part of their time, their energies, and sometimes their entire lives, to the service of the missions.

This section concludes with a reminder that "serious preparation is needed for all workers for evangelization . . . [especially] for those who devote themselves to the ministry of the Word." Preachers and catechists are mentioned specifically.[7]

Clearly, Pope Paul VI acknowledges the role of the laity in both the Church and the world. In reading his exhortation, one gets the impression that he genuinely values the contributions laypeople make in both areas of life. Furthermore, he recognizes that laypersons may "consecrate . . . their entire lives" to ministry (specified by him as in the missions). But perhaps most important for our study is the method he proposes for a discernment of what new ministries are needed: attentiveness to the present needs of the Church and the world, and to our tradition, will make adaptation possible.

THE REVISED CODE OF CANON LAW

The revised code represents one way in which the teaching of the Second Vatican Council receives further official explication. As John Paul II has said, it is "an important element in implementing the spirit and teachings of Vatican II."[8] As with the document, *Church*, the code begins with the People of God. "The 'rules of office' are here rather than in a special clergy section, showing clergy as part of the community and opening up offices to anyone, lay or cleric, with the proper qualification."[9] Whereas traditionally holy orders was seen as the chief sacrament of ministry, here "it is through baptism that we first become empowered by Christ to be His ministers," and to share in the priestly, prophetic, and kingly *munera* of Christ.[10] The Christian faithful are called to share in the mission and ministry of the Church; all have a right and an obligation to develop the charisms received through baptism. "We have not just the right, but the obligation, to participate in and through the Church in her works of liturgy, charity and ministry, and the obligation to work for justice in the world."[11]

There are some specific canons which are applicable to our study. One, canon 517, allows that "due to a dearth of priests a participation in the exercise of the pastoral care of a parish is to be entrusted to a deacon or some other person who is not a priest." Canon 228 allows qualified laypersons to assume ecclesial offices and functions and to serve as experts and advisors to pastors. Canon 231 states that laypersons "who devote themselves permanently or temporarily to some special service of the Church" have a right to decent remuneration," including pension, social security, and health benefits. Canon 230 treats the lay ministries of lector and acolyte, the offices of lector, commentator, cantor, and others and the possibility of serving as a minister of the Word, presiding at liturgical prayer, conferring baptism, and distributing communion.[12] Other canons allow for additional non-ordained ministries: chancellor, notary, procurator-advocate, promoter of justice, defender of the bond, judge, diocesan business managers, extraordinary ministers of the

Eucharist, canonically missioned teachers of theology, missionaries, and catechists.[13] Obviously, the Code both writes in law various principles and ministries named in council documents, and includes others apparently not yet envisioned in the 1960s, during the council. However, as noted in chapter 5, the code is more conservative in its treatment of lay ministry than was the council, indeed, more conservative than Pope Paul VI in *Evangelii Nuntiandi.*

THE SYNOD ON THE LAITY

In October of 1987, bishops from throughout the world gathered in Rome for a world synod on "The Vocation and Mission of the Laity in the Church and in the World." It is helpful to consider the dialogue about ministry which the synod gave rise to in two phases, before the synod, and at the synod. The treatment will be at some length because it gives a valuable perspective on the way those involved in the synod were striving to understand how the Church should respond to the new lay ministries. It gives a snapshot of the process of discernment, of the Church striving to incorporate the new, in the light of the tradition.

BEFORE THE SYNOD

The first part of the preparation for the synod consisted in the publication of the *Lineamenta* and its use in the consultations with laity conducted by conferences of bishops in various parts of the world. In the United States, over 200,000 laypersons participated in the five consultations with the bishops who would be representing the United States church. Certain themes that arose in these dialogues are of value as we strive to understand the response of the Church to the new lay ministers. In summarizing them, Robert Kinast, the facilitator of the consultations, said:

> These faithful have a very strong sense of their share in the mission of Jesus and the church by virtue of their baptism. Very few persons mention the lack of ordained priests as the primary reason for lay ministry . . . There is no desire to replace priests or to take over traditional "priestly" work, but there is a desire to contribute all that lay people can, which will enable priests to

concentrate on their spiritual-liturgical roles. There is uniformly high regard for the contributions of lay ministers and a positive feeling about the development of lay ministry so far. Generally these faithful want lay ministers who are adequately trained and compensated for their work . . . they assume that ministry must be collaborative if it is to fulfill the mission of the church.[14]

Although the focus of this volume is on the church in the United States, it is worth noting that the consultations in general reported the increased involvement by laypersons in the programs, activities, liturgical life, leadership roles, and ministries of the Church. There is great variation in the forms of participation. The need for a clarification of the term *ministry* and a better theological understanding of this concept was mentioned in many reports. While some thought the term was being used too widely, "many reports and speeches stressed that these ministries and functions must be seen as arising from the vocation and mission of the lay person, as received in baptism and confirmation, and not as mere expedients to supplement the shortage of priests."[15]

The second step in the preparation was the publication of the working paper, by the General Secretariat of the Synod of Bishops. This document, which incorporated responses to the *Lineamenta* from bishops around the world, was to serve as the starting point for dialogue at the Synod. Kinast offered a review of the paper, in light of the United States consultations. One point he made is of importance for our study:

The main thrust of the working paper is toward the laity's role in the world. There is no rescinding of the laity's role in the church, but this document gives more attention to the traditional secular role of the laity. The thrust of the lay consultants in the United States is more toward church ministry than social mission. Consequently, a number of concerns which arise in church ministry are not dealt with or not treated very thoroughly.[16]

Peter Hebblethwaite commented that there is an ambivalence in the paper regarding lay ministries, an uncertainty as to whether they are good or bad, especially because of the warning of the dangers of clericalizing of the laity.[17] Nonetheless, the United States bishops took as one theme, addressed at the synod, "the parish as the primary focus in the United

States for spiritual development, ministry and reaching out in mission to the world." This included "attending carefully to the pivotal role of the pastor, emerging lay ministries and collaboration in ministry."[18]

The working paper affirmed some points and raised some questions relevant to the new ministers. The document affirmed that many charisms are given to the laity, and that all who have received charisms have a right and duty to exercise them; ecclesiastical authority has the task of judging the genuiness of the charisms. (This, of course, was affirmed in more than one Vatican II document.) Furthermore, the charismatic action of the Spirit is "linked to the rise of ministries in the church." The document seems to connect these ministries to the official roles of lector and acolyte. It also names as a need "clarification regarding the non-ordained ministries," especially a need "to define the difference between the tasks commonly assumed by the laity and those of ordained ministries." The document posed the questions: Who can authorize the creation of such ministries in the Church? What ought to be the manner of entrusting the laity with non-ordained ministries? (A liturgical rite or simply by a juridical act?) What ought to be the duration of such ministries and the manner of discontinuing them?[19] Clearly, the working paper recognized that lay ministries legitimately exist in the Church, and that there are unanswered questions about the ways in which the official Church can and should be responding to them.

THE SYNOD

The synod was truly a gathering of representatives from all the continents of the world. The great majority were bishops, but the convocation also included sixty lay auditors from forty-four countries and all five continents. Faced with a vast topic, obviously they could only deal with some dimensions. The Relator's Report, provided to begin the discussion, included several points relevant to our concerns. One theme it presented was "Ministries of Lay People in the Church Today." It stated that it is clear that in many regions of the world ministries are assigned to the laity. It presented the need for the synod to explain what the Church understands by the term *ministry*, and the differences that can exist in the same ecclesial ministry. Furthermore, it said that there was a need to clarify which offices assigned to the laity can be numbered among the ministries. On women, there were some concerns relevant to ministries, for example, the question of how can the charisms and services proper to women be more fully developed and acknowledged in the Church.[20]

The initial phase of the synod's work allowed each participant who wished to speak a maximum of eight minutes. It was in this listening phase that the work of reflecting together on the topic was begun. Some interventions are of particular interest for our purposes. Cardinal Ratzinger offered four levels of meaning of the word lay: theological (the distinction of cleric and layperson), models of spiritual life (embracing a wide variety of spiritualities), historical and eschatological (focused toward the coming of the kingdom), and sociological and functional. Of this last level he said that "whoever assumes a full-time permanent function within the Church is not 'in this sense' a lay person" because the specific problems faced in reference to the Church are not problems of the laity per se.[21]

On the topic of ministries assigned to laypeople, the interventions from bishops all over the world help to highlight the complexity of the present situation. Archbishop Pimenta of India emphasized that "lay ministry has to be oriented not only to altar or parish, but to a large extent to the crying needs of the people at large." On the other hand, Cardinal Malula of Zaire defended the role of the *mokambi*, laymen responsible for a parish, a ten-year-old development in his country. Bishop Santos Villeda of Honduras described the work of the 10,000 *Delegados de la Palabra de Dios* who serve not only as ministers of the Word but also facilitators of the basic communities and, often, extraordinary ministers of the Eucharist. Bishop Giraldo Jaramillo of Colombia referred to John Paul II's statement in Mexico that these ministries do not transform laypersons into clergy, but that that those who receive them must be considered as archetypes of the participation of all the faithful in the salvific mission of the Church. He indicated that persons should be called by the bishop for a ministry, and this should normally be exercised within a parish. Cardinal Hume, of England, said that ministry "should be applied only to the service of those who act in a specific way in the name of the Church community, and are authorized by the bishops." These could include instituted ministries like lector and acolyte which presuppose a certain permanence and prior training, whereas commissioned ministries would be temporary within the local church community. Father Salaverri Aranegui, SM, of Spain, suggested that certain characteristics of those ministries exercised by brothers and sisters could help to describe and lay foundations for lay ministries. They should be based on baptism and confirmation; be part of the salvific action of Christ; be an approved mission from the Church; there should be continuity in exercise; and there should be adequate formation. From the United States, Archbishop Mahony noted the expansion of full-time pastoral positions held by laity, and favored reserving the title of minister for those who occupy some formal position in church service. He thought that we may need to proceed with the suggestion of Pope Paul VI in *Ministeria Quaedam* regarding the establishment of other offices in the Church. He also stressed the need for adequate preparation and appropriate skills and dispositions to work in harmony with others. These points made by a few synod participants from various parts of the globe suggest the complexity of a world Church striving to discern a new reality.[22]

The next phase of the synod began with a twenty-eight page summary of the interventions, presented by the Relator of the Synod, Cardinal Hyacinthe Thiandoun. He presented twelve sets of questions which served as the basis of discussion in the twelve groups formed according to language preference. The groups included both synod fathers and lay auditors. One set of these questions, number 6, bears directly on our issue:

> Which functions should be called "ministries" and which "offices" and "tasks"? What is the competent authority which can decide or permit these ministries in the church? In what way can non-ordained ministries be conferred on lay people? Is a liturgical act necessary or is the juridical one sufficient?

Another set of questions asked whether women can have access to non-ordained ministries and the diaconate.[23]

The actual discussion of these questions in the groups elicited many and varied responses; sometimes groups could not come to a consensus. English Group C concluded, "In the light of the many differences in the needs of varied cultures, the Group believes that issues raised under question 6 in the Relation would, at least for the present, be better addressed at the level of each episcopal conference." They agreed that issues of women and ministries, in which local culture must be taken into consideration, also should be handled by the local episcopal conference. On the other hand, English Group B gave specific recommendations:

[E]stablish special "instituted ministries" fully open to both men and women for those who are called by the Church to serve either full-time or in a major capacity over a fairly long period of time, [and] recognize "commissioned ministries" to cater for specifically local needs, whether of the local church community or of the general community served by the Church.[24]

Each of the twelve groups came to its own answers. And yet, despite the many differences, Peter Hebblethwaite observed that in the English, Spanish, and French-speaking groups (nine in all) one could see a consensus emerging regarding lay ministries, and regarding women. However, when the English, Spanish, and French-speaking groups were asked "at the 11th hour" to produce a single synthetic "language group" document from their respective reports, much of the specificity disappeared.[25] Finally, a consensus listing of fifty-four propositions were developed by the synod and forwarded to the pope. "The new homogenized propositions were indeed based on the scores of resolutions hammered out in the small groups. But everything specific, and certainly everything at all controversial, had been removed from this list which was now presented for the Synod's vote."[26] The changes can be traced in regard to the issue which concerns us in this study:

The first draft of the propositions recognized the power of episcopal conferences to establish lay ministries within the limits set by Canon Law. This provision was canceled in the second and final drafts. Instead there is the statement: "The Church has need of the participation of a greater number of laity in parochial activities so that a process of evangelization suited to present-day circumstances may be put into effect. Such lay tasks do not require sacred orders." The synod does, however, request (in Proposition 18) a timely revision of Paul VI's *Motu Proprio Ministeria Quaedam* issued after Vatican II—the document which still regulates lay ministries in the post-conciliar Church.[27]

The synod concluded with the release of a "Message to the People of God" at the close of the gathering. Under the heading "Ministries and Services," the document said that all the local churches owe a debt of gratitude to the lay faithful who have gone forth, together with clergy and religious, to build up the church. It affirmed that today lay Christians have "a fuller participation in the life of the church and her action in the world."[28]

CONCLUSION

What is most significant about the synod is the work the assembly did together. It is clear that lay ministry is an important part of its lived experience in many parts of the world Church. It is also clear that there was not unanimity about language to use to describe what is happening, nor about how the Church should respond to the new developments in her midst. Many of the synod participants took positions similar to that of Archbishop James Hayes, then head of the Canadian Conference of Catholic Bishops: "the local church will have to be given the freedom to make decisions within the episcopal conferences according to cultural circumstances."[29]

CHRISTIFIDELES LAICI

On December 30, 1988, Pope John Paul II issued his *Apostolic Exhortation on the Vocation and Mission of the Lay Faithful in the Church and in the World*, based on the work of the 1987 Synod of Bishops. A lengthy document, it can clearly be traced to the dialogue at the synod; both themes from the speeches of the bishops and the majority of the final propositions are found in its pages. Overall, the exhortation explores the participation of the laity in the Church's life, in her communion, in the Church's mission, and in the importance of their formation.

Various themes relevant to our study are treated; only a brief overview is possible. The pope affirms that a diversity of ministries, gifts, and ecclesial tasks exist in the Church today, even as they did in the period of the New Testament. These ministries are the gift of the Spirit, and "even in their variety of forms a participation in Jesus Christ's own ministry as the good shepherd who lays down his life for the sheep . . . [and] the humble servant who gives himself without reserve for the salvation of all." He states that while the ordained ministries are in a primary position, the lay faithful also participate in the priestly, prophetic, and kingly mission of Christ. Therefore, "[t]he pastors ought to acknowledge and foster the ministries, the offices and roles of the lay faithful that find their foundation in the sacraments of baptism and confirmation, indeed, for a good many of them in the sacrament of matrimony."[30]

As he begins to explore the ministries of laypersons, John Paul II especially commends the roles of the laity in liturgy and its preparation. However, while stating that because of pastoral necessity laypeople may be entrusted with certain offices and roles that are connected to the ministry of pastors (for example, to distribute communion or exercise the ministry of the Word), here he is more cautious. Whenever laypersons act in this way, they do so only because of the official deputation given by the pastors, under the guidance of ecclesiastical authority. As one commentator says, "The consequence of this is that no matter how much pastoral work one does or how competent one becomes, the non-ordained person never 'forms' or 'rules' a community as a leader in the sense in which a cleric does."[31] As the exhortation states, "a person is not a minister simply through performing a task, but through sacramental ordination." The pope voices the concerns he heard at the synod:

> . . . about a too-indiscriminate use of the word ministry, the con-
> fusion and the equating of the common priesthood and the min-
> isterial priesthood, the lack of observance of ecclesiastical laws
> and norms, the arbitrary interpretation of the concept of "sup-
> ply," the tendency towards a "clericalization" of the lay faithful
> and the risk of creating, in reality, an ecclesial structure of paral-
> lel service to that founded on the sacrament of orders.

Nonetheless, the pope does say that it is necessary to respect the ministries, offices, and roles in the Church that are rooted in the sacraments of baptism and confirmation. When he describes these, he stresses that they ought to be exercised in conformity to the specific lay vocation, which is focused on "the vast and complicated world of politics, society and economics as well as the world of culture, of the sciences and the arts, of international life, of the mass-media."[32] At this point, because John Paul II quotes Paul VI only in regard to the laity's role in the world, omitting the section on ministries in the Church, he seems to be saying that lay ministry is only exercised in the secular world. The tone is far more cautionary than in *Evangelii Nuntiandi*.

The pope acknowledges the discussion on "the lectorate and the acolytate" held at the synod, and reports that a commission has been established to respond to the recommendations that *Ministeria Quaedam* be reconsidered. The task of the commission is "to provide an in-depth study of the various theological, liturgical, juridical and pastoral considerations which are associated with the great increase today of the ministries entrusted to the lay faithful." The pope cautions again that the essential difference between the ministerial priesthood and the common priesthood as well as the difference between the ministries derived from the sacrament of orders and those derived from the sacraments of baptism and confirmation must be respected.[33]

Charisms are then considered. Whereas recent theological writing roots ministries in charisms, John Paul II says: "The Holy Spirit, while bestowing diverse ministries in church communion, enriches it still further with particular gifts or promptings of grace called charisms." They are ordered to "the building up of the church, to the well-being of humanity and to the needs of the world." On the one hand, charisms demand that those who have received them exercise them; on the other hand "the discernment of charisms is always necessary." Therefore, "no charism dispenses a person from reference and submission to the pastors of the Church."[34]

Two other themes of *Christifideles Laici* are particularly relevant for our study. The first is that of collaboration. Though developed only modestly, the pope speaks of the principal of collaboration in a positive way, and encourages episcopal conferences "to evaluate the most opportune way of developing the consultation and the collaboration of the lay faithful, women and men . . . so that they may . . . manifest better the communion of the whole church."[35]

The topic of the formation of the lay faithful is treated at much greater length. The pope says, "The fundamental objective of the formation of the lay faithful is an ever-clearer discovery of one's vocation and the ever-greater willingness to live it so as to fulfill one's mission." Emphasis is placed on spiritual and doctrinal (including social doctrine) formation, as well as cultivation of human values. Formation is seen as especially important for two groups: first, those "who have responsibilities in various fields of society and public life" and as for the second, John Paul II says:

For the purpose of a truly incisive and effective pastoral activity, the formation of those who will form others is to be developed through appropriate courses or suitable schools. Forming those who in turn will be given the responsibility for the formation of the lay faithful constitutes a basic requirement of assuring the general and widespread formation of all the lay faithful.[36]

Who these persons who "will be given responsibility for the formation of the lay faithful" are is not specified.

An interesting note is sounded by Pope John Paul II when he considers the role of the Christian family as the "domestic church" and the natural and fundamental school for formation in the faith. "Father and mother receive from the sacrament of matrimony the grace and the ministry of the Christian educators of their children, before whom they bear witness and to whom they transmit both human and religious values." This use of the term *ministry* was already found in *Familiaris Consortio* (article 53).

Certainly, the exhortation represents a strong affirmation of the laity, of their place in the Church, of their part in her mission. But the focus is on their role in the world. The assessment of their part in the ministry of the Church notes dangers, confusions, and violations of ecclesiastical laws and norms. (Only the ministry of parents to their children seems to be fully affirmed.) It seems as though Pope John Paul II heard the fears and concerns about the new ministries that were expressed by the synod participants, but did not hear the recommendations for various ways of responding positively to this new reality which they also expressed.

THE ROMAN INSTRUCTION

In November of 1997, a Roman document, *Some Questions Regarding Collaboration of Nonordained Faithful in Priests' Sacred Ministry* was made public. It was approved by Pope John Paul II, and was signed by the heads of eight Vatican offices. Its primary emphasis was on the distinction between the ministry of priests and that of laypeople. From the standpoint of a reflection on the new lay ministers, some points are particularly relevant. The document begins with a statement of the call to all members of the Mystical Body "to participate actively in the mission and edification of the People of God," rooting the call within the mystery of the Church. Furthermore, it states that the call has been heard. Quoting *Christifideles Laici*, it says:

> This is witnessed, among other ways, in the new manner of active collaboration among priests, religious and the lay faithful; by active participation in the liturgy; in the proclamation of the word of God and catechesis; in the multiplicity of tasks entrusted to the lay faithful and fulfilled by them; by the flourishing of groups, associations and spiritual movements as well as by lay commitment to the life of the church and in the fuller and meaningful participation of women in the development of society.

This acknowledgement and affirmation of the multiplicity of tasks and services fulfilled by laity is clear. Again quoting *Christifideles Laici*, the document says that the foundation of the ministries, offices, and roles of laity is in baptism and confirmation, and for many, matrimony.[37]

In contradistinction to these areas of complementary activity, the Instruction says that "there exists a more restricted area, namely the sacred ministry of the clergy," in which laypeople, including vowed religious, "are called to assist." A key point in the document is that:

> . . . it is necessary that all who are in any way involved in this collaboration exercise particular care to safeguard the nature and mission of sacred ministry and the vocation and secular character of the lay faithful. It must be remembered that "collaboration with" does not in fact mean "substitution for."

More positively, they state that in many particular churches collaboration "has borne an abundance of good fruits while at the same time being mindful of the boundaries established by the nature of the sacraments and of the diversity of charisms and ecclesiastical functions. . . [including] in situations of a shortage or scarcity of sacred ministers." In situations of scarcity "faithful are called to assume specific duties which are as important as they are sensitive." Gratitude for such lay involvement is expressed, but it is noted that is some areas of the world "certain practices have often been developed which have had very serious negative consequences and have caused the correct understanding of true ecclesial communion to be damaged." It is to address such problems that the document was promulgated.[38]

The second part presents theological principles; these are not new, but given the weight of the document are worth outlining. "The common priesthood of the faithful and the ministerial or hierarchical priesthood . . . differ essentially and not only in degree . . ." Central to the difference is the conferral of "sacred power," which is to be exercised with a "character of service." The ordained minister "exercises the functions of teaching, sanctifying and governing the faithful." "Only in some of these functions, and to a limited degree, may the non-ordained faithful cooperate with their pastors should they be called to do so by lawful Authority and in accordance with the prescribed manner." Again quoting *Christifideles Laici*, they say, "The exercise of such tasks does not make pastors of the lay faithful, in fact, a person is not a minister simply in performing a task, but through sacramental ordination." The fear that certain practices "can encourage a reduction in vocations to the (ministerial) priesthood" is named. This is given great significance because "were a community to lack a priest, it would be deprived of the exercise and sacramental action of Christ, the head and pastor, which are essential for the very life of every ecclesial community." Although laypeople may collaborate in the ministry proper to the Church's pastors, "the non-ordained faithful do not enjoy a right to such tasks and functions," and they must be exercised within the parameters of canon law. The section concludes:

> Where the existence of abuses or improper practices has been proved, pastors will promptly employ those means judged necessary to prevent their dissemination and to ensure that the correct understanding of the Church's nature is not impaired. In particular, they will apply the established disciplinary norms to promote knowledge of and assiduous respect for that distinction and complementarity of functions which are vital for ecclesial communion.[39]

The final section of the document is called "practical provisions." It contains no new teaching, but draws on canon law and prior documents to deal with a range of particular issues. Concerns include use of the term *ministry*, which does not sufficiently elucidate the difference between baptismal and ordained priesthood; assumption of titles such as pastor, chaplain, coordinator, or moderator; reservation of the homily at Mass to priests; centrality of a priest as pastor of a parish; reservation of membership on the presbyteral council to priests; pastoral councils and parochial finance councils as advisory, and that *vicars forane* be priests; that the prayers of the liturgy proper to the priest be pronounced only by him; that Sunday celebrations in the absence of a priest follow instructions; that extraordinary ministers of Holy Communion function only when they are actually necessary, and within certain parameters; that the anointing of the sick be performed only by priests; that priests and deacons should preside at funeral rites; and that "supplementary" assistance be provided by "lay faithful of sound doctrine and exemplary moral life" who "possess that level of formation necessary for the discharge of the responsibilities entrusted to them."[40]

Is the institution an affirmation or critique of lay ministry as it has developed in the United States? Bishop Hoffman, a canon lawyer, went to Rome to receive the document on behalf of the United States Bishops' Conference. He returned the day of a long-scheduled workshop for bishops, the purpose of which was to give an overview of the work of the Subcommittee on Lay Ministry, and to seek response to the efforts as of that time of the ongoing project. The workshop schedule was changed so that Bishop Hoffman could address the group, because of the relevance of the Instruction to the agenda. He explained that countries from around the world were invited to be present, to receive the document, and to hear presentations, but not to suggest changes. As he listened, he judged that the document should not be read through the lens of lay ministry. While it is a response to "new forms of pastoral action," the needed lens is "the pivotal role of the ordained ministry in the ecclesiology of the Roman Catholic Church." He stated that apparently in some places in the world that is becoming more obscure. Bishop Hoffman pointed out that the document is not primarily theological, but rather liturgical-canonical, and that it is not new law. Bishop Hoffman also later addressed the conference, adding additional perspective. He gave some history of the document, dating back to a talk given by Pope John Paul II in 1994. He explained that the pastoral provisions are concerned with those actions that obscure or make unnecessary the work of the ordained priest; the document is not intended to disvalue the positive ministry of laymen and laywomen. Bishop Hoffman judged that the work of the Subcommittee on Lay Ministry, of which he was a member, was within the guidelines provided in the document.[41]

A second perspective on the document was offered by Bishop Hubbard who published the diary of his *ad limina* visit to the Vatican in his diocesan newspaper. Based on meetings with Cardinal Ratzinger (Congregation for the Doctrine of the Faith) and Cardinal Francis Stafford (Congregation for the Laity), he concluded that the document was prompted by European concerns, and not meant to apply to the American situation. Furthermore, he said "the instruction, while reminding us of some fundamental theological and canonical distinctions between the ordained and non-ordained, is not truly adequate for our situation in the United States." He said further that "modification and clarification needs to be made in light of our lived pastoral realities."[42]

Despite such judgments by bishops, many lay ministers expressed deep dismay at the document's seeming description of lay ministry as being only by exception, for special need, temporary. Some noted that the cultural norm for the title of those who offer pastoral care in health care institutions and prisons is, precisely, chaplain, and that the title Director of Religious Education followed thirty years of practice and the guidelines of many dioceses. Others observed that various church documents, from the council and since, were considerably less restrictive regarding lay ministry than the instruction. (Actually, the introduction to the document itself, when quoting *Christifideles Laici*, is considerably more positive in tone than the later sections.)

So again we may ask, is the document an affirmation or critique of lay ministry as it has developed in the United States? The document's intent was to emphasize the role of the priest, in the face of abuses of norms from canon law. The original draft was more negative and critical than the final document. In the consultation, bishops reported the positive developments in lay ministry in the United States, and stated that the draft would negatively impact the morale of lay ministers. The final document does offer positive valuation of and express gratitude for lay ministry. Nonetheless, it is often experienced as a critique, indeed, a severe critique, by lay ministers in the United States. For bishops, it is important to understand this. For lay ministers, it is important to put the document in the context of a world Church. The new reality that has emerged in the Church is not yet clearly defined and understood.

THE UNITED STATES BISHOPS

EARLY RESPONSES

In 1977, the National Conference of Catholic Bishops changed the name of one of their committees from the Committee on the Lay Apostolate to the Bishops' Committee on the Laity. The reason: "the new name reflected the expansion of the Committee's pastoral concerns, moving beyond that of organizations and movements, although including them, to the new emerging lay ministries . . ." They began publishing a newsletter, for the purpose of bringing together "the many diverse lay individuals and groups who work to further the mission of the Church," including lay ministers, members of lay organizations, members of parish or diocesan staff, and the "'person in the pew' living a Christian presence in the world."[43] Developments in lay ministry which they noted included lay missionaries, usually young adults working for a few years; laity, especially young adults, preparing in seminaries and divinity schools for service in the Church; and laity, usually adults with some experience, participating in the approximately sixty diocesan ministry formation programs.[44] When Cardinal John Dearden addressed Pope Paul VI on behalf of the Midwest bishops, he said,

> At the same time that the number of our clergy has diminished, there have been called forth in the church new types of ministries involving both religious and laity. Through broad collaboration, works of education and charity abound.[45]

CALLED AND GIFTED: THE AMERICAN CATHOLIC LAITY

In 1980, the NCCB commemorated the fifteenth anniversary of the proclamation of the *Decree on the Apostolate of the Laity* by issuing their fairly short but significant reflection on the role of the laity. The document opens with a prayer of praise for what is happening among the laity, and the statement of their desire to describe what they have been experiencing and learning from the laity. In light of the focus of this book, it is significant to note that one of the four calls of laity named is the call to ministry. The call is rooted in the charisms received; "baptism and confirmation empower all believers to share in some form of ministry." This ministry is both Christian service in the world and ministry in the Church. The bishops expressed gratitude to the many volunteers and part-time workers who serve parishes and dioceses. Then they add:

> Growing numbers of lay women and men are also preparing themselves professionally to work in the church. In this regard religious sisters and brothers have shown the way with their initiative and creativity. Ecclesial ministers, i.e., lay persons who have prepared for professional ministry in the church, represent a new development. We welcome this as a gift to the church. There are also persons who serve the church by the witness of their lives and their self-sacrificing service and empowerment of the poor in works such as administration, housing, job development and education. All these lay ministers are undertaking roles which are not yet clearly spelled out and which are already demanding sacrifices and risks of them and their families. As lay persons increasingly engage in ecclesial ministry, we recognize and accept the responsibility of working out practical difficulties such as the availability of positions, the number of qualified applicants, procedures for hiring, just wages and benefits.[46]

PREPARING LAITY FOR MINISTRY

Having recognized the importance of this new development, the emergence of "ecclesial ministers," the first concern shown by the committee was for information about the ways in which they were formed for ministry. This led to a study done with the Office of Research of the Conference, in conjunction with the National Association for Lay Ministry and the National Pastoral Planning Conference. This study summarized information about 164 programs (only programs of two or more years duration were included) in 123 dioceses, of which 40 percent granted an academic degree. Over 3,500 people were studying in degree programs, and 7,000 in non-degree programs; the majority of those in the degree programs were "continuing their development in a church career," whereas those in non-degree programs were preparing for volunteer church service or marketplace ministry. In the degree programs, two-thirds were laywomen, one-third vowed religious and clergy; all but 10 percent of the non-degree participants were lay. Of the faculty, 40 percent were clergy, 35 percent lay, and 24 percent vowed religious. Eighty percent of the programs had started between 1976-1986. Twice as much time was given to spiritual formation of participants in non-degree programs as in degree programs; only about 10 percent of program time was given to field experience, in all programs.[47]

What is particularly notable about this early report is how quickly programs had multiplied, and how many people were involved. Clearly something new was unfolding; Catholic academic institutions and dioceses had initiated something now involving many laity as students and also as teachers. The researchers noted:

> It seems clear that programs of ministry preparation for laity have moved beyond training for a specific ministry with its limited implications to the wider possibilities of ministerial education and formation. Programs are offering a broad base of study in theology, scripture, spirituality, Christology, and ecclesiology that give laity a basis upon which they can develop shared responsibility with clergy and vowed religious for the mission of the Church.[48]

CALLED AND GIFTED FOR THE THIRD MILLENNIUM

To commemorate the thirtieth anniversary of the *Decree on the Apostolate of the Laity* and the fifteenth of *Called and Gifted*, the NCCB issued a new pastoral statement. Here they revisit the four "calls" of their previous document and "update them in light of Church teaching, pastoral practice and changing conditions in the world." Once again, they affirm ecclesial lay ministers, "professionally prepared lay men and women offering their talents and charisms in the service of the Church." Some roles at liturgy that are specified are cantors, music directors, readers, eucharistic ministers, altar servers, and laity responsible for leading Sunday worship in the absence of a priest. Other ministries mentioned are the teaching of youth and adults; serving in peace and justice networks, soup kitchens, and shelters; in marriage preparation, bereavement programs, and ministry to the separated and divorced. Those laity who provide daily pastoral leadership of a parish in the absence of a resident pastor and persons providing leadership in Catholic institutional ministries such as social service and health care are also named. The bishops conclude,

"Indeed, the pastoral needs of this moment are being ably and generously served by many kinds of ecclesial lay ministers."[49]

The bishops recognize several challenges in the present situation. First, they see a need to develop and commit the resources necessary to help laity, both paid staff and volunteers, prepare for church ministry. Second, they recognize that it is often difficult for lay ministers to support themselves and their families, and say that it is necessary to practice justice and provide a living wage. Third, they acknowledge the need to incorporate minority lay ministers into ecclesial leadership. Fourth, they feel challenged to ensure that the Church be a good steward of its human resources, and "recognize that God is blessing the Church with lay vocations to ministry." Finally, the challenge they see which "undergirds all of the above" is "the need to foster respectful collaboration, leading to mutual support in ministry, between clergy and laity for the sake of Christ's Church and its mission to the world." The bishops pledge that as an episcopal conference they "will expand our study and dialogue concerning lay ministry in order to understand better the critical issues and find effective ways to address them."[50]

THE SUBCOMMITTEE ON LAY MINISTRY

In the fall of 1988, the Bishops' Committee for Pastoral Research and Practices began a joint project with other conference committees to study new developments in ministry. The focus was to be collaborative ministry; one dimension was to be full-time ecclesial ministers, both clergy and lay.[51] Eventually, the committee determined that there was a need to examine the rapidly expanding practice of hiring laypeople and religious for pastoral positions in parishes. The goal was refocused to include part-time personnel, in order to study some ministries (such as music) which are usually part time. (It also was narrowed to lay ministers, including vowed religious, only.) The study was undertaken by the National Pastoral Life Center, under the direction of Philip Murnion. It included a review of earlier studies, a variety of consultations, surveys of an initial sampling of parishes, further surveys of those parishes with lay pastoral ministers, and on-site visits to fifty-two parishes.[52] The result was the publication in 1992 of *New Parish Ministers: Laity and Religious on Parish Staffs*, which was drawn upon extensively in the first part of this book.

When Monsignor Murnion initially presented his findings to the Committee on the Laity an observer noted a certain sense of euphoria in the group. The committee realized that the report contained much good news: the pastors, the parishioners, and the new ministers themselves were very happy with their work.

EARLY WORK

An outcome of the study was that in March of 1994 the Laity Committee established the Subcommittee on Lay Ministry, "to study the emerging data, experience, issues and questions pertaining to lay ministry in the church." Chaired by Bishop Straling, the membership on the committee included bishops from other ministry-related committees, in order to maximize possibilities for dialogue about the relationship of lay ministry and other dimensions of the Church's life. *New Parish Ministers* was seen as foundational to their work. The subcommittee was asked to determine, what are the key questions for lay ministry, and what questions can be addressed by bishops, and how. One conclusion at the end of the meeting was, "The overall intent. . . would be to insure the future quality of parish ministry and staffing."[53]

The early work of the subcommittee reflects the efforts of the bishops to understand the nature of the new development they were addressing. Some questions focused on the role of the parish life coordinator (variously named, but referring to those described in canon 517.2): "is there a theological basis for having anyone other than a priest in the position of pastoral leader of a parish?... are there different interpretations of Canon 517.2 . . ." Others looked at lay ministry in a broader sense: "what are the merits of using people who have university degrees in pastoral ministry versus using volunteers and giving them formation through diocesan programs?... whether the term 'pastoral ministry' or 'collaborative ministry' or just 'ecclesial ministry' would be better than 'ecclesial lay ministry'?" There was a clear intent to build on the research in *New Parish Ministers*, with the continued inclusion of vowed religious, but also an expansion to include some diocesan ministries.[54] At the same time there was often an uncertainty about focusing on a smaller group of lay ministers. On the one hand, there was concern that this might serve to diminish emphasis on the laity's role in the transformation of the world. On the other hand, there was concern that singling out some might seem to diminish the importance of all laity sharing in the mission of the Church, and could lead to creation of an elite group. Gradually the work of the subcommittee focused on the smaller group of lay ministers. It is worth noting that the kinds of questions raised by the subcommittee in the early stages of its work would emerge again with other groups in the future, including the theologians at the colloquium.

The subcommittee obtained a Lilly Endowment grant, and in 1996 began a project, "Leadership for Ecclesial Lay Ministry." Originally intended to take three years, the project was eventually extended to four. By distributing a survey to bishops, lay ministry graduate programs and professional associations representing lay ministers, they sought to identify priorities for the work of the subcommittee. The issue given highest priority was the theology of lay ministry. Second was the formation and education of lay ministers. Other issues ranked high were: the relationship between lay ministers and ordained ministers; greater attention to the multicultural dimension of the Church; financial concerns and human resource items; the term *lay minister*; and the need for a clearer definition and understanding. These would set the agenda for the activities of the subcommittee.[55] The fact that bishops' conferences in other parts of the world have also been pondering these issues in light of their own pastoral situation and needs would also be part of what the committee studied.

The survey work was complemented by five focus groups, with a total of thirty-three bishops, held in different sections of the country. This venue allowed bishops, in small groups, to surface their concerns about many issues, some with a theological focus (for example, lay ministers need to be called, or sent, by the Church), some very practical (for example, the need for the diocese to be protected from potential suits). Often in the discussion no distinction was made between professional ministers and parishioners; when considered, professionalism tended to be viewed quite negatively. There was also some real questioning about lay ministers who pursue education on their own in graduate programs. Issues the subcommittee had discussed arose in these groups also, for example, the tension between the impact of encouraging lay ministry in the Church on the ministry of laity in the marketplace, and concerns about the limited number of minorities becoming lay ministers. What the groups demonstrated was the concern the bishops have about the issue of lay ministry, and their affirmation of the need for the conference to address these issues.[56]

FORUM FOR LAY MINISTERIAL ASSOCIATIONS

In addition to focusing the concerns and needs of the bishops, the sub-committee also consulted extensively with various individuals, leaders of organizations and associations, and directors of both academic and diocesan programs. For example, in March of 1996 a Forum for Lay Ministerial Associations brought together representatives of twenty-one professional associations and organizations for a day of dialogue with four bishops from the subcommittee. The day began in a very formal, even constrained way, but as the conversation unfolded a fuller exchange occurred. The professional associations raised trust and credibility, as well as communication, as major issues. Individuals in the group shared the stories of their lives in ministry, their ongoing efforts to discern what God was calling them to, their conviction, as one said, "that my ministry is not like a coat that I take off, but is a part of myself." The bishops listened, and the group said that they felt listened to and included in the process. One result was that the subcommittee decided to have a second meeting the following year, and to ongoingly communicate with the associations in various ways. When the second group was convened a year later, the conversation began with a degree of openness and ease more like the end of the first meeting than the beginning, even though more than a third of the participants were new. Clearly, the communication achieved at the first meeting had an impact. A second result of the meeting was the effort of the subcommittee to struggle with the meaning of "vocation" as it might apply to the ecclesial lay ministers. The bishops recognized the dynamics of vocation, of call, in the stories told, certainly out of their own experience and that with their priests, and sought to understand and contextualize what they had heard.[57]

THEOLOGY AND RELATIONSHIPS

The issue of a theology of lay ministry surfaced often in the work of the subcommittee. The theological colloquium, which was convened in May of 1997 to address this concern, is discussed in chapter 9. Also of significant concern was the question of the relationship of priests and lay ministers. The complexity of the issue was highlighted in a structured discussion facilitated by Monsignor Philip Murnion, who identified the factors affecting relationships, including theology, attitudes/personality, skills, and structures.[58] Relevant here is a finding in the Murnion and

DeLambo report: "The pastors are more likely than the pastoral ministers to see the basic relationships as those of a team vs. staff, than do the parish ministers. They are much more likely (58.3 percent) to see the situation as one of collaboration than do the parish ministers (31.5)."[59]

MULTICULTURAL CONCERNS

An ongoing concern of the subcommittee was the issue of multiculturalism. This first arose from the data in the Murnion study indicating that minorities were significantly underrepresented among the new parish ministers. Dr. Zoila Diaz was invited to join the subcommittee as an advisor to assist in reflection on multicultural issues. Dr. Diaz gave a presentation to the group outlining some of the challenges of developing lay leaders in non-dominant-culture communities. In addition to language, factors such as diverse styles of leadership, varying role expectations for men and women, economic constraints, and limited education represent difficulties in the development of minority leaders. She recommended that all ministers be trained to serve diverse cultures.[60]

In their continued effort to understand and receive input from minority groups, the subcommittee convened a forum of representatives from various ethnic communities in March 1998. Seventeen individuals, many of whom were from diocesan offices, and others in higher education, gathered. The communities represented were African American, Cambodian, Filipino, Guatemalan, Haitian, Korean, Mexican American, Native American, Nigerian, and Puerto Rican. The day was preceded by an evening reception, and included liturgy (with attention to multiculturalism), small group and large group sharing of stories, group analysis seeking common themes, and closing prayer, drawing on diverse cultural customs. In small groups they were invited to share with the bishops, staff, and advisors their experiences and/or perceptions of ministry within their community, the gifts of that community that relate to ministry, how ministry needs are being met and whether they are being met by choice or because of a lack of other options, and how ministry leaders are identified and supported. Many felt that those from their communities are not invited to leadership within the parish, diocesan, or national structures, and that resources are often lacking for training programs and appropriate materials. Representatives noted that volunteers are of primary importance in their communities, and that often they themselves had begun as volunteers, responding to a call to service rather than planning a profession or a career. Furthermore, leadership emerges more from the recognition of a person's gift than from the attainment of a credential, a charismatic more than an academic base. The diversity within the ethnic communities was stressed. Representatives said that there are unique traditions and perspectives which are lost when all minorities are seen only as being different from the dominant culture. Their desire is for inclusion, not assimilation.

Recommendations to the committee included that the definition of ecclesial lay ministers reflect the multicultural, pluralistic reality of the church in the United States and deliberate, intentional recruitment of individuals from diverse backgrounds to participate as students and as teachers in lay ministry formation programs. They also recommended that all seminarians and ministry students be required to experience, minister within, and be educated about diverse ethnic groups.[61] When the subcommittee published *The State of the Questions*, important conclusions were drawn from this consultation. For example, they said that the bishops' conference should explore the development of policies and strategies to identify, support, and properly prepare lay ministers from all cultural groups, and not only to serve within their own communities, but for the wider Church. They also emphasized that all ministry training must be done with an awareness of the many cultural contexts within the Church.[62]

A CONTINENTAL DIALOGUE

The subcommittee desired to examine our experience of new ministers in the United States by placing this in a larger context. Therefore they invited bishops from the Canadian Conference of Catholic Bishops (CCCB) and the Latin American Bishops' Council (CELAM). One bishop and a laywoman from CCCB, five bishops (including two archbishops) from CELAM, seven bishops from the subcommittee, and staff and advisors, attended the two day dialogue. Simultaneous translation in three languages was provided. Each visiting bishop described the lay ministry scenario in his own country, naming as well cultural factors that present challenges to the mission and ministry of the church. The composite picture was one of great vibrancy and diversity. Some snapshots from their much fuller descriptions provide evidence of this. In Brazil, there are 300,000 catechists, and new forms of pastoral service such as prison ministry and justice work focused on land distribution are emerging. Ministries are categorized as recognized (a service in the community), entrusted (some formal conferral), official (by installation, for a service that is stable, with responsibilities), and ordained. In the recent past, the church in Colombia has prepared and installed many lectors and acolytes (for women, they used canonical mission), but fearing a clericalization of the laity now emphasize parish renewal. Stable ministries have arisen out of this; in ten dioceses (not all in the country) over 200,000 serve in a variety of roles. Ecuador has more than 1,000 persons involved in recognized ministries; at the beginning they did everything, but gradually their work has been specified. While Venezuela has been reluctant to institutionalize lay ministry, there has been extensive development in the barrios and rural areas where laity give life and activity in the absence of priests. The developments in Canada are similar to those in the United States. Most ministers work in parishes, but the role of school chaplain, which requires a mandate from the bishop, is prevalent.[63]

The Latin American bishops reported on the work of CELAM, especially a lay ministry conference held in 1995. Noting the diversity in different countries, they had decided to focus on the most urgently needed ministries that are in accord with canon law: Ministry of the Word (lectors), Ministers of the Eucharist (acolytes), and Ministers to the Sick (a general ministry of charity). Of primary concern is the adequate theological and pastoral preparation of all ministers.

> The important thing is to begin defining roles, formation requirements, conditions for admissions, rites for institution, evaluation procedures, and organization of lay ministries. In other words, we need to structure lay ministries.

CELAM speaks of ministries confided to the laity, viewing this as better terminology than lay ministry.[64]

In the dialogue that followed the reports, many points were raised which helped to highlight differences in culture and in approaches in the local churches. The church in Latin America is very poor and deeply imbedded in the larger culture, unlike the situation in North America. Latin American culture is marked by a stability of local communities, and a high valuation of relationality as a mode of working; North American culture is marked by mobility and individualism. The Latin American bishops spoke often of mission, of a ministerial church, of communion. All bishops present were concerned about adequate preparation for lay ministers, and a theology which adequately grounds their life and work. The relationship between priests and laity is also a concern in both the North and the South. The relationship between lay ministers and bishops seems quite defined in South America; one bishop said that his parish visitations are one week long, allowing him time to visit with each lay minister. Latin American bishops said that very few lay ministers were paid, and that while many are women, women do not have official mandates. While the feminization of ministry and the effect of lay ministry on vocations to the priesthood are concerns mentioned in the United States, this is not true for those from South America. In the United States, formal education, organizational patterns of social life, professionalization, and specialization are valued.[65]

The experience of the continental dialogue reinforced an understanding of how culture-specific developments in ministry are, and yet how many common themes emerge. The dialogue helped to demonstrate that lay ministry, and even the language to be used in naming it, is still in a process of development, and that both theological understanding and pastoral practice are unfolding.

Consultations with Priests and Deacons

In 1999, the subcommittee held two consultations with priests, and a third with priests and deacons, in different parts of the country. Participants emphasized the necessity of clear distinctions between ordained and lay ecclesial ministers and the complementary and collaborative, not competitive, differences of their roles. Education, formation, helping discernment of a call to ministry and church recognition of vocation were also seen as important. However, some do not believe that establishing an ongoing relationship between bishops and lay ministers is as important as some bishops and lay ministers have indicated.[66]

Report of the Subcommittee

The original subcommittee presented its findings to the Conference of Bishops in November of 1999. A draft was submitted to all members beforehand, representatives briefly outlined central points, and small group and plenary session discussions were held. In the discussions, bishops raised many of the questions which the subcommittee originally had asked themselves, including whether emphasis on lay ecclesial ministry were to the detriment of the secular vocation of the laity, or to the ministry of all the baptized. Nonetheless, in feedback sheets received from the bishops, all of the subcommittee proposals were affirmed. They gave the highest priorities to scholarly research and writing about the theology of ministry, and continued study of the relationship between the lay ecclesial minister and the bishop, including the theological and pastoral aspects.[67]

The report of the subcommittee is organized around the six issues originally identified by the survey of the bishops. Each section includes conclusions, followed by background information, especially what was learned relative to that topic through various activities of the subcommittee. In addition, Appendix I gives the proposals the bishops were asked to vote on and Appendix II the questions the subcommittee posed to them; Appendix III gives a chronology of the work of the subcommittee.

First. Regarding the term *lay ecclesial minister*, the report states it is chosen to stress that the persons named remain lay, and that their work is an expression of the legitimate vocation of all laity. Ecclesial denotes that their ministry is not undertaken as a personal initiative, but under the supervision of the hierarchy. It is used to identify a broad category of persons, not as a job title. Identity as a lay ecclesial minister is partly a question of personal awareness and intentionality, partly a matter of recognition by church authority. A list of characteristics (though not really a definition) is given indicating that the person is responding to the gifts of baptism and to a call to ministry, is prepared for a ministry of leadership in a public role conferred by ecclesiastical authority, and is installed by the bishop (or his representative) to perform ministry in a stable manner as a staff person or a volunteer.[68]

Second. The subcommittee notes that because the phenomenon being dealt with is, in many ways, new, their conclusions regarding a theology of lay ecclesial ministry are a starting point for discussion more than a final word. The foundations for lay ecclesial ministry are found in understanding of the Church as a *communio*, in mission, and of the baptized as sharing in the three-fold ministry of Christ, through the gifts of the Spirit. Their ministry is as laity: sharing in Christ's ministry, according to their own secular character, serving the transformation of the world by building ecclesial communion. And, they are ecclesial ministers, called to a ministry within the Church, a ministry that is publicly recognized and authorized, with duties and responsibilities which for the majority of them can be considered proper to the laity. Because of the charisms they have received they have the right and duty to use their gifts and to be incorporated into the life of the Church.

Further conclusions about a theology of lay ecclesial ministry are far-ranging. They state that the Church is impoverished when persons of diverse cultures are not designated as lay ecclesial ministers. Lay ecclesial and ordained ministry complement each other; ordained ministers are to acknowledge and promote the service of lay ecclesial ministers, and both need to work collaboratively. Such collaboration does not diminish either the sacramental character of ordination nor the secular character of the laity. The role of bishops in relation to lay ecclesial ministers includes fostering and guiding their gifts, encouraging all vocations and fostering collaboration by acting as a center of unity, seeing that they have the needed education and formation, and affirming the distinctive character of their role. The subcommittee states that it is important to distinguish tasks undertaken by lay ecclesial ministers that are proper to the laity, and those proper to the ordained. For the former, recommended language is entrusting, commissioning, or instituting. Also, conferring offices and installing can be used for the former as well as for the latter. In the past ministries have changed over time, so bishops are encouraged to be faithful to the needs of faith communities today when considering desired ministries. While calling on the bishops and their leadership to structure the new ministries, the report also states that lay ecclesial ministers should be designated by the diocesan bishop (or representative) to their ministerial assignments within the diocese.

As also relevant to a theology, the subcommittee reflected on our Church's experience of lay ecclesial ministry. They affirmed it as a grace-filled work of the Spirit which many experience as a call, a vocation; the entire Church has the responsibility to foster, nurture, encourage, and help discern all vocations. Reflection on these realities calls for the balancing of fidelity to Scripture and Tradition with the charismatic activity of the Spirit. The need to be aware of developments in theology and practice in other countries is also acknowledged.[69]

Third. Throughout the project, the issue of the preparation of lay ecclesial ministers was recognized as important. Quoting Pope John Paul II, the subcommittee states that intra-ecclesial work "should be undertaken only by men and women who have received the necessary training in accordance with clearly defined criteria." They note that a growing number of dioceses have developed standards and certification processes. They recommend that there be dialogue among the various agencies of formation within a region, promoted by the bishops. The importance of continuing education is stressed, and the value of laity, religious, deacons, and priests experiencing it together is presented as helpful for building relationships for collaborative ministry. Tuition assistance and scholarships are encouraged. The experience of a call to ministry is said to be "worthy of respect and sustained attention."[70]

Fourth. The issue of the relationship between lay ecclesial ministers and ordained ministers is seen primarily in regard to the bishop. Stating that this needs "further attention and clarification," the subcommittee concludes that it should be expressed in rituals of installation and commissioning as well as in the administrative structures of the diocese. In order to maintain the distinction between ministries proper to laity and those ordinarily reserved to the ordained, appropriate titles, rituals, and canonical and liturgical forms should be used for the installation of all ecclesial ministers. Clarification of titles is needed, as is appropriate incorporation of lay ecclesial ministers within the consultative structures of the diocese. The concern that giving attention to lay ecclesial ministry will detract from vocations to the priesthood needs to be acknowledged and addressed.[71]

Fifth. The topic "Financial and Human Resource Issues" is addressed in the report in various ways. Studies of the new parish ministers demonstrate that formal job descriptions and contracts, performance evaluations and staff meetings, which are standard human resource practice, are increasingly found. Some dioceses have begun to develop grievance and due process procedures; consultation with experts from NACPA is recommended when doing this. The portability of pensions is named as a need, as well as procedures "that guarantee that policy and not personal biases determine continued employment or termination." Finally, the subcommittee supports "the development of comprehensive, integrated personnel systems" for clergy, religious, and lay who serve together in one setting—not for the same policy, but consistent policies.[72]

Sixth. When focusing on multicultural issues, the subcommittee commented on the rich traditions varied cultural groups have to offer the

Church, and concluded, "We believe that greater numbers of lay ecclesial ministers should be drawn from the communities they serve." They also stressed the need for "policies and strategies designed to identify, support, and properly prepare lay ministers who come from all the cultural groups within our Church" and that "all ministry training be done with an awareness of the many cultural contexts within our Church."[73]

With the publication of the report, *State of the Questions*, the work of the original subcommittee was complete; their tenure of six years was unusually long for the conference. At the present time, dioceses and other organizations are using the document in many and varied ways, evidence of both the importance and the reception of their work. A new subcommittee has formed. It is continuing the work begun, especially through regional consultations with bishops and other key persons gathered to dialogue about the report, and lay ecclesial ministry in their region. The first consultation was held in San Antonio for Region X, in October, 2001;[74] a second is scheduled for Region VII, in Chicago, and a third planned for Region II.

INDIVIDUAL UNITED STATES BISHOPS

Many individual bishops in the United States have been reflecting on these issues and taking initiatives in their own dioceses. For example, in 1994 Joseph Cardinal Bernardin issued a pastoral letter addressing the two issues he thought most important for focused strategic planning in his diocese; one was ministerial leadership. He said, "The well-being of the life of this local church is directly related to the number and quality of its ministers." Acknowledging the value and importance of the ministry of priests and vowed religious, he affirmed that participation of laity in ecclesial ministry is theologically based, and "such participation should be encouraged, therefore, even if the number of priests were plentiful." In light of the diminished number of priests, he said the need is even greater, and that collaboration is essential. He also focused on recruitment, initial and ongoing formation, and accountability (standards for all candidates for ministry, and evaluation of priests, deacons, and professional ministers).[75]

On Holy Thursday, in April 2000, Cardinal Roger Mahony and the priests of the Archdiocese of Los Angeles issued *As I Have Done for You:*

A Pastoral Letter on Ministry. The history of the letter begins with a Priests Assembly in 1997, focused on the nature of the ordained priesthood in the light of contemporary challenges. The group reflected on their lives and work; most expressed a great sense of satisfaction in their ministry. The challenges discussed included the burdens of administration, the declining number and rising ages of priests, the multicultural nature of the diocese (for which a growing appreciation was noted), and the flourishing of the gifts of the lay faithful. In the course of the assembly the decision was made that the priests and the archbishop would together write a pastoral letter on ministry, "articulating a clear vision of ministries, ordained and non-ordained, and inviting local communities to begin to plan for the future of ministry in the archdiocese." Discussions at two annual convocations of priests, as well as within the deaneries, further explored the challenges. In the fall of 1998 a report was published in the diocesan paper, calling "for input from individuals, parishes, and other constituencies within the archdiocese about the present and future of ministry." Born of dialogue, the letter invites all in the archdiocese into the process of reflection, and of planning for the future.[76] Calling for collaboration of all, a process of collaboration was followed in developing the pastoral. The fact that it was issued by the archbishop with the priests of the archdiocese (a first) is in itself notable.

The letter invites to "a major reorientation in our thinking about ministry as well as in our ministerial practice."

> This necessitates four things. First, it must be recognized that lay ministry rooted in the priesthood of the baptized is not a stop gap measure . . . Second, there is a pressing need for greater collaboration and inclusivity in ministry . . . Third, there is a need for a clear understanding of the nature of lay ecclesial ministry on the part of the baptized and those who have received the sacrament of Holy Orders . . . Finally, there is a need for a common foundational theology as the basis for the formation of seminarians, deacons, religious and laypersons for ministry, as well as for the development of more collaborative skills on the part of the ordained.[77]

The letter begins with two snapshots of a composite parish in Los Angeles, one in 1955, the second in 2005. The two are contrasted. In the first, the primary work was sacramental, educational, and devotional, and was performed by a number of priests and the sisters in the school. The second snapshot pictures a richly multicultural parish, the many laity who have a strong sense of their baptismal call and an awareness that all in the parish are responsible. There is a diverse staff—both multiculturally and in terms of church state in life, multiple ministerial endeavors, and a complex program—in scheduling and range of activities.[78] This second picture presents the challenge for that particular "parish," and each of the parishes in the archdiocese.

The second half of the letter outlines the theological grounding for a shared ministry, and a series of exercises designed to help each parish plan for a collaborative, inclusive ministry. Theologically, the emphasis is on the centrality of baptism, and the rootedness of all ministry in Christ and the Spirit. Multiple ways that laypersons witness, worship, and serve are outlined, and the particular "vocation of full-time Church service," "professionally trained or otherwise properly prepared women and men, including vowed religious, who are in positions of service and leadership in the Church." This lay ecclesial ministry "emerges from a personal call, requires appropriate formation, and is undertaken with both the support and the authorization of competent Church authority." The letter states that greater attention and support for lay ecclesial ministry is needed, through public recognition and authorization within a particular ecclesial community. The role of the priest is carefully delineated as well, but for the purposes of this study need not be presented here. The exercises invite the exploration of present reality through a process of first seeing and understanding, then understanding and judging, then deciding, and finally, acting.[79]

In this letter lay ecclesial ministry is placed in a larger context— theologically, that of ministry, and pastorally, that of a multicultural diocese in which many ministries are flowering. The vision presented calls, of necessity, for collaboration in ministry, and invites all into a process of theological reflection designed to assist each parish in concretizing the vision.

Bishop Matthew Clark focuses precisely on the issue of lay ecclesial ministry which he explored in an address, "The Relationship of the Bishop and Lay Ecclesial Minister." Noting a 35 plus year history of lay ecclesial ministry in his local church, he said, "we have so much more growing to do fully to integrate these ministers into the ecclesial life of the Diocese of Rochester." A central concern is "establishing a vital, ongoing relationship between us [that is, bishops] and lay ecclesial ministers," which "is necessary to the very life and mission of the church of the future." He notes the difficulty of discerning a pattern for this relationship of the bishop and lay ecclesial ministers, because the experience is "still too fresh and evolving." However, he asserts that the work must be begun.[80]

Drawing a parallel with the relationship between bishops and priests, Bishop Clark named four aspects of developing this relationship. First, he roots his vision theologically, in an understanding of Church in which communion is central, and from which mission follows. Second, he stresses that "all relationships in the church are both personal (because we are in communion with each other) and ministerial (because our communion is directed to mission)." The relationship of bishop and ministers requires a loving communion focused on mission, toward fostering the communion and mission of the diocesan church. The bishops' task is "overseeing and coordinating the good order and functioning of ministry within his diocese." Therefore, Bishop Clark suggests that the term *diocesan ministerium* be used to refer to "all those who exercise in the local church an official ecclesial ministry, whether they are ordained or not." He sees the episcopal role as "discerning, fostering, ordering, structuring and empowering qualified ecclesial ministers' gifts on behalf of the local church over which he presides."[81]

To this end, structures of communion are needed—"organizational mechanisms that help ensure that ministry in communion thrives in fidelity to the Spirit's gifts." (He says that these structures are particularly relevant when the inevitable challenges of being in relationship arise.) Several examples are offered. One is ways of fostering collaboration among deacons, lay pastoral leaders, religious, and priests. In his own diocese these include twice a year meetings of all involved in pastoral ministry at special ministry days, in order to work together on common pastoral strategies. A second is ways of fostering competence for all ministers, including guidelines requiring graduate degrees for certain positions and certificates for others and financial assistance for study. Still another need is for structures of communion that foster recognition of lay ecclesial ministry, including a ritual for designating a person as an ecclesial minister. He says that structures of communion are also needed to foster equity for lay ecclesial ministers, including adequate salary, benefits, appreciation and spiritual life, and diocesan policies such as standard human resource practices, grievance procedures, and portability of pension benefits. Finally, Bishop Clark says that because ministry is never simply a job, "We need a spirituality to sustain us." He quotes Pope John Paul II in describing this spirituality of communion, which includes "the ability to see what is positive in others... [to bear] each other's burdens... resisting... competition, careerism, distrust and jealousy... to make room for all the gifts of the Spirit... an organic blending of legitimate diversities . . ."[82]

The work of Cardinals Bernardin and Mahony and of Bishop Clark represents bishops who have a very positive valuation of the emergence of lay ecclesial ministers in the Church. Not all bishops share these views. For example, Bishop DiMarzio issued a pastoral letter, "Laity in the New Millennium." His topic is not ministry, nor lay ministry, but the broader conception of the laity's role in the Church. Bishop DiMarzio emphasizes the secular role of the laity, stating that the parable of the vineyard "stresses that there is a place for all of God's people in the vineyard, which is the kingdom of God in the world." He emphasizes the differences between the lay vocation and that of the ministerial priesthood, because though equal they are dissimilar, and sees a need for "more specificity about the identity of the laity and their primary role." The laity's mission is understood as being "accomplished primarily by engaging in the temporal affairs of the world." This is related to the call to holiness of all Christians; their holiness consists in a gift of self. "In the case of the laity, the gift of self takes place in family life and employment in the world. Without work in the world there is no holiness for the lay person because there would be no occasion for the gift of self." The value of the letter is its affirmation of the importance of the lay vocation and the reflections on the evangelization of the world, as well as its overview of the programs educating the laity in the diocese of Camden and the need for collaboration in pastoral ministry.[83] But there is no place in this vision for the role of the laity described by the Subcommittee on Lay Ministry as ecclesial lay ministers, called to their ministry in the Church.

Bishop DiMarzio's letter is also representative of the view of many bishops in their emphasis on the mission of laity to the world, and on the "secular character" of laity, both described in council documents and official writings since then. The concern about a blurring of the lay and clerical distinction is also relevant, echoing the Roman Instruction of 1997.

This overview documents the writings of some individual bishops. In addition, there are pastoral responses of many kinds in individual dioceses, shaped by bishops' desires to respond to the new reality of lay ministry. Efforts include guidelines for formation (especially for the role of pastoral associate) and for certification as a minister of the diocese (a different process from the granting of a certificate at the end of a program of study), mechanisms for incorporation into the organizational life of the diocese (examples include a diocesan council of lay ecclesial ministers and a diocesan *ministerium* for all ministers), and programs of financial aid designed for graduate tuition assistance.

CONCLUSION

In the last ten years, the bishops, individually and as a conference, have given considerable attention to the new ministers in the Church. They build on the documents of the Council and others promulgated since the Council. It is clear that for the most part they endorse and support the emergence of these new ministers, even as they struggle to understand what this means in light of church teaching, and how to respond pastorally to the reality in their own dioceses and in our country. The work of the subcommittee has provided significant leadership in this effort. The broad consultation and dialogue which they have both undertaken and sponsored has contributed greatly to the articulation of the issues, and some ways of understanding and responding to them. However, it must be noted that their report names the state of the questions. There is much work still to be done; the ongoing leadership of the bishops is very important.

NOTES

1. David N. Power, *Gifts That Differ: Lay Ministries Established and Unestablished* (New York: Pueblo Publishing Company, 1980), pp. 3–6.
2. *Ministeria Quaedam*, in Flannery, pp. 427–432.
3. Power, *Gifts*, p. 6.
4. Articles 18–24.
5. Articles 59, 66–70.
6. Article 73. It is worth noting that this quotation is used in the Universal Catechism (#910), in the discussion of the laity's participation in Christ's kingly office. Numerous canons are also quoted in the section on the lay faithful, including those regarding lectors, acolytes, catechetical formation, and the teaching of the sacred sciences (#903 and #906).
7. Ibid.
8. Quoted by James Provost, ed., in *Code, Community, Ministry* (Washington, D.C.: Canon Law Society of America, 1983), p. v.
9. Mary Moisson Chandler, *The Pastoral Associate and the Lay Pastor* (Collegeville, MN: The Liturgical Press, 1986), p. 26.
10. Provost (1988), p. 287. "Through its various documents, Vatican II made munus a significant ministerial word. However, the words *munus* and *munera* do not have precise English translations. Following the practice of some writers, in this study both words will be incorporated into English usage as they are and not cited as Latin." Elissa Rinere, "Conciliar and Canonical Applications of 'Ministry' to the Laity," *The Jurist* 47 (1987) n. 7, pp. 205–206.
11. Chandler, pp. 35–36.
12. *Code of Canon Law* (Washington, D.C.: Canon Law Society of America, 1983).
13. Cf. Richard G. Cunninghan, "The Laity in the Revised Code," in *Code, Community, Ministry*, pp. 32–37. See also Elissa Rinere, "The Term 'Ministry' as Applied to the Laity in the Documents of Vatican II, Post Conciliar Documents of the Apostolic See and the Code of Canon Law," (Unpublished dissertation, Washington, D.C.: The Catholic University of America, Canon Law.)
14. Robert L. Kinast, "U.S. Consultation: A Report," *Gifts*, Winter/Spring 1987, p. 11. A helpful summary of responses to the *Lineamenta* by

episcopal conferences throughout the world is given by Gerard O'Connell, "The Synod of Great Expectations," *The Month*, February 1988, pp. 530–539.

15. O'Connell, p. 537.

16. Robert L. Kinast, "The Working Paper and the U.S. Consultation," *Gifts*, Summer/Fall 1987, p. 10.

17. Peter Hebblethwaite, *National Catholic Reporter*, May 29, 1987, p. 26.

18. Archbishop John May, Joseph Cardinal Bernardin, Archbishop Rembert Weakland, and Bishop Stanley Ott, "What We Have Heard and What We Will Say," *Gifts*, Summer/Fall, 1987, p. 11.

19. "Working Paper for the 1987 Synod of Bishops," *Origins*, May 21, 1987, p. 10.

20. Gerard O'Connell, "The Synod on the Laity: Dichotomies or Distinctions?" *The Month*, March 1988, pp. 572–577.

21. Ibid., pp. 579–580.

22. Gerard O'Connell, "The Synod on the Laity: Riches in Diversity," *The Month*, May 1988, pp. 694–696.

23. O'Connell, "The Synod on the Laity: An Unfinished Agenda," *The Month*, August/September 1988, pp. 869–870.

24. Ibid., p. 872. The views of Cardinal Hume, a member of this group, which he had presented in an intervention, can be discerned here.

25. Peter Hebblethwaite, "Reports Reveal Curia Derailed Lay Synod," *National Catholic Reporter*, February 5, 1989, pp. 7, 26, 28.

26. Janet Somerville, "On Finding Pearls in a Fogbank," *Catholic New Times* (Canada), November 22, 1987, p. 6.

27. Sean O'Riordan, "The Synod on the Laity, 1987," *The Furrow*, January 1988, vol. 39, no. 1, p. 11.

28. *Origins*, November 12, 1987, vol. 17, no. 22, pp. 387–388.

29. Mary Frances Coady, "Burning Questions Unanswered at Synod," *Catholic New Times* (Canada), November 22, 1987, p. 1.

30. Articles 21, 22.

31. Susan Mader Brown, "The Most Precious Fruit Desired," *Canadian Catholic Review*, November 1989, pp. 371–372.

32. Article 23.

33. Brown, commenting on this section says, "A lay person can on occasion fulfill part of the pastoral role of a cleric, but to function in this way is not to exercise a 'lay' ministry any more than for a

priest temporarily to run the family business while a parent is ill is to exercise a 'pastoral ministry,'" p. 372.

34. Article 24.
35. Article 25.
36. Articles 58, 59, 63.
37. In *Origins*, November 27, 1997 (vol. 27, no. 24), pp. 397–399. A helpful reflection on the document is offered by Richard Gaillardetz, "Shifting Meanings in the Lay-Clergy Distinction," *Irish Theological Quarterly* 64, 1999, pp. 115–139. He explores differing perspectives on the question in council documents, one of which emphasized a contrasting approach. He suggests that current Church reality with diverse ministries such as those of DRE's and permanent deacons cannot be explained from this position and calls for a fuller pneumatological approach to resolve tension. The argument from "repositioning" presented here is expanded in his Collegeville seminar paper, as outlined in chapter 9 of this volume.
38. Ibid., pp. 399–400.
39. Ibid., pp. 400–402.
40. Ibid., pp. 402–407.
41. *Origins*, November 27, 1997, pp. 399–401, and personal notes.
42. *The Evangelist*, March 5, 1998.
43. "Introduction: To Build and Be Church," *Gifts*, Bishops Committee on the Laity (Washington, D.C.: United States Catholic Conference, 1983), p. 2.
44. Dolores Leckey (executive director of the staff working with the Bishops Committee on the Laity), "Developments in Lay Ministry," *Origins*, vol. 8, no. 16, 1978, p. 246.
45. "Midwest Bishops at the Vatican," *Origins*, vol. 8, no. 3, 1978, pp. 43–44.
46. *Called and Gifted: The American Catholic Laity*, National Conference of Catholic Bishops (Washington, D.C.: United States Catholic Conference, 1980), pp. 1, 4–5.
47. Suzanne E. Elsesser and Eugene F. Hemrick, *Preparing Laity for Ministry* (Washington, D.C.: United States Catholic Conference, 1986), "The Report at a Glance," pp. 1–4.
48. Ibid., "Introduction."
49. *Called and Gifted for the Third Millennium*, National Conference of Catholic Bishops (Washington, D.C.: United States Catholic Conference, 1995), pp. 1, 16, 17. Note the change in nomenclature,

from ecclesial ministers in the 1980 document to ecclesial lay ministers in 1995. One reason is that priests, of course, are also ecclesial ministers.

50. Ibid., pp. 17–18.

51. Minutes, Contemporary Lay Pastoral Ministry Project, September 21, 1988.

52. Murnion, pp. 1–3.

53. Minutes, NCCB Committee on the Laity, Subcommittee on Lay Ministry, June 20, 1994. (Henceforth, Minutes.)

54. Minutes, November 14, 1994.

55. *Lay Ministry Update: A Newsletter for U.S. Bishops.* Sponsored by the NCCB Subcommittee on Lay Ministry, vol. 1, no. 1, January/February 1996 and vol. 1, no. 3, May/June 1996.

56. *Lay Ministry Update*, vol. 1, no. 4, July/August 1996.

57. Minutes, March 17, 1996, and personal observations.

58. Minutes, November 9, 1996.

59. Murnion and DeLambo, p. 58.

60. Minutes, March 16, 1997.

61. Minutes, June 1998, and *Lay Ministry Update*, March/April 1998.

62. *The State of the Questions*, p. 55.

63. *Lay Ministry Update*, Summer 1998, and personal notes.

64. Ibid.

65. Ibid., and *State of the Questions*, p. 59.

66. *Lay Ministry Update*, Summer 1999 and *State of the Questions*, p. 47.

67. *Lay Ministry Update*, November/December 1999. Another structure for inclusion of lay ecclesial ministers is found in Oakland. Bishop Cummins formed a consultative body of lay ecclesial ministers similar to and collaborating with the Presbyteral Council, the Deacons Council, and Diocesan Pastoral Council.

68. *State of the Questions*, pp. 7–8.

69. Ibid., pp. 14–21.

70. Ibid., pp. 25–27.

71. Ibid., pp. 42–43.

72. Ibid., pp. 48–49.

73. Ibid., pp. 54–55.

74. For a brief overview of the consultation, see *Lay Ministry Update*, November/December, 2001.

75. *Decisions for the Future of Our Church*, Joseph Cardinal Bernardin, Spring 1994 (no publication information given), pp. 1–3, 6–9.

76. Chicago: Liturgy Training Publications, 2000, pp. 14–17.

77. Ibid., pp. 15–16.

78. Ibid., pp. 4–13.

79. Ibid., pp. 18–36. See also Cardinal Mahony's remarks, "Charting a Course for Participation in Ministry," *Origins*, April 5, 2001, vol. 30, no. 42, pp. 669–676.

80. Bishop Matthew Clark, "The Relationship of the Bishop and Lay Ecclesial Ministers," *Origins*, vol. 30, no. 42, April 5, 2001, p. 677.

81. Ibid., p. 678. Bishop Delaney of the Diocese of Forth Worth has such a "ministerium" in his diocese.

82. Ibid., pp. 678–681.

83. "Laity in the New Millennium," *Catholic Star Herald*, January 4, 2002, pp. 9–13.

✠

PART THREE

An Agenda
for the Future

INTRODUCTION

In many ways, the Second Vatican Council is the precipitating event for the development of lay ministry today. Therefore, it is fitting that a methodology that emerged in the Council suggests a way for reflecting more deeply on the reality of the new ministers in our midst, and then asking the question, what do these developments call us to, as a Church. The method is utilized in the final document of the council, the *Pastoral Constitution on the Church in the Modern World.*

Some history helps to set the context. Initially, laity had no role in the work of the Council, not even as consultors. It is almost as though the initial work of the Council, the constitutions on the Liturgy and the Church, needed time to be interiorized, time for the implications to emerge. In a Church which is not simply clergy and laity, but first and most important, People of God, the idea of a role for the laity became clearer. By the time of the third session when the pastoral constitution was discussed, the role of laity as official participants, both by their presence and through their voice, was helping to shape the perspective of the bishops. The focus of attention in the document is *ad extra*, turned toward the world, and not considering only the inner life of the Church.

The document begins with a reminder that the Church always has "the responsibility of reading the signs of the times."[1] The vision is of the need to discern how God is acting in human history, how human deeds and human action are embodying the ideals of the gospel.[2] So the introduction to the constitution first ponders the situation of humanity today. At the time the document was written and debated, some thought that such a description would be useless, because it would only be valid for a few years; others thought it inappropriate to include this in a theological document. Nonetheless, this is the method of thinking adapted both in the opening section, and in the introduction of the different chapters of the second part. "(T)he basic attitude . . . [is] one of facing reality, of looking at the facts before making a judgment." (In some ways, the method is similar to that developed in the Christian Family and Young Christian Workers movements, "see, judge, act.")[3]

Pope Paul VI advocated using such a method for reflection when he analyzed the development of diversified ministries among the laity. He noted that laypeople may feel themselves called to service side-by-side with the ordained ministries, offering a particular service to the Church. He acknowledged that the story of the origins of the Church is very illuminating, and that the experience of ministries at that time can be helpful to us today. However, he cautions that,

> Attention to the sources has to be complemented by attention to the present needs of mankind and of the Church. To drink at these ever inspiring sources without sacrificing anything of their values, and at the same time to know how to adapt oneself to the demands and needs of today—these are the criteria which will make it possible to seek wisely and to discover the ministries which the Church needs and which many of her members will gladly embrace for the sake of ensuring greater vitality in the ecclesial community.[4]

Pope Paul VI helps us realize more fully that this present reality comprised of both the new ministers themselves and the present needs of humanity and the Church calls for our attention. Church tradition may illuminate our present experience, may be helpful to us today—but may not hold the answer to the demands and needs of our times. Rather, Paul VI alerts us to the fact that present needs and demands call upon us to adapt ourselves, even as we maintain the values of our tradition.

The method described in the teachings of Paul VI and the Council shapes this book. Part I presented the reality of the new ministers and the response thus far of the Church to this development. The effort was made to relate this as descriptively, as objectively, as possible. (Of course, disposition, life experience, predilections all do color how we see, even what one sees, and bias certainly entered in unseen!) Part II turned to our tradition, both Scripture and recent church teaching, to understand better the Church's experience and understanding of ministry. In Part III the task now is to reflect on what has been presented and to try to discern, is this of God? What does it mean?

NOTES

1. *Pastoral Constitution on the Church in the Modern World*, 4.
2. M. D. Chenu, "The Signs of the Times," in *The Church Today: Commentaries on the Pastoral Constitution on the Church in the Modern World*, Group 2000, eds. (New York: Newman Press, 1968), p. 137. "It is as earthly events—with everything that implies—that they are signs. It is as such that the Church finds them open to the Gospel and to grace. They must be respected and expropriated."
3. Abbe Francois Houtart, "Suggestions for Doctrinal Development," in *Vatican II: An Interfaith Appraisal*, John H. Miller, ed. (Notre Dame: University of Notre Dame Press, 1966), p. 546. "This method of thinking, perhaps new for some theologians, should be more greatly developed in other theological fields, too, for example, ecclesiology: the study of the different institutions of the Church (the parish, religious congregations, the Roman Curia, the lay apostolate) . . ." (p. 547).
4. *Evangelii Nuntiandi*, 73.

CHAPTER SIXTEEN

THE INTERSECTION OF PRESENT EXPERIENCE AND THE TRADITION

INTRODUCTION

Our tradition is a living one, rooted in the experience of the historical Jesus and those who first gathered in community around him, and animated through the centuries by the Spirit of the Risen Lord. Therefore, we may look for the action of our living God in our collective story as well as in our present experience as a Church. Indeed, we may look at all of human history, past and present, for signs of God's work among us, the God who creates and liberates and sanctifies. As we try to answer the question, are the new developments in ministry part of God's unfolding plan in our community, we need to ponder both our present lived experience and our prior history, both the scriptural record and the further unfolding of our story as encoded in history and official documents. It is as the new realities and our prior history intersect that we can try to discern: is this development faithful to our past? how has the past inspired and shaped it? how does the past critique what is happening? are there ways in which the present experience is a new evolution, a new expression, born of the Spirit?

DIVERSE MINISTRIES AND MINISTERS

THE MINISTRY OF THE CHURCH

The dominant image of the Church that has emerged from the Second Vatican Council is that of the People of God. The council fathers used many images to reflect on the mystery of the Church, but this one is sometimes named as one of the great achievements of the council. It is certainly the one that has captured the popular imagination. Implicit in the image are two perspectives on ministry—historically, it focuses on the communal life of the immediate followers of Jesus Christ, wherein all shared in diverse ways in building up the community; today, it focuses on the shared mission of the whole community in the ministry Jesus began, and which is continued throughout history in the power of the Spirit.

In the period before the council, the understanding of ministry, and of the apostolic tradition, was of a singular reality, vested in its fullness in the bishops. Today the focus is on the whole Church as the recipient of the mission and ministry of Jesus, and of the apostolic tradition. The ministry of individuals, whether ordained or not, can only be understood when situated within "the context of the ministry of the whole Church of Christ. It can . . . only be understood as ministry in service to the Church, and within the Church, to enable it to exercise its common priesthood."[1]

It is within this context that the unfolding of lay ministry in the Church is understood today. For example, the report by the United States Bishops National Advisory Council gives as the explanation for the expansion of lay involvement since Vatican II "the heightened awareness of the Church as a community of believers."[2] This understanding flows from the teachings of Vatican II, perhaps most especially, chapter 2 of the *Dogmatic Constitution on the Church*.

The data regarding the new ministers presented in chapter 4 suggest that they are instrumental in developing a more ministerial church. They invite people into various roles, and the people say yes. They also form committees, planning teams and advisory boards, giving a broader group of laity a part in shaping and implementing the mission of the local community.

Furthermore, one could view the new parish ministers as themselves a sign of the ministry of the whole Church. The great majority of them had prior involvement in ministry, usually as volunteers, before they began their salaried work. Many now work only part time, combining their ministry with other responsibilities. Overwhelmingly, they agree that they would work as volunteers, if they left their church positions. A significant number each year do leave salaried church work, returning to the ranks of "ordinary" laity.[3] These facts, especially when viewed together, help to show how these people blur, in their persons and their work, the once sharp distinctions between those who minister and those who are ministered to. They are a sign of the ministry of the whole Church.

The emergence of lay ministers from the community has precipitated much recent theological discussion. O'Meara's perspective is helpful for describing the new ministers. He holds that the Spirit is given to the Church, and ministry is grounded in the response of an individual to the call of the Spirit. The Spirit gives charisms to the community and the individual, which result in ministry, in service. "A sign of living as a Christian is to have at times in one's life charisms which are ministry . . . There can be charisms ranging from momentary inspirations to life-long decisions fraught with risk."[4] The new ministers have had more than momentary inspirations—but their present form of ministry is not a permanent option for many of them. They are part of the whole community, which is gifted by the Spirit to serve the Kingdom.

One danger that exists is that the understanding of ministry, which the scriptural tradition and Vatican II affirm as belonging to the whole Church, again be narrowed to a few ministers—clergy and the new ministers. Two facts noted in one study could contribute to this: the great emphasis placed on professional training and competence by lay ministers (a good in itself, but it could make professional and minister co-extensive) and their tendency to confer primarily with the pastor and staff in making decisions in their work. At the present time, this narrowing does not seem to be occurring—but it could.

A parallel exists in regard to the role of the assembly and of special ministers in liturgy. The *Constitution on the Sacred Liturgy*, article 14, affirms that "the entire body of the faithful has been summoned to participation in it as the priestly people of God. . . " And yet, article 29 names laypeople with a special role in the liturgical celebration: servers, readers, commentators, and members of the choir.[5] It is possible (and in some parishes is the case) that the special roles become, virtually, the only ones, with the laity in general passive spectators at liturgy. However, the problem is not the special roles themselves, but the way they are performed. For the whole community to share actively in liturgical celebration, and in ministry, requires understandings, attitudes, and practices by special ministers that foster the participation of all.

DIVERSE MINISTERS

The history of ministry can be viewed in two ways. O'Meara takes one perspective, saying that throughout the history of the Church there has been an expansion and a diminution of numbers and kinds of ministers. For example, for him, the growth of the monasteries and subsequently of the mendicants each represented an expansion of ministers.[6] This view is rooted in his definition of ministry, which stresses that it is public activity on behalf of the community[7]—he does not add the word *official* to his definition. In the second perspective the emphasis is on official ministry in the Church. From that viewpoint, Coriden sees the present dispersion of ministerial roles as something unparalleled since the third century. He says that there has been, since the fourth century, a limitation and diminution of ministries, which went hand in hand with their absorption into priestly office. For him, only a symbolic residue of a once broader ministerial life remained, in the minor orders.[8]

While O'Meara's view is more comprehensive, taking into account many aspects of the Church's experience in the New Testament and subsequent history, Coriden's view is representative of ideas that have shaped the understanding of ministry in the Church, even until today. That is why the contemporary "explosion of ministries" is greeted with such excitement, and why lay ministers see their involvement as radically new. Therefore, while affirming the broader definition of O'Meara, Coriden's perspective will be used to focus the diversity of ministers in the Church today.

First, we know that there are significant numbers of laypersons in the Church in leadership roles, performing many functions which twenty-five years ago were almost always performed only by clerics. Second, contemporary theologians, the American bishops, and the lay ministers themselves view their work precisely as ministry. Third, in a way not known since our earliest history, authority in the Church is shared with women in ministry. Finally, while the largest number of the new ministers are religious educators, pastoral ministers, and youth ministers, there are diverse roles exercised in different parish communities. In addition, the many Catholic institutional ministries (chaplains, campus ministries) add to this diversity.

One characteristic of the New Testament period was that different roles were emphasized in different churches, for example, scribes in the Matthean community. Furthermore, one of the teachings of Vatican II was the affirmation of the uniqueness of the local church, and its part in evolving appropriate responses to the gospel. The kinds of roles that have grown up in the American church reflect concerns and styles of this culture. The emphasis on children and youth both in parishes and on campuses, the use of such skills as administration, program development, and pastoral counseling are all very American. They are an expression of ways the American Church sees and responds to contemporary pastoral needs.

There is another aspect of the diversity of ministers which is also related to American culture. In the United States, we are experiencing an increasing specialization in all of the professions, and much of the work of labor. Medicine, for example, now utilizes teams of doctors with varying specialties as well as various technicians and nurses in the treatment of each major disease. Hospices work with teams that include a nurse, a social worker, and a chaplain. The chaplain is expected to have specialized training and competence. In light of cultural developments it is interesting to note that lay ministers in one study chose as the primary explanation for their employment: "there is a recognized need for certain areas of specialization which laity are trained for." Their second reason expresses a similar perspective from a theological standpoint; "there is recognition of a variety of gifts given to various members of the community."[9] That they see the second most important source of their authority as their professional training and competence is a related finding.

While is it true that in the New Testament period we do not find a clarity regarding functions, it does appear that, for example, there is a difference between the central functions of the prophets and the teachers, or the prophets and the deacons. And, in a society as complex as our own, diversification of roles, to some extent by functions, is taken for granted. However, one survey shows that when given a list of eighteen possible functions in ministry, most parish ministers checked most of the functions, suggesting little differentiation in practice. Another survey indicates that while some differentiation in leadership for areas of ministry can be discerned related to roles, there is far more overlap in terms of involvement in various areas.

However, the New Testament provides another insight regarding diversity of roles: sharp delineations generally did not occur. This is seen, for example, in the fact that various ministers probably presided at Eucharist. Today, too, DRE's, pastoral associates, and youth ministers share many areas of responsibility, both in individual parishes and also in these fields in general. However, without any delineation, theological confusion and ministerial burnout occur.

One aspect of the development of lay ministry is disturbing: poor parishes are not served by employed lay ministers. The issue is certainly at least in part an economic one. As the pattern of more lay ministers and fewer clergy becomes more pronounced in the future, this will be a serious problem. Just as the Church has found ways in the past to fund an official ministry in every parish, she will need to find ways to address this question as well.

In conclusion, it is clear that a perception of the past, that the sacrament of orders had swallowed all ministries, is not true today. The diversity of ministers, men and women, found in the Church bears a resemblance to the diversity in the New Testament period. And, as in our earliest history, the rapid evolution presents a scenario in which much is not yet well differentiated.

DIVERSE MINISTRIES

Contemporary theology has different ways of schematizing the many ministries of the Church, the diverse ways she builds up her own life and serves the world. Whether the highly nuanced development of Cooke or the pastorally focused presentation of *A Vision of Youth Ministry*, each provides a way of listing discreetly what in the New Testament was generally described phenomenologically. Here, five "namings" of ministries, chosen from five distinct sources, will help illuminate contemporary developments: ministry as sacramental/liturgical, as stewardship of the tradition, as community building, as prophecy, and as caring for society.

From the sociological viewpoint, the picture of ministry that emerged as particularly Roman Catholic (and Orthodox and Anglican-Episcopal as well) was that of ministry as sacramental-liturgical.[10] Here, the role of priest is emphasized, and, generally speaking, other functions are considered less essential than the primary exercise of the priest's ministry, celebration of the Eucharist. When parish lay ministers were surveyed, overwhelmingly they saw the celebration of the Eucharist as the most important function of the priest's ministry. Preacher (probably meaning homilist at liturgy) was named second. The function named most often as essential for their own role was teacher; this was fifteenth in their listing for priests. The understanding operating here could be this: the priest's functions are those forbidden to lay ministers. And conversely, those functions important in the ministry of professional church workers are not central to priestly ministry. Theologically, this is not a sound way to resolve the issue. But, since practice does influence theology, it could become the basis of an inadequate theology of ministry.

A second ministry of the Church is stewardship of the tradition. This is a ministry distinct from both supervision and leadership in the community; the teachers of the early church were described as performing this ministry.[11] It is particularly focused on the handing on of the tradition. The roles of many of the new parish ministers have this as an essential characteristic. The value that they give to the function of teaching, and the focus of their responsibility on children and youth, and, increasingly, adult formation, indicates this. This ministry was a particular function of the teacher-scribe of Matthew, a distinct ministry with its own valuation in the community. Perhaps today we need to recognize particular ministers as responsible for this function. The established lay ministry of lector could be developed along these lines, a development which the South American bishops are exploring in their conference.

The ministry of community building is described by Cooke. He sees the creation of a community as the continuing work of the Church.[12] Vatican II stresses the communal life of the Church in its choice of the image, People of God. The lay ministers surveyed saw community builder as their primary function—and the second most important for priests. The high valuation placed on this function is rooted in biblical and Vatican II teachings. However, the experience of contemporary life in the United States highlights the need for this work. In our highly mobile society, many experience loneliness and alienation. Ethnic neighborhoods, which once provided a communal focus, have declined, and geographically (and in many others ways) American Catholics have moved into the mainstream. (The pattern in Hispanic and new immigrant communities is different.) Sociologists today speak of associational (meaning intentionally chosen) rather than communal churches.[13] Reading the signs of the times suggests that ministers must intentionally build community, just as reading Scripture and Vatican II suggest that they should. Their high valuation of community building shows that lay ministers know this. Liturgists and music ministers, DRE's and youth ministers, priests and pastoral associates all contribute to community building.

Prophecy was an important ministry, especially in the New Testament period, and surely prophets have continued to be active in the Church throughout our history.[14] However, prophecy is not seen by lay ministers as essential for their work, and is accorded last place for priests. The functions of teaching and priesthood on the one hand, and prophecy, on the other, while they can be combined in one person, do have a basic tension between them. For example, for lay ministers, employed by pastors and parish communities, and with little security in their position, the function of prophecy would be a difficult one to undertake. (Of course, it is never easy!) In the past, great prophets have often been members of communities of vowed religious. Perhaps that will be the usual context for this ministry. However, in the ordinary life of the community, the function of prophecy may well be exercised by various individuals, at different times. The key issue is an awareness of the importance of prophecy in the Church and an attentiveness for the voice of the prophet, a task for all ministers. This very perspective helps to keep alive the realization of diverse ministries in the community, and the role of the whole community in ministry.

Ministry as caring for society is the image presented by Kinast. Many new ministries in the Church offer pastoral care to human need. Murnion's study indicates that the increasing numbers of pastoral associates often have responsibility for social services, home visiting, and ministry to the elderly. Some communities have ministers responsible for counseling, care of the sick, and social action. Those who minister within Catholic institutions such as hospitals, AIDS's hospices, and inner-city schools are "caring for society." Older ministries which are now often formalized and bureaucratized under the umbrella of "Catholic charities" are institutional ministries which serve "the world," as are the majority of inner-city Catholic schools. Even in missionary work, much activity is focused toward the human, social needs of those the missionaries wish to evangelize. Such ministries blur the distinction between ministry to the church community and ministry to the world. They represent an aspect of ministry with a long history in the life of the Church, but one which the *Pastoral Constitution* of Vatican II calls us to with particular urgency, in our service not only within the Church, but to the world.

In conclusion, it is clear that today there is a great diversity of ministries. A question which emerges from such an overview is, what is proper to the ministry of the priest? Greater clarity about the ministries of the laity will require further specification of the ministry of the ordained.

MINISTRY AS *DIAKONIA*

The most distinctive aspect of the New Testament record regarding ministry is its choice of language: ministry is *diakonia*, service. Vatican II articulated this value in many ways. One striking example is the designation of bishops as "servants to their brethren,"[15] a change from language emphasizing powers to one emphasizing service. Contemporary theologians clearly emphasize the servant dimension of ministry.[16] The impact of this theological emphasis can be observed by contrasting the 1972 and 1977 publications of the United States Catholic Conference on priesthood. In the former, the idea of service is not really developed; the latter is entitled *As One Who Serves*, and has this as its central theme.[17] There is evidence of the valuing of the ideal of service by lay ministers. There is also evidence of some attitudes that are in tension with this ideal.

In the New Testament, ministry is service of Christ and of one's brothers and sisters. It is true that a manifestation of service of Christ will be precisely in service of others. However, the central role given by lay ministers to personal faith, vocation, and ministry is suggestive of the underlying motivation, service of Christ. Perhaps it is because this is so that 90 percent of parish ministers say they are happy in their work, despite the significant frustrations that are sometimes present.

Service has as an essential quality of attentiveness to the needs of others. The etymology of the word *ministry*, rooted in the idea of serving at table, or being at the disposal of others to serve their needs, underlines this aspect of the meaning of service. Eighty-seven percent of youth ministers said that they were drawn to their work because of their concern for youth and their needs. In identifying what gives general guidance to how they plan their work, 55 percent of parish ministers named the needs of the people first, 87 percent ranked this in their first three choices; only 6 percent omitted it entirely.

Studies have not been done that evaluate how ministers learn about the needs of the people, nor how accurate their reading of the needs are. Those are questions related to the effectiveness and genuineness of service, and certainly would be fruitful issues to investigate. However, one finding in relation to parish ministers indicates that some recognize the importance of evaluation by those who are served; they seek evaluation from committees of parishioners, those who attend programs, the teens worked with, or the religious education board. Furthermore, when asked whose evaluation is most sought, those directly served was ranked highest, with 25 percent of the group placing this first. Additional evidence of the value lay ministers place on service is found in the locus of attention they have in regard to praise, critique, evaluation, and valuing of work done. Here, it is those they directly serve who are named most frequently, and parishioners in general who are the third most often indicated.

However, there are some findings that suggest a tension in regard to the ideal of service. In Scripture, service is seen in contra-distinction to emphasis on rank and status. The model is Jesus, dressed as a servant, washing the feet of the disciples at the Last Supper. When the parish ministers were asked how their work situation could be improved, one-fourth named as their first choice: "that my efforts are valued." An additional one-fourth ranked this second or third, making it the highest ranked answer to the question. Furthermore, the third ranked item was "that people thought more highly of my role"; here the issue of status is even clearer. (Granted, this was a forced-choice question, in that the issue was ways work could be improved.) Similarly some of the reasons given for developing competency standards include both the idea of providing greater clarity for the new roles, and increasing the status of the positions.

These issues of clarity of role and greater valuing of the new position are related to the fact that, in Power's terms, the work of the new ministers is "unestablished ministry." Kinast deals with a result of this in a perceptive manner. The context is his assessment of why laity have claimed the word ministry to describe what they do. He thinks an initial reason is that it suggests that their work is important. He says that they need others to recognize that importance, and support them in their work. However, he thinks that growth will come when the lay ministers can move beyond acceptance and evaluation by others, from "importance" toward "authenticity."[18] Perhaps the fact that Murnion finds the youth ministers, who are the youngest of the new ministers, least satisfied in their ministry is related to this need for affirmation, need for recognition, which reasonably would be most keenly felt by younger people.

Recognition is a human concern. (Granted, in the fullness of grace, one can transcend it.) How can the ministry of these lay ministers be truly recognized if a theology of priesthood is not developed, which differentiates but values the roles of clerical and lay ministers? How can lay ministers be affirmed if there is no formal recognition of their work by the community? How can they be fully recognized if appointment to their role is not ritualized in some way? The context proposed here is precisely service: recognition, so that people can be freed to focus their attention more completely on service. Personal spiritual growth is most important, but external forms can assist the possibility of that growth.

In conclusion, today we have recovered an understanding of the centrality of service, so much so that Vatican II recasts the traditional language of powers in the language of service. Both theological and pastoral writings emphasize *diakonia*. In the work of the lay ministers there are clear signs of the high value they place on the ideal of service to the community. However, there are also some signs of attitudes that could hinder the genuine performance of service. The journey toward servanthood is a central aspect of spiritual development. However, it is a journey, as is that of metanoia, which is never completed in this lifetime.

Ministry as Collegial

The centrality of collegiality, or co-responsibility, is clearly attested to in Scripture. An overemphasis on the hierarchical nature of the Church had overshadowed our appreciation of this principle of New Testament ministry, but the *Constitution on the Church* reaffirms its importance. As both the theological and pastoral literature of the post-Vatican II period show, what is affirmed in the council documents about the relationship of the pope and the bishops is gradually applied to the relationships among all members of the People of God.

The idea of collegiality is one that is particularly appealing to Americans. This point was made by Bishop James M. Malone, speaking as the United States delegate at a synod, in Rome:

> The expressions of collegiality in the episcopal conference of the United States are not just instances of those gimmicks and pragmatic contrivances for which Americans are thought to have a penchant . . . We see collegiality as embodied in our conference as an important service to evangelization.

How we relate to one another and work together as a conference does, indeed, reflect some typically American values and procedures. But wholesome values and procedures from our culture serve ecclesial communion and the proclamation of the Gospel of Jesus Christ, just as the wholesome values and procedures of any other peoples and cultures.[19]

However, at the present point in our history, we are only beginning to develop the kinds of practices and structures that could make us a really collegial Church.

An example of increased collegiality is found in the ways that the new ministers work with their pastors and the people. They affirm that they are delegated authority by the pastor, pastoral team, or parish council in their area of responsibility. In one study, 77 percent say that to a great extent they are granted authority for their work and that the large majority of staff members, parish leaders, and parishioners accept their authority. The number saying their authority is accepted very little or not at all is negligible. Furthermore, the new ministers invite others into ministry, and many say yes. Clearly both the leaders and the people are open to shared responsibility.

When analyzing other data a more mixed picture emerges. In making decisions in their work, the most valued voice is that of the pastor. Other professionals are second, along with parishioners. Furthermore, in making decisions, only 19 percent include parishioners in their decision-making process. This suggests a kind of behavior typical of many professionals, who most value the voice of other professionals. It is not a fully collegial style of ministry.

On the other hand there are various decision-making groups that lay ministers work with, have formed, and see as desirable. Seventy-five percent have personally formed some type of group for shared decision making. By these efforts, they are fostering collegiality. But, if they don't sufficiently value the work of these groups, as their tendency to make decisions with fellow staff members suggests, this could be a negative rather than positive development, breeding disillusionment and frustration in the people.[20]

One cause of difficulty for collegial working together is the varying educational settings for lay ministers and priests. Traditional seminaries are more hierarchical in their organization, and hence their modeling, than newer educational settings in dioceses and universities. The socialization processes differ; consequently, behavioral expectations differ. As we strive to become more collegial, more collaborative as a Church, bridging such differences will be important.

In conclusion, we see that today, the logical outcome of a Church that is the People of God is being explored by experimenting with various collegial practices and structures. A collegial style is rooted in our scriptural tradition and affirmed by the council. However, there are tensions between lay ministers' ideal (they highly value collegiality in the Church) and their practice (only a small number make decisions with parishioners). Another example is their desire to work with shared decision-making groups, and their commitment to form them, yet their penchant for actually making decisions with the pastor and/or staff. Neither the lay ministers nor the universal Church have yet embodied the fullness of the vision of a collegial community, in which all the baptized actively participate.

CHARISM AND ORDER

CHARISM

Vatican II develops the scripturally rooted concept of charism, especially in the *Constitution on the Church*. For example, we read: "There is only one Spirit who, according to His own richness and the needs of the ministries, distributes His different gifts [i.e., charisms] for the welfare of the Church."[21] It is apparent from reading the commentaries on the documents that the Fathers struggled with the idea of gifts given to the laity, and at times seemed afraid to affirm them.[22] However, that the whole People of God is gifted by the Spirit with charisms is a teaching of the Council, even if the link with ministry is often not made.[23]

In relation to charisms given to individuals, the Church has two responsibilities. "They [pastors] must make a judgment about the true nature and proper use of these gifts, not in order to extinguish the Spirit, but to test all things and hold fast to what is good."[24] While the first point is clearer—pastors must judge the genuineness of charisms, and their proper use—a second point is also made here: the gifts are not to be extinguished. Translated colloquially one could say: those with gifts should not have wet blankets thrown on them, or, gifts must be fostered, even as a flame must be fanned so it will not go out.

Most lay ministers do not hesitate to affirm their charisms: 74 percent say they have charisms; only 6 percent say they do not. It would be interesting to study further those who say that they are unsure. We cannot affirm our own gifts unaided. The scriptural tradition and the early church stress the role of the community in discerning the genuineness of a charism. Vatican II stresses the role of the pastors in this respect. Perhaps those who say they are unsure about having a charism have not been affirmed in their ministry.

Of course, it would also be worth studying further those who say they *do* have a charism, to discern whether the judgment is simply their own, or one confirmed by the Church. To some extent, it would seem that confirmation is present, because the great majority had worked in the Church as volunteers, priests, sisters, or seminarians before their employment. In effect, that was a period of testing. Second, the great majority were invited into ministry, an implicit recognition of some gift. Third, in one study only 10 percent had been employed for less than one year. Therefore, the commitment by the parish, whether formal or informal, has been ratified, a sign of affirmation of charism, whether named as such or not. Charisms are an aspect of the baptismal call, and the origin of ministry. Lay ministers say that their authority for their work derives from their baptism. Two-thirds of the group named this among their first three choices, when rank ordering reasons for their authority. They did not see their authority as derived from the priest.

There is a danger in an overly individualistic emphasis on charism, in that the individual charismatic may undervalue the role of the community in naming, nurturing, judging, and using charisms. Perhaps an understanding of the danger lies behind the hesitation with which Vatican II handles charisms. Two findings in one study suggest possible cause for concern.

First, when naming that which gives general guidance to the planning of their work, the second highest ranked reason is their own faith. Sixteen percent of the group named this first, 58 percent included it in their first three choices; only 17 percent omitted it entirely from their ranking. Furthermore, comparatively speaking, the tradition of the Church and the teachings of the pope and the teachings of the bishops were omitted from their choices by 37 percent, 51 percent, and 47 percent, respectively. Especially in light of the role lay ministers play in the stewardship of the tradition, that so many completely omit these items from their ranking is sobering.

Second, when ranking what gives them authority for their work in the Church, the third ranked reason is vocation. For priests, they give this as the first ranked reason. While we do not know how the lay ministers understand this term, its usual association with a personal call from God to the individual is certainly a possible interpretation.[25]

In conclusion, in Scripture, charism and ministry are intimately linked. At Vatican II, hesitantly, the gifts of all, clergy and laity, were affirmed. In the lived life of the community, the charisms of the laity are implicitly affirmed, because lay ministers are employed in ministry. The self-understanding of lay ministers includes an affirmation of their own charisms, and, for most, a rooting of their ministry in baptism. However, emphasis by some on personal faith and vocation could indicate some over-individualization of ministry. Perhaps this emphasis is inevitable while there is no formal way of incorporating the new ministers into the body of official ministers.

ORDER

The concept of order may be understood either in a broad sense, to designate a regulation of ministries, or in a narrow sense of the designation in the community for a particularly defined official ministry. Until recently, questions of order predominantly involved the narrower definition of the word. In recent years, new questions began to emerge, arising from the actual life experience of the Church—the reality of lay ministers active in the mission of the Church. The issue now involves the broader understanding of order, the regulation by the Church of her ministries.

Is the Church regulating the new ministries? In the case of parish ministers, the fact that they are employed by pastors and accepted by the people represents a certain recognition and affirmation of their ministry. The relationship of the Church to some other ministers, hospital chaplains, for example, is more ambiguous. Whereas at one time a hospital would hire a Catholic chaplain who was ordained (whose ministry, therefore, was regulated by the Church), today they may hire lay Catholic chaplains, whose credentials may be CPE (Clinical Pastoral Education) and a master's in theology, but who have no official link with the bishop.

Dioceses have certainly exercised a central role in the formation and credentialing of lay ministers. The majority of lay ministers hold diocesan certificates for their work. This means, first, that diocesan offices have recognized the significance of the grassroots development of lay ministry, and have moved to provide a regulatory mechanism (an ordering) for these ministries. It also means that the lay ministers have taken part in the programs offered—often funded by the parishes. The regulation offered by the diocese is accepted by the ministers, and the parish community. Murnion and DeLambo have noted that between 1992 and 1997 parish ministers report considerably more diocesan involvement in their placement than had been true five years earlier. This includes things such as recruitment, training, screening, and continuing education.[26]

Despite these facts, it would seem that most lay ministers would welcome another way of designating them as official ministers: 74 percent said they would choose a rite of installation for their role, if one were available. People who plan to stay indefinitely in ministry are especially interested in a rite of installation. An increasing number report some form of ritual designation, but no uniform and official mode is used.

Clearly, some ordering is present; however, a central aspect of ordering is not developed. The relationship of the new ministers with the bishop, and therefore, with the local church, is not established. Priests are ordained for a particular diocese, and pledge obedience to their bishop. Priests coming to a new diocese must seek the bishop's acceptance of their ministry. Lay ministers including parish ministers, chaplains, and Catholic school principals, have no formal relationship with the bishop or the diocese, and often receive no orientation to the life of the local church within which they minister.

But a further question is—should these lay ministers be ordained? Schillebeeckx examines what he calls the anomaly of the pastoral workers of our day, who function as leaders of communities, but "are not recognized as such theologically or in church order." His context is an exploration of the right of the community to Eucharist, but his discussion goes beyond this, probing the inconsistency of ministers who are accepted by the community, who perform ministerial functions, and yet who are not officially recognized by the Church.[27] The logic of his argument is that since these pastoral workers function as leaders of communities, they should be ordained.

O'Meara also raises the question of the appropriateness of ordination for persons involved in various aspects of the Church's ministry. What is distinctive about his approach is his analysis of a number of ministries, such as education and peace and justice, in addition to the ministry of leadership stressed by Schillebeeckx. His point is that, if a certain ministry is considered important by local or regional churches and particular ministers are prepared educationally and willing to make a lengthy commitment, they should be ordained. But they should be ordained precisely for a particular ministry.[28] What this implies is a variety of focal points within the sacrament of order, so that it includes more than priesthood, the deaconate, and the episcopate.

Do the lay ministers want to be ordained? The majority say no, they do not wish to be ordained priests. However, 15 percent of the women and 25 percent of the men said yes—if priests could marry. The question of ordination to a specific ministry, in O'Meara's sense, has not been explored in sociological studies. However, in light of the fact that the majority of those surveyed would choose a rite of installation, there probably would be an openness to this possibility.

The issues of installation or ordination have to do with the institutionalization of particular roles in the life of the Church. A related issue is the legal status of lay ministers, both in regard to the security of their positions and the financial remuneration for their work. From Vatican II, we read:

> The pastors of the Church should gladly and gratefully welcome these lay persons [who offer their personal service to apostolic associations and activities] and make sure that their situation meets the demands of justice, equity, and charity to the fullest possible extent, particularly as regards proper support for them and their families.[29]

The new Code of Canon Law also addresses this issue. "Canon 231, paragraph 2, talks about the right of laypeople who work for the Church to a living and family wage and to health insurance benefits and social security benefits."[30] Financial remuneration for lay ministers varies widely. One-third of the parish ministers do not find their salaries adequate for their needs. Fringe benefits are also a source of concern. Catholic lay ministers are not accorded official status civilly, unlike, for example,

Jewish cantors and some Protestant lay ministers, and therefore the Internal Revenue Service disallows tax-free housing for them. Their reason is that the Catholic Church does not have an official lay ministry.

A related issue is the availability of an effective due process procedure, for the protection of lay ministers. Many lay ministers do not know of such a procedure; perhaps some dioceses do not have one. Furthermore, they often do not see existing procedures as effective. Coriden states the problem succinctly:

> Any person assigned to an ecclesiastical office (now defined as "any function which is conferred with stability and is to be exercised for a spiritual purpose"—*Presbyterorum Ordinis*, 20) has the right to hold and exercise that office against any arbitrary intervention; the minister should not be transferred nor have his/her ministry curtailed without a showing of cause that such action is for the good of the community.

Only if a due process procedure exists is a mechanism for a showing of cause available.[31]

Of course, related to due process would be the establishment of an effective evaluation procedure for lay ministers—indeed, for all ministers. Again the point is well made by Coriden:

> Ministerial offices are not sinecures. Effective performance must be somehow measured and demonstrated. There is a grave need in the Church to develop good processes and accurate criteria for evaluation of performance in pastoral office. Accountability means periodic review of the minister's performance—by the minister, by the community served, and by peers . . . Standards should be carefully formulated . . .[32]

In conclusion, it can be seen that at the present time the Church is indeed regulating, to some extent, the new ministerial roles that have been assumed by laypersons. However, the lay ministers themselves, and various theologians, see a need for a more formal, official ordering of these ministries, whether by installation or ordination. Congar says:

. . . [n]ot only is there a distinction between personal life and public functions, but between the two you have the whole order of ministries, not only the ministries instituted as sacraments, strictly sacerdotal or episcopal ministries, but also those stemming from charisms sanctioned by a consecration of the Church. There is the ministry of teaching, a ministry to the sick, of liturgical action, of Catholic action, of missions and so on. These are true ministries. We should restore to our ecclesiology this notion of ministry, which in fact has been too monopolized by the priesthood of the ordained. I would have no objection to seeing these ministries consecrated by liturgical ceremonies and eventually by the imposition of hands, which is a polyvalent ceremony . . .[33]

CHARISM AND ORDER

Having considered each of these issues separately, it is also helpful to consider charism and order in relation to each other. Both principles were clearly present in the New Testament churches—even if one or the other received greater emphasis. We have seen that both charism and order are operative in the ministries of the laity. In fact, if, as was noted, one danger is an individualization of ministry, it is precisely its ordering by the Church that will preserve the communal character of these ministries.

However, in the ordering there is always a danger that legitimate charisms not be recognized, because of the limitations inherent in a human Church.

There is a contradiction, an opposition between [the Church's] constitutive moments: institution and prophecy. The Church needs an institutional ministry: this is its historical flesh and blood; without the institution there would be neither prophecy nor charism. But when the institution is touched by sin (and being borne by men, it is impossible for it not to be) the contradiction is produced: the institution pronounces charism its enemy . . . The verdict of the ministry on a particular charism is not infallible. This is possible because the Spirit, not the institution, is the origin of charism.[34]

All ministers need to understand this limitation of the Church, and even while willing to submit to the proper authorities, must be willing to maintain a vision of the service they are called to offer. Needless to say, assistance in discernment of spirits in such a situation is important.

Furthermore, the category of charism is more central to the life of the Church than that of order—especially when ministry is viewed as part of a theology of grace. The centrality of God's action in the life of the individual and in the community, an action of the Father, of Jesus, of His Spirit, as the sources of ministry, are what is at the center of the experience of ministry.[35] This centrality must be safeguarded.

One practical application of this is that those whose ministries are regulated, by informal or formal means, have a duty to discern, nurture, and safeguard the charisms of all in the community. An essential insight of our time is that the entire Church is ministerial. A role of designated ministers is precisely to enable the entire Church to minister.

In conclusion, there is a priority of charism, but a necessity of order, which is also an action of grace. This perspective is summarized well by O'Meara:

> Recalling the Pauline motif of building up the Body of Christ, the churches and their leaders find their office as a service of an active grace, a diaconal charism.[36]

NOTES

1. Alan C. Clark, "Forward," *Modern Ecumenical Documents on Ministry* (London: SPCK, 1975), p. viii.

2. "The Thrust of Lay Ministry," *Origins*, March 13, 1980, p. 222.

3. Robert Kinast perceptively comments: "And for those who do not stay in formal church ministry or who cannot find suitable work there, they can bring to secular occupations a new level of theological and ministerial competence. If this were to happen, it would represent a unique fulfillment of the original intent of Catholic Action. . . ," *Caring for Society: A Theological Interpretation of Lay Ministry* (Chicago: The Thomas More Press, 1985), p. 250.

4. O'Meara, 1983, p. 69.

5. Ibid., pp. 144 and 148.

6. O'Meara, 1983, pp. 95–128.

7. Ibid., p. 142.

8. James Coriden, "Ministry," *Chicago Studies* 15 (Fall 1976), p. 305.

9. Commenting on the redistribution and decentralization of ministerial functions, Coriden says, "It is impelled by a keener sense of need for more specialized and expert pastoral ministry, by an appreciation for individual charism, by an increased sense of co-responsibility and participation, and by a heightened awareness of the meaning of the baptismal commitment and membership in the Church," "Ministry," p. 306.

10. *Ministry in America*, David S. Schuller, Merton P. Strommen, and Milo L. Brekke, eds. (San Francisco: Harper & Row, 1980), p. 65.

11. Dillon provides this descriptive, "Ministry as Stewardship of the Tradition in the New Testament."

12. Cooke, chapters 1–7 (Part One), pp. 33–215.

13. "Communal and Associational Churches," James D. Anderson and Celia Allison Hahn in *Alban Institute Action Information*, September 1980, pp. 1–5.

14. Avery Dulles, "The Succession of Prophets in the Church," in *Apostolic Succession: Rethinking a Barrier to Unity*, Hans Küng, ed. (New York, Paulist, 1968), pp. 52–62.

15. *Church*, 18, p. 37.

16. See chapter 11.

17. *The Priest and Sacred Scripture* (Washington, D.C.: United States Catholic Conference, 1972); United States Catholic Conference, 1977.

18. Pp. 60–62. He says: "As lay ministers appropriate and exercise their gifts it becomes less important that others acknowledge their ministry. . . Of course, no one reaches such a level alone or all at once. Affirmation and support and feedback from others help to insure that one's actions are prompted by the Spirit and do liberate according to God's purpose. At this end of the continuum more energy can be spent exercising one's ministry and less energy spent securing recognition of one's ministry from others" (pp. 61–62).

19. "Synod Takes on Personality, Direction," *National Catholic Reporter*, December 6, 1985, p. 16.

20. Thomas Sweetser has indicated that there is often resistance by parishioners to decision making by their peers. They often view the pastor and staff as the ones who properly have power ("The Parish as Faith Community," *Chicago Studies*, vol. 16, no. 2, Summer 1977, p. 241). This does make the lay minister's task more difficult.

21. *Church*, article 7, pp. 20–21.

22. For example, Klostermann, p. 303.

23. Osiek develops this point well, especially pp. 41–42.

24. *Apostolate of the Laity*, p. 493.

25. Hervé-Marie Legrand comments on the modern conception of vocation as "too subjective, too individual, too little ecclesial." He sees it, objectively as "the appeal the community addresses to one or several of its members which it considers suited to the ministry, even if they have never wanted it." See "The Presidency of the Eucharist According to the Ancient Tradition," *Worship*, vol. 53, no. 5, September 1979, p. 438.

26. Murnion and DeLambo, p. 65.

27. Schillebeeckx, *Ministry*, pp. 140–141. For a fuller development, see chapter 8.

28. O'Meara, 1983, p. 152. For a fuller development, see chapter 8 of this volume.

29. *Laity*, article 22, p. 512.

30. Bertram Griffin, "The Parish and Lay Ministry," *Chicago Studies*, vol. 23, no. 1, April 1984, p. 56.

31. "Ministry," p. 313.
32. Ibid., p. 312.
33. *An Interfaith Appraisal*, p. 272. In "Pathfindings," he makes a similar point: "The plural noun [ministries] is essential. It signifies that the Church of God is not built up solely by the actions of the official presbyteral ministry but by a multitude of diverse modes of service, more or less stable or occasional, more or less spontaneous or recognized and when the occasion arises consecrated, while falling short of sacramental ordination," p. 176.
34. Dussel, p. 530.
35. O'Meara, pp. 176–184.
36. Ibid., p. 21

CHAPTER SEVENTEEN

NEXT STEPS

INTRODUCTION

Just as the discernment process outlined earlier in the book has been the work of many individuals and groups in the Church, so too decisions about what to do next in response to the new ministers will require action by many. This concluding chapter will suggest some possible next steps which build upon the work of discernment and analysis the Church has been engaged in. It takes as its starting point the conviction that the new ministers represent a genuinely new reality in the life of the Church. In the past, new forms of ministry arose at different points in history: when ministers lived in monasteries and rectories, the itinerant orders were born; when vowed religious lived in cloisters, active orders were founded to work in society. Today, over 30,000 laypeople are employed as ministers in parishes (an increase of 35 percent in the five years between 1992 and 1997), and many more in other settings, in leadership roles which once would have been performed only by priests. These ministers say they are called, define their work as ministry and claim their baptism as their authorization. Pastoral leaders have invited them into ministry, and the people are accepting them as chaplains, pastoral leaders, teachers, spiritual guides, counselors, and more. Although their emergence is not simply related to the decline in the number of priests and vowed religious, in light of that decline their service in the Church is invaluable. Colleges and universities, seminaries and dioceses, have prepared them for their role. Canonists, various church associations and organizations, liturgists, bishops, and theologians have all sought to understand and support this new reality. God promised, "I make all things new" (Rev. 21:5); in our time, new ministers have been called forth by the Spirit in the Church. What further response is needed to this new reality?

322

LIVE WITH THE AMBIGUITIES

Lay ministers working in the Church today are called to live with many uncertainties, ambiguities, and tensions. Some prepare for professional ministry, often bearing all or much of the cost, without clarity about employment possibilities; all serve the Church without official recognition; many strive to minister collegially with some who do not recognize their roles as ministerial; all minister in the Church without clear definition of their place; some serve long years and then are fired, often with no demonstration of cause. Furthermore, they work side by side with priests, for whom the patterns of employment, recognition, and ministerial identity are very clear indeed. On the other hand, they live side by side with family, friends, neighbors, for whom the dynamics of uncertainty, risk, and lack of recognition inherent in these examples is a fact of modern life. In light of these realities, the lay ministers are called to live with the ambiguities, indeed, to ponder them deeply so as to recognize the basic contours of human life present within them. (It is easy to say, "we have here no lasting city," but harder to make the connection between the impermanence of daily life and the invitation within it to live toward eternal life.) At the same time, they are called to grow in their ministerial identity, focused on the deep meanings of why they serve, whom they serve, and to what end. The ambiguities have the potential of contributing to spiritual growth.[1] But there is also a call to work toward a fuller acceptance of lay ecclesial ministry, to work toward a more just ordering of ministry, including the theological, organizational, and relational adjustments needed so that right relationships and just structures will be possible.

DEFINE THE NEW MINISTERS

This task will be a difficult one, for many reasons. It calls for delineation, establishment of boundaries, judgments about who falls within and who without the definition. Perhaps this is always difficult, but today cultural and ecclesial factors make it particularly hard. American society emphasizes egalitarianism, and often resists that which is perceived as in any way creating a special class. The Church today is struggling to reduce a once-deep division between clergy and laity, and resists development of distinctions. Often the new ministers desire to be defined only as lay minister—and emphasize that all in the Church are called to ministry. And, because this new reality has emerged without prior definition, we are confronted with a multifaceted development which poses many challenges to definition.

Why define? Why not simply allow the situation to continue as it has begun? Several reasons are worth considering. The first is drawn from leadership theory, which differentiates formal and informal leaders.[2] The latter are all those who perform leadership functions which assist a group in performing its task. In healthy groups, informal leadership is exercised by various persons at various times. In a vibrant Christian community, this is certainly true. A formal leader, on the other hand, is the one who is designated in some way as the leader, one who is granted the right and the responsibility of leading the group. The act of designation makes clear who has this right and responsibility for leadership. Furthermore, standards can be set which indicate appropriate qualifications, such as age, educational background, and appropriate experience, for one who would be designated as a leader. The advantage for a designated leader is that one does not have to begin by demonstrating competence and winning credibility, but can move forward leading the group in performing its task. (Experienced lay ministers who have observed the ready acceptance of newly ordained priests by the people, and compared this with the much longer, slower acceptance of their own often more mature leadership will recognize this illustration of leadership theory in their own experience.) The advantage for the community is that leadership can be exercised more effectively, assisting the group in its mission.

Another reason is from psychological theory, which holds that leaders are more effective when they are more differentiated from the group. This does not mean that a person should be separate from the group, but rather that the distinct role of the leader as not simply a member of the group must be adequately internalized by the leader.[3] Differentiated does not mean better than, though in a society and Church resistant to hierarchilization this may be the fear. We need a way for our new leaders to think of themselves in relation to those they lead which honors their being part of the group (for example, we are all the People of God) and yet allows for that differentiation which assists effective leadership.

Perhaps a helpful context for this analysis is the *Oxford Dictionary* definition for distinction: 1) One of the parts of a whole; a division, section; a class or category. . . 2) the action of distinguishing; the perceiving, noting or making a difference between things; discrimination. . . 3) something that distinguishes; a distinguishing mark, quality, or characteristic. Designation, differentiation require the making of distinctions. Just as the *Constitution on the Sacred Liturgy* identified some distinct ministries within the worshipping assembly, so the Church needs to identify new, distinct ministerial roles within the community. The new ministers are a category within the whole People of God; it will be necessary to perceive or note the differences between them and the community. What may be the distinguishing mark, quality, or characteristic?

Historically, it is through ritual that we have established distinctions in the Church: the ordination of a deacon, the public vows of a religious. Such rituals serve both the community and the minister, the process of designation allowing ministry, especially leadership in ministry, to proceed more effectively.[4] But in the present situation in which many new ministers have emerged and are exercising ministry without a formal ritual of installation, a prior task will be, precisely, definition. Who should be designated? And, as what?

The new ministers themselves, through their professional organizations, have been attempting definition in various ways, at times describing functions to be performed, at times competencies needed for a role. They are defining the roles that have emerged in the church in the United States, for example, director of religious education or youth minister. However, neither the language used nor the descriptions sufficiently root their definitions in the tradition of the Church.

Two other beginning attempts at definition made by the official Church more deliberately focus on the tradition. The first is the work of the bishops of South America, who are describing lay ministries in three categories: ministries of the Word, the Eucharist, and charity.[5] The first two they connect to the official lay ministries of lector and acolyte. The second attempt at definition is that of the United States bishops, who in 1980 used the title ecclesial ministers to describe "lay persons who have prepared for professional ministry in the Church." In 1995 they modified this language, saying ecclesial lay ministers, and listed a broad range of roles such as cantors, eucharistic ministers, teachers of young people, pastoral leadership of a parish, and serving in soup kitchens.[6] The title "ecclesial ministers" is more scriptural, and does not have the narrow connotations that lector and acolyte presently have in our country, but it does not indicate any specificity of ministry. Nor, given the variety of roles cited in the 1995 statement, is there clarity about whether ecclesial lay ministers are actually differentiated from the lay faithful in general. One weakness of this approach is that it does not functionally define the ministry these persons do. However, as the profiles of parish ministers show, the existing roles usually encompass a variety of ministries, and people move from one role to another as their journeys and local needs draw them in new directions.

The most recent document which offers a "definition" of lay ecclesial ministers is *The State of the Questions*. It identified characteristics which include: a fully initiated lay member of the Christian faithful (including vowed religious), responding to the gifts of the Spirit given in baptism and confirmation; one responding to a call to participate in ministry; one with the needed formation and education; one engaged in a specific ministry of ecclesial leadership, with community support and recognition, whose role is conferred by ecclesiastical authority, installed by the bishop or his representative; one committed in a stable manner who is either paid or a volunteer as a leader in a particular area of ministry. However, it then says "it is highly desirable that each of them be present to some degree in every minister," and that who fits into the category is determined by "the needs of the local church as well as the perspective and authority of its diocesan bishop." In other words, the document offers a description of some who might be designated lay ecclesial ministers by their bishops.[7] The paradox is that the language is now being used by people in the field to describe many different categories of lay ministers, from all ("it is the new word for lay minister," someone said) to a few, but in fact individual bishops have not officially designated lay ministers. The document offers what may be an ideal, but it does not *define*, as in "to fix or mark the limits of, demarcate; to make distinct, clear, or detailed in outline" (Webster's). By contrast, deacons are defined; one knows who is and who is not a deacon, and when and how one becomes a deacon. The clarity in relation to deacons (for the modern Church, a new reality since the council) stands in significant contrast to the ambiguities relative to the new lay ministers.

One aspect of the United States bishops' 1980 definition bears further reflection, "professionally prepared." (The 1999 *State of the Questions* does not use this language.) This emphasis is congruent with both the high level of education of increasing segments of American society and the norms of preparation for priests in this country. The Master of Divinity is the generally accepted credential for both Catholic and Protestant ordination. The majority of women religious in the United States are professionally credentialed for their varied ministries. In an increasingly educated society, it is appropriate that religious leaders have professional education, and this could serve as one norm for defining the new ministers. However, there are ways in which this norm would not be helpful. As we have seen, many of the new ministers acquire a credential of some kind only after they have been involved in a leadership role in ministry for some time. Furthermore, in minority communities, professionally prepared, employed lay ministers are not usual, though ministries are performed and leadership provided by gifted persons.

Another norm drawn from the Church's tradition which would be useful for a definition is what we could call stability. (The *State of the Questions* includes this characteristic in its description, speaking of "performing the duties of ministry in a stable manner.") Through our history this has developed in different ways. Benedictines emphasize a stability of place; both men and women belong to a particular monastery and only move if they go to establish a new house. Diocesan priests, too, are ordained for a particular place, a particular local church. Stability is not only a matter of space, but also of time; it is served by the fact that priests and deacons are ordained for life. Of course, the very founding of the itinerant orders, beginning with Francis, reminds us that the norm of stability is not an absolute, as does the tradition of temporary vows in religious life. In contemporary society, with its high level of mobility and lifespans many times what they were in the past, stability is recognized as being more problematic for us today.

What definition, then, might be helpful? First, the recognition that among the lay faithful there are those who are called precisely to full-time ministry in the Church. Although as members of families, citizens, neighbors, and at times persons of leisure, they live and function "in the world," their work is not within the "secular" realm. (A dichotomous view of world/Church, secular/sacred is not faithful to the vision of a God incarnate in human history, but as we have noted in earlier chapters this language does inform much reflection, official and other, about the laity, and so it is necessary to work with the existing terminology.) Some theologians (for example, Cardinal Ratzinger) would say that such a commitment to full-time ministry indicates the person is not lay, theologically speaking, and some (for example, Thomas O'Meara) propose they be ordained to a diaconate.[8] However, at this point in the history of the Church, there are many reasons why official lay ministers would be desirable.[9] For one thing, an additional category of ministers could help lessen the lay-clerical dichotomy. In addition, in the secularized culture of the United States, indeed, of much of the West, individuals who in their persons bridge the sacred-secular dichotomy would be valuable signs. Also, this would be in accord with our tradition which has evolved various classes of ministers at different points in our history, from monks to apostolic orders. It would give emphasis today to the diversity of ministers and ministries, which has been part of our history from the beginning.

The most helpful way to designate lay ministers as official ministers would be to petition Rome for another category of official lay ministers, a possibility already proposed in *Ministeria Quaedam*. Of course, this would only be a possible direction if women, too, would be admitted to official ministry. While the present regulation regarding lectors and acolytes excludes women, the 82 percent of the new ministers who are women calls for a way to include them. However, even if this were not granted at this time, the United States bishops could evolve a way to define and grant a semi-official status to the group. (This would parallel the semi-official standing of sisters and brothers.) A ritual of designation of some kind, common to all the dioceses of the United States, could be devised. The ritual would indicate that the person was formally authorized as a publicly recognized minister in the community.

This definition, then, envisions an official ministry entrusted to laypersons, a ministry rooted in their baptism that does not change their lay status. There is one role, however, presently held by laity which needs to be considered separately, that of the pastoral administrator of a parish without a resident priest pastor. In *Christifideles Laici*, Pope John Paul II affirms that pastors "ought to acknowledge and foster the ministries, the offices and roles of the lay faithful that find their foundation in the sacraments of baptism and confirmation." Many of the roles held by laity, as described in chapters 1 to 4, fit this description. However, then the pope says,

> When necessity and expediency in the church require it, the pastors according to established norms from universal law, can entrust to the lay faithful certain offices and roles that are connected to *their* [emphasis added] pastoral ministry but do not require the character of orders . . . [Here the Code is quoted, per exercising the ministry of the word, presiding over liturgical prayers, conferring baptism and distributing holy communion.] The task exercised in virtue of supply takes its legitimacy formally and immediately from the official deputation given by the pastors as well as its concrete exercise under the guidance of ecclesiastical authority.[10]

In light of Pope John Paul II's analysis, it would seem that the role of the pastoral administrator is significantly different from that of, say, a director of religious education. The latter role has its foundation in baptism; the pastoring of a parish, the role of primary leader in a church community on a day-to-day basis, properly belongs to the ordained. A layperson may be entrusted with that role, but only due to necessity, expediency, in virtue of supply. To group this role with the other emergent roles is to confuse two realities. That there are not sufficient priests to pastor all of our parishes is sad. That there are many new ministers filling various new roles in the Church is an "explosion of ministries" and a reason for joy. Ideally, pastoral administrators should be ordained; ideally, the new ministers should be officially designated. That an officially designated lay minister might serve as a pastoral administrator is reasonable. But if pastoral administrators were no longer needed, it would not mean that the new ministers were no longer needed.

A second aspect of a definition is that these new ministers would generally be professionally prepared, holding an advanced degree suitable for their work. However, it would be helpful to have a flexible approach to this. One interesting model to consider is found in Canon 9 of the Episcopal church which provides for the raising up of indigenous clergy "in communities which are small, isolated, remote, or distinct in respect of ethnic composition, language or culture." These priests are authorized to serve in their home parishes only, and are expected to work under mentors and to earn most or all of their living outside of the church.[11] Within the category of those who are designated as official lay ministers, the majority would be professionally prepared, but some could be designated for service of the community within which they emerged as leaders, or to which they were sent for particular reasons. On the one hand, such an approach risks the creation of two classes of ministers. On the other, it provides a way of responding to both the particular needs of minority communities and what now exists in terms of new ministers. The need is clear, and pastoral effort to minimize the human tendency to rank differences would lessen the risk.

Third, new ministers defined as part of this category would be those who chose to make a stable commitment to ministry. This need not be a life-time commitment, but would be for a set number of years. We have an ecclesial model for this with the temporary profession of vowed religious, and a societal one with term contracts for university professors. In both instances, three and seven year commitments are usual. In the case of professionally prepared ministers, the commitment would be to the local church; others could commit themselves to their home community.

What name should such a newly defined group be given? Lay ecclesial ministers has been chosen by the United States bishops, and is helpful.[12] The words are derived from Scripture (with the addition of the modifier lay) and are fairly straightforward in what they connote—those who serve within the Church, but are not ordained. Furthermore, this name is not presently used in such a way that deciding who would be so called would require taking the name away from someone who now holds it. It could be helpful to add a specification to this title, which would use ecclesial language for further defining a person in relation to his or her actual role and functions, and area of competence. For example, the titles "lay ecclesial minister for chaplaincy" or "lay ecclesial minister for teaching" may be somewhat long, but they do give greater clarity.

Who should be so named? Those who are professionally prepared (or designated for a particular community), who commit themselves to a period of service of some duration, and who are accepted by their bishop to be ritually designated as an official lay minister. The last part of this definition will be explored further in the sections that follow.

ESTABLISH A RELATIONSHIP WITH THE BISHOP

As the new ministers have emerged from the community, various ways of appointing them to their roles have unfolded. As we have seen, in parishes pastors generally do the hiring, sometimes in consultation with representative parishioners. (Increasingly diocesan offices offer various kinds of assistance in this process.) Occasionally, the appointment to the parish position is ritualized through a blessing or commissioning, using a format developed in the parish. Occasionally a bishop has adopted a ritual mode of appointing new ministers, sometimes modeled on the rite for the installation of a pastor. In hospitals and hospices, Catholic lay chaplains are hired by the institution. Similarly, in Catholic institutional ministries such as colleges and social service agencies, the search process and hiring procedures of the institution govern the manner of bringing new leadership personnel into their roles. There is a certain strength in this pattern, in that local communities and individual institutions, the ones most in touch with actual needs, are the primary agents in hiring. However, the Catholic Church through history has not been shaped by a congregational model, but rather by a model of local church, with the bishop as the center of unity. Presently, most bishops play little or no part in the incorporation of laypersons into the ministry and mission of their local churches.

This issue has theological, relational, and organizational aspects, all overlapping, but which for clarity can be somewhat separated conceptually. Theologically, O'Meara's presentation of the three interdependent sources of ministerial authority provide a framework for an analysis. He sees gifts or charisms, given by God (the Creator, in calling a particular person into being, the Spirit, in baptism) as one source. However, gifts must be discerned, so a validating call by the community represents a second source. But still authorization is not complete; a confirming recognition by an appointment to a leadership role is the third source.[13]

In a Church which has as one aspect of its life hierarchical organization, it is the third step that "inserts" an individual into the ordered life of the institution. (This can be understood as the repositioning delineated by Gaillardetz, outlined in chapter 9 of this volume.) This represents an acknowledgment of the reality that while ministry is not simply dependent on hierarchy, those involved in "official" ministry are under the authority of the hierarchy. (One must say "official" because at the present time the new ministers are not part of the official ministry of the Church, though that is the direction this argument proposes.)

Another way of conceptualizing this is in the traditional terms regarding official ministry in the Church, "called and sent." One is called by God, and perhaps by the community, and the community validates the call. Then one is sent by the official Church—designated, delegated in an official manner for a particular role in the Church. Although one could say that presently pastors fulfill this function when they hire lay ministers, traditionally it is the function of the bishop. The situation of persons serving in other roles, such as that of campus minister or hospital chaplain is even less clear than that of parish ministers, in terms of authorization from the official Church. Theologically, the situation of new ministers serving in roles once reserved to clergy, by tradition if not by law, calls for a way to establish a relationship of the bishop with the new ministers. A further question would be, which roles require such authorization? This will be explored further below.

Another way to consider the issue of the relationship of new ministers with the bishop is in terms, precisely of relationships. We realize today how much influence our social place has on our understandings, values, and attitudes. In part that is because our place somewhat determines our relationships, who our conversation partners are, and therefore how our vision of reality is shaped. If laypersons exercise significant leadership in the Church, what is their social place? If it is not in some way with other official ministers, bishops, priests, and deacons, their understandings, values, and attitudes will not be influenced by those relationships. (And conversely, neither will the other official ministers be influenced by them.) Furthermore, over time many will experience anger at the injustice of the marginalization they experience, in relation to the other formal leaders in ministry. This is, of course, a sensitive issue. Ministers are to be part of the community they serve, not over or against the community, but walking the journey of faith in the midst of the people. And yet, as leaders, their role is different, and differentiation is needed. In that differentiation, some identification will, naturally, be made with others in similar roles. (The various organizations of, for example, youth ministers and prison chaplains, attest to this.) However, without identification as well with the larger body of official ministers, fragmentation rather than unity is fostered. Because a primary function of the bishop is as the center of unity within his diocese, it is the establishment of a formal relationship with the bishop that will contribute to a greater unification of all the official ministers in the local churches. In a Church striving to be a *communio*, working to be collaborative, such unity is essential. Furthermore, a relationship will allow the bishop to offer the support, encouragement, and affirmation that the ministers indicate is a high-priority need.[14] Vatican II called on those in authority to judge the genuineness of gifts, not to extinguish the Spirit, but to hold fast to what is good. The role of the bishop in affirming the ministers in his local church is important.

Finally, one could consider this issue at the organizational level. A task of the bishop is leadership of the diocese in its fulfillment of its mission. To do this, the bishop delegates various tasks of leadership to others in the diocese—pastors, heads of various diocesan offices, directors of different institutional ministries. Generally, priests have been prepared for such roles through earlier work assignments that were often chosen precisely to test and develop leadership potential. As an institution, the Church has a responsibility to steward human resources in this way. Today, however, some of the roles once filled by priests are often being filled by laypeople, but seldom have such leaders been deliberately groomed for their jobs, as part of a comprehensive vision of the personnel available to the bishop to help in the work of that local church. Of course, here, too, there are dangers. "Careerism" is a term used pejoratively in church circles, and there is a danger that individuals could develop a careerist mentality. Also, in a highly mobile society, many lay ministers do move from one diocese to another. Especially in light of the fact that so many new ministers are married, job changes by spouses would have an impact on this. Nonetheless, the issue of the relationship of the new ministers with the bishop is important, organizationally speaking, and does require creative resolutions.

How should a relationship of the bishop with the new ministers be established? The first step could be that the bishop call individuals to lay ecclesial ministry. In light of the 30,000 plus persons already serving in ministry, initially dioceses would need to work with these individuals. Persons who had been professionally prepared, as well as those who would serve a specific community (as described above), and who wished to commit themselves for a set period of time to minister in the diocese could present themselves to be officially installed as lay ecclesial ministers. It is the bishop who would call and send the ecclesial minister. A part of this process should be an evaluation by the bishop of the readiness of the person for lay ecclesial ministry, in terms of educational and formational background and appropriate personal and spiritual maturity. This would be the pattern especially in regard to people already serving in ministry in the diocese. The question of calling new people into ministry would be the second phase of formalization of lay ecclesial ministry. It would require participation in a diocesan formation program of some kind, in the way that deacons often are required to begin. Suitable candidates could be encouraged to pursue graduate study, preparatory to being called as lay ecclesial ministers. Individuals who had served in other dioceses, and those completing studies, could take part in an additional diocesan formation program of some kind. The purpose would be to provide orientation to the local church, to develop relationships with other of its ministers, including the bishop, and to continue the growth and development of the individual—personally, spiritually, and ministerially.

One way that this model could be implemented would be for the local community or institution to play a primary role in hiring the individual deemed to have the background, experience, and personal gifts most suitable for the particular position. Of course, that could mean that a person so chosen would not be accepted as a lay ecclesial minister, for whatever reason, by the bishop. Nonetheless, this pattern would be helpful in giving flexibility to the parish or institution, and to the individual minister. It would also mean that while the bishop authorized a lay ecclesial minister ("sent" the person) for his or her role, the responsibility for placement of lay ecclesial ministers would not rest with the bishop, giving him flexibility as well.

Which roles should require, at least ideally, that they be filled by a lay ecclesial minister who stands in an established relationship with the bishop of the diocese in which the person is hired? Two types of roles would benefit significantly from this clear authorization. In the first group are those called upon to in some way represent the official Church, not only to Catholics whom they serve, but in a wider institutional sense. For example, Catholic chaplains in prisons and hospitals, campus ministers in colleges and universities (Catholic or not), and leaders of Catholic institutional ministries all serve as representatives of the Church within and beyond their institutions, in relationship to other professionals and the general public. This issue is quite complex; some recent legislative actions suggest, for example, that Catholic social service agencies are not necessarily seen as performing a work, a ministry of the Church. This could mean a serious erosion of the witness dimension of such service, intended as a continuation through time of the ministry begun by Jesus. Perhaps the fact of the diminishment of the number of ordained and vowed persons involved in institutional ministries contributed to such a perception. The appointment of official lay ministers to roles of leadership in these settings would augment the sign value of the service as, precisely, a ministry of the Church.

The second group of roles that would benefit from official authorization are those that call upon the minister to be a formal leader and/or teacher in the community, persons responsible for the calling forth and formation of other lay faithful for diverse roles in ministry. For example, a director of religious education who does not simply coordinate a program, but prepares catechists and designs catechetical experiences for adults and children is a teacher in the biblical sense, and should be authorized for the role. Similarly, a pastoral associate responsible not only for visiting the sick but also for calling forth and forming individuals to share in this ministry is indeed building the community and should be delegated this task by the bishop.

Could vowed religious be lay ecclesial ministers? Should they be, if they fulfill certain roles? As we have seen, many of the new ministers are sisters, and some are brothers. It has been said that although religious are lay theologically, they are part of the official Church, sociologically. Their leadership is more readily accepted by others. Furthermore, the institutional ministries of religious orders have an official relationship with the bishop of the diocese they are in. Nonetheless, it would be helpful if vowed religious were designated as lay ecclesial ministers and officially appointed to roles of leadership in parishes, diocesan offices, and at least those institutional ministries that are not missions of their own order.

The task of determining which roles require authorization will be a difficult one. It would be most helpful if the answers were discerned through dialogue between leaders of groups representative of the various new ministers and the bishops. It would also be helpful if it were the Conference of Bishops (rather than individual bishops) that made such decisions, especially in light of the high level of mobility in our society.

RITUALLY CELEBRATE

One of the great riches of the Roman Catholic Church is its tradition of ritual. So many have experienced a new flowering of the tradition through the various celebrations which are part of the RCIA. Catholics instinctively ritualize, which is why so many blessing and commissioning services have been "self made" by and for the new ministers. University and diocesan programs often conclude with a commissioning ritual, and religious communities sometimes send members forth to a new ministry with a service of blessing. At times parishes commission a new minister as he or she assumes responsibility for a role. The very fact that so many forms have emerged attests to their power. This was cogently described by a long-time church minister who explained that he held an M.Div. and had served in parishes for many years. He said that, despite all that history, "my sending ceremony for Maryknoll was the most exciting thing for me . . . to be sent by your community in mission is incredibly powerful."[15] Of course, such a ritual is important for the community as well, because it clarifies that there is a vital relationship between the community and the minister. This relationship is captured by the words of Pope John Paul II who said that laity who perform ministry are not clergy but archetypes of the participation of all the faithful in the salvific mission of the Church.[16] The participation of the community in a ritual celebration serves this vision, as they pray for one entrusted with a special role and responsibility within their midst.

Ideally, the ritual celebration would be an official installation as a lay ecclesial minister. This, as noted above, would require permission from Rome to add this ministry to the existing ministries of lector and acolyte, and acceptance of women into official ministry. The recent document from the Canon Law Society advocating opening the deaconate to women[17] suggests that theologically and canonically opening official ministry to women should not be insurmountably difficult.

In the meantime, it is not enough to simply have parish-based blessings and commissionings, because these do not establish a relationship with the bishop. If the bishops' conference defined lay ecclesial ministry and delineated the roles which should require that those who fill them be lay ecclesial ministers, they should also establish a ritual for designating a person as a lay ecclesial minister. The bishop would be the presider at such a celebration; the ritual would establish and define the relationship of the lay ecclesial minister with him. However, the communities in which the ecclesial ministers (will) serve also should be a part of the celebration, since the relationship is with them as well.

Such a ritual would install individuals as lay ecclesial ministers and depute them to a particular place and role in ministry. In other words, one would not be a lay ecclesial minister without a community in which to minister. This follows in the ancient tradition of being ordained for a particular community of faith. The installation would have a term: perhaps three years at first, then seven years. For serious reasons this could be abrogated, as religious vows may be. Such official appointment could be preceded by two or more years of working in a ministry role and discerning readiness for ritual installation. Religious life has a testing period, postulancy, which suggests such a model. The installation would make clear that the lay ecclesial minister is at the service of the Church, and has a formal and stable relationship with the bishop and the community in which he or she serves in a committed fashion. This would establish a reciprocal responsibility between the lay ecclesial minister and other official ministers in the community and the diocese. This model would work most readily in a parish setting; adaptation for institutional ministries would be needed.

CONTINUE WORK BEGUN

As shown in part one, many individuals and groups have contributed to the emergence of the new ministers, and to the understanding and support of this new reality. Continued reflection and discernment are needed to assist the ongoing development of this new group in the history of ministry.

The fact of the new ministers poses questions to scripture scholars. Are there models and norms that have not yet been fully explored which can illuminate further our new experience? Can we learn more about couples involved in ministry together in the New Testament period? What lay ministries existed in the period of the Hebrew Scriptures which could show us strengths and weaknesses, tensions and fruitful sharing, between laity and priests that we could learn from? What more can we discover about women in ministry? Both conceptual clarity and spiritual models can be sought in a further study of the Scriptures.

Similarly, the reality of the new ministers poses questions to theologians, canonists, and liturgists. Certainly, further historical study will be helpful, again in an effort to uncover models and norms, and to critique present developments. Further reflection on the present reality itself is needed, as we strive to discern the work of the Spirit in the life of the Church today. We cannot simply put new wine into old wineskins.

The Christological, ecclesiological, and pneumatological context and implications of this new reality need to be explored, so that both the new ministers and the larger Church may root the understanding of their ministry deeply in our theological tradition. Such rooting is important for a fullness of spiritual development, as well as conceptual clarity. Since the present Code of Canon Law is narrower in its definition of official ministry than was Vatican II, reflection on how to work with and change these limitations is needed, so that law would more fully serve the actual life of the community. Liturgists could study what kind of installation ceremony would be fruitful and appropriate, and also consider whether lay ecclesial ministry implies a role in some liturgical celebrations. More interdisciplinary reflection, such as that modeled by the Dayton and Collegeville gatherings, would be especially helpful.[18]

Professional organizations and associations of lay ministers have very worthwhile agendas to which they are committed and that require ongoing effort. Three actions are particularly important for them to address. One is greater collaboration among these groups. Networking initiatives and mutually supported projects have been begun, but continued work in these areas is needed. The development of the common competencies is an example of such work. Second, the activity of these groups would benefit from a more ongoing dialogue with the theological tradition—with theologians, liturgists, and canonists. The perspectives of organizations and associations of lay ministers have been deeply shaped by their life in the Church, but the language and reference points they use do not always communicate this to clerical ministers, whose socialization often differs from their own. The differences that shape laity and clergy can be fruitful, giving the Church the richness which diversity promises to us. But the ways in which those differences can be complementary need sufficient commonality of language and experience to be understood. Third, these groups are well placed to initiate studies and to pilot projects focused on leadership by laity in minority communities. Granted that the middle-class, professional model of the new minister is not prominent in minority settings, what is emerging? What can be developed? What support of these developments is needed, from the lay groups and the larger Church? The organizations and associations can serve as advocates—but only if we are clearer about what would be helpful.

As we have seen, colleges, universities, and seminaries have made significant contributions to the development of the emerging new ministers. The proposal that the new ministers be officially recognized suggests several questions for the educational institutions. One is, does the curriculum adequately prepare the individual not only to minister in a particular role, but also to officially represent the Church? This question focuses two realities: adequate understanding of the tradition and appropriate identification with the role of public minister in the Church. Adequate understanding of the tradition requires some assessment of the prior preparation of each student, the prior experiences that have shaped (or not yet shaped) Catholic identity. It also requires evaluation of the curriculum, to determine how well it fosters appreciation of the breadth of the tradition, as well as critical appraisal of how it has developed over time. In addition, appropriate identification with the official Church in order to fill the role of public minister with integrity requires further assessment of the curriculum. Second, what is the role of the educational institution in the personal and spiritual formation of pastoral ministers? As we have seen, some institutions believe it is not their role to form ministers personally and spiritually. As the educational institutions ponder this question, models from other professional educational programs could be helpful. For example, in the preparation of professionals in the fields of psychology and social work, considerable personal formation is included; similarly, dimensions of the preparation of nurses can be viewed as spiritual formation. What can, and should, educational institutions do, and what should be the role of the parish and diocese in relation to their efforts? Related to this is the question of discerning readiness for study for pastoral ministry. Can academic norms alone be sufficient? What is the responsibility of the institution in determining that an individual has at least a reasonable possibility of being accepted for official ministry? And in this age of occasional abuse of individuals by those in the helping professions, is formal psychological assessment needed so as to offer some protection to those who will be served?

Third, how can the educational institution foster the attitudes and skills needed for collaborative ministry? It has been said that "there is no more important issue facing the American Catholic Church than . . . the integration of the new ministers in the ongoing life of dioceses across the country."[19] Much of the work of integration is the task of priests and bishops, but the role of lay ministers will also be important. The ability to work collaboratively includes recognition of diverse roles and functions, and the degree of authority appropriate for each. It also requires such skills as conflict resolution and shared decision making. However, the more subtle issue of socialization to being part of a group bears examination in this context. Strong identification with a group sometimes finds expression in attitudes of opposition to members of another group. The lay-clerical tensions that have been part of the history of the Church can become focused between ministers in today's Church. For the educational institutions, the question of creating sufficient dialogue among the various groups in ministry is an important one, and bears directly on the development of the attitudes and skills needed for collaboration. Fourth, what educational enrichment can be offered to those already employed in ministry, or who demonstrate significant leadership potential yet do not meet the requirements for admission to a degree program? Colleges and universities have, in fact, developed many successful initiatives, including institutes and certificate programs, designed to assist the ongoing development and credentialing of diverse populations. Usually these efforts add responsibilities to faculty, and are not as financially remunerative for the institution as degree programs. It can be particularly helpful if such programs are developed in concert with diocesan leadership so that the educational institution receives support for its efforts on behalf of the Church, and the programs are well focused to meet local needs.

Finally, how can the educational institutions further assist in the empowerment and education of multicultural leaders for our multicultural Church? Additional research on patterns of leadership in various ethnic and racial communities, especially church communities, would be helpful. Further studies of styles of learning among different groups, and the piloting of educational offerings using appropriate learning methods, would also be valuable. The utilization of leaders from the diverse groups as teachers and visiting lecturers would be important, too. The educational institutions and lay organizations and associations are potential partners in this kind of effort.

DEVELOP SUPPORT SYSTEMS

One of the great strengths of religious orders is the community living which characterizes them. It is clear that a life of shared prayer and shared mission has nurtured individuals, allowing vision to grow and ministry to flourish, despite hardships. In recent years, some diocesan clergy have sought to deepen communal ties, forming various kinds of priest support groups. Other ministers have recognized this also; for example, spiritual directors often belong to peer supervision groups. In the larger culture, there are myriad forms of support groups, collectively attesting to the value of coming together with people-like-us to gain strength and clarity of vision.

Certainly, the new ministers do belong to professional organizations and associations. But some of the data in the surveys causes one to ask whether the groups may be too functionally focused, and may not really be giving the kind of support that is needed. The ministers report that they are concerned about burnout, they seek affirmation for their work, they are uncertain about whether they will continue in ministry. What is needed?

The married ministers affirm that they turn to their spouses for professional, emotional support in their work. One expects that they do receive this. But in Catholic circles there is little attention to the particular stresses for couples involved, through one partner or both, in professional church ministry. Protestant work in this area[20] alerts us to the fact that this is insufficiently addressed. When individual couples struggle alone with issues, they often don't have a name for the problem, and don't realize they are not the only one facing that particular difficulty. Training programs, retreat days, support groups, reading lists would all be helpful.

Young single ministers face a particular support difficulty. At a time of life when interaction with peers is very important, the fact that most ministers are older is an initial difficulty. Second, in an age when many young adults are alienated from the Church, these ministers probably experience more incredulity from friends about their vocational choice than they do helpful support. The assistance of mentors and skilled supervisors is needed. Opportunities to be part of occasional or ongoing support groups for their ministry would be valuable. Probably they would benefit from help from more mature ministers in beginning such groups, which ideally would include people in different roles (to avoid all "shop-talk"). Groups would need to be small enough for real sharing, yet large enough to include varying perspectives.

Two developments in the Church have potential for providing good, ongoing support for the new ministers. The first is the initiative on the part of many religious orders to extend their community life to include associates. The growth rate of membership has been phenomenal, from an estimated 6,000 in 1990 to 25,500 in 2000, with an additional 2,700 in formation.[21] Associate programs provide initial formation and ongoing opportunities for shared prayer and the sharing of faith journeys, including ministry.

The second development is the decision by religious orders to be more intentionally collaborative with laity, especially those who share in their ministries. To support this effort, days of prayer, common visioning and planning initiatives, and skill building workshops of various kinds have been held by groups such as the Jesuits, the Franciscans, and the Salesians for those who minister with them in their institutions. The importance of developing collaborative communities is not just that effective ministerial teams are built this way, but also that individuals are provided the personal and spiritual support they need for ministry.

To a certain extent, the task of building a necessary and suitable support system belongs to each minister. But this is a task for the Church as well, a task that has always been at the heart of its ministry, building up the community and supporting its leaders. Dioceses, colleges, universities, associations, organizations, religious orders, the "wisdom community" among ministers, all need to consider how to develop more effective support systems.

CONTINUE TO SERVE

We began by focusing on the new ministers and will end there as well. What next steps would be fruitful for them, their ministry, and the life of the Church? There are four aspects of ministry that we have explored, which the new ministers must continue to emphasize in their pastoral practice.

One: ministry belongs to the whole Church, not a particular group. Official ministers have as a primary function the recognition of the charisms of all the people, and the development of pastoral practices that will enable and sustain the exercise of those charisms. It is the responsibility of official ministers to recognize and rejoice in the diverse ministers and ministries of the Church. Studies of the new ministers show that they call many others into ministry; their efforts should continue, and grow.

Two: ministry is *diakonia*, service of the people, service of the local community. Human needs for rank, status, recognition, and even affirmation are secondary to this central dimension of ministry. Discernment of spirits, personal and communal, is needed, if service is to grow in authenticity. Concrete ways of accurately understanding the needs of the people, and of evaluating efforts in meeting them, are also called for.

Three: ministry is collegial. Although it is often easier to just do it oneself, an exercise of ministry faithful to the biblical tradition calls for efforts at being the Body of Christ organizationally and programmatically, as well as spiritually. Experimentation with new processes of decision making and evaluating is needed, and the ongoing development of skills for collaboration necessary. Spiritual growth is both a requirement for and a result of efforts at working collaboratively.

Four: the horizon of ministry is the Kingdom. The Church does not exist for herself. Although the lay ministers have, as their primary task, work for the building up of the community, that work itself must have a focus beyond the community. Some ministers, such as teachers and pastoral leaders, have a responsibility to enable the Church to perform her ministry of service to the world. Some, such as hospital chaplains and prison ministers, offer the service of the Church to the world.

As the new ministers reflect on their own experience, and the response of the Church to them, they are called to joyfully celebrate all that is. And as they experience the difficulty of what is not yet, they are called to live in a spirit of hope for all that is still to unfold, firm in the belief that God is with the Church.

CONCLUSION

On the twenty-sixth Sunday of the year, the Church brings together two readings, Numbers 11:25–29 and Mark 9:38–43. The first tells the story of the seventy elders whom Moses gathered together around the tent. Yahweh came down in the cloud, and the elders received some of the spirit that was on Moses, so as to share in his leadership. When the spirit came on them, they prophesied. Furthermore, two men who had been chosen, but who were not present at the tent, also began to prophesy. Some cried out to Moses to stop these two. Moses replied: "If only the whole people of Yahweh were prophets, and Yahweh gave his Spirit to them all!"[22]

And in Mark, we read of an apostle coming to Jesus and telling him that "a man who is not one of us" is casting out devils in the name of Jesus. Jesus replied: "You must not stop him: no one who works a miracle in my name is likely to speak evil of me. Anyone who is not against us is for us."[23]

In the time of Moses, in the time of Jesus, and even today, the Spirit breathes where the Spirit wills, always making all things new.

NOTES

1. For a fuller treatment of this theme, see Zeni Fox, *Forging a Ministerial Identity* (Chicago: National Association for Lay Ministry, 1999).
2. See, for example, Ronald A. Heifetz, *Leadership without Easy Answers* (Cambridge, MA: Harvard University Press, 1994).
3. E. H. Friedman, *Generation to Generation: Family Process in Church and Synagogue* (New York: Guilford Press, 1985).
4. A very helpful reflection on this process of "repositioning" is offered by Gaillardetz: see chapter 9 of this volume for commentary, and his "Shifting Meanings in the Lay-Clergy Distinction" in *Irish Theological Quarterly*, 64, 1999, pp. 115–139.
5. *Lay Ministry Update*, vol. 2, no. 1, January/February 1997, p. 2.
6. *Called and Gifted*, and *Called and Gifted for the Third Millennium*, as discussed in chapter 14.
7. *State of the Questions*, p. 8.
8. See the discussion in chapter 8. Also note O'Meara's qualification of this idea in his revised volume.
9. Osborne's treatment of lay ministry emphasizes the validity of a vocation and mission within the Church that is properly lay, especially pp. 596–600.
10. Article 23.
11. Garret Keizer, *A Dresser of Sycamore Trees: The Finding of a Ministry* (San Francisco: Harper, 1991), p. 209.
12. As noted in chapter 9, some theologians do not find this language helpful. See also James Heft, "Toward a Theology of Ecclesial Lay Ministry," p. 44: "To be a 'layman' in some fields means to be an amateur. Ministry that is 'lay' then becomes, accordingly, associated with the work of amateurs," p. 84.
13. Whitehead, *Alternative Futures*, develops these ideas, p. 155.
14. The *ministerium* and the Lay Ecclesial Ministry Council described in chapter 15 are examples of structures which further this relationship.
15. Conversation with Gary Lee, October 1996.
16. Address in Mexico City.
17. See chapter 5.
18. See chapter 9.

19. Conversation with Fred Hofheinz, Program Director, Religion, Lilly Endowment, Inc., March 13, 1997.
20. The Alban Institute has reported on such research through the years.
21. *The Associate*, Summer 1996, p. 2, and the 2000 CARA/NACAR survey as reported in a conversation with Sister Ellen O'Connell, coordinator of the North American Conference of Associates and Religious, February 15, 2001.
22. Numbers 11:29.
23. Mark 9:39–40.

INDEX